Lexical Errors and Accuracy in Foreign
Language Writing

SECOND LANGUAGE ACQUISITION
Series Editor: **Professor David Singleton**, *Trinity College, Dublin, Ireland*

This series brings together titles dealing with a variety of aspects of language acquisition and processing in situations where a language or languages other than the native language is involved. Second language is thus interpreted in its broadest possible sense. The volumes included in the series all offer in their different ways, on the one hand, exposition and discussion of empirical findings and, on the other, some degree of theoretical reflection. In this latter connection, no particular theoretical stance is privileged in the series; nor is any relevant perspective – sociolinguistic, psycholinguistic, neurolinguistic, etc. – deemed out of place. The intended readership of the series includes final-year undergraduates working on second language acquisition projects, postgraduate students involved in second language acquisition research, and researchers and teachers in general whose interests include a second language acquisition component.

Full details of all the books in this series and of all our other publications can be found on http://www.multilingual-matters.com, or by writing to Multilingual Matters, St Nicholas House, 31–34 High Street, Bristol BS1 2AW, UK.

SECOND LANGUAGE ACQUISITION
Series Editor: David Singleton, *Trinity College, Dublin, Ireland*

Lexical Errors and Accuracy in Foreign Language Writing

María Pilar Agustín Llach

MULTILINGUAL MATTERS
Bristol • Buffalo • Toronto

Library of Congress Cataloging in Publication Data
A catalog record for this book is available from the Library of Congress.
Lexical Errors and Accuracy in Foreign Language Writing/María Pilar Agustín Llach.
Second Language Acquisition: 58
Includes bibliographical references.
1. Language and languages–Study and teaching. 2. Rhetoric–Study and teaching.
3. Vocabulary–Study and teaching. 4. Second language acquisition.
I. Agustín Llach, María Pilar
P53.27.L49 2011
418–dc22 2011015600

British Library Cataloguing in Publication Data
A catalogue entry for this book is available from the British Library.

ISBN-13: 978-1-84769-417-1 (hbk)
ISBN-13: 978-1-84769-416-4 (pbk)

Multilingual Matters
UK: St Nicholas House, 31–34 High Street, Bristol BS1 2AW, UK.
USA: UTP, 2250 Military Road, Tonawanda, NY 14150, USA.
Canada: UTP, 5201 Dufferin Street, North York, Ontario M3H 5T8, Canada.

Copyright © 2011 María Pilar Agustín Llach.

All rights reserved. No part of this work may be reproduced in any form or by any means without permission in writing from the publisher.

The policy of Multilingual Matters/Channel View Publications is to use papers that are natural, renewable and recyclable products, made from wood grown in sustainable forests. In the manufacturing process of our books, and to further support our policy, preference is given to printers that have FSC and PEFC Chain of Custody certification. The FSC and/or PEFC logos will appear on those books where full certification has been granted to the printer concerned.

Typeset by Datapage International Ltd.
Printed and bound in Great Britain by the MPG Books Group.

Contents

Acknowledgements vii
List of Abbreviations ix
Introduction xi

Part 1: Lexical Competence and Lexical Errors
1 Vocabulary Acquisition in the Second Language 3
   Theories of Vocabulary Acquisition in the Second Language 4
   Vocabulary Acquisition by Young Learners 13
   L1 and L2 Vocabulary Acquisition: Similarities
   and Differences 17
   Conclusion 19

2 Variables Affecting Lexical Production 21
   Overview of Variables Affecting the Production of
   Vocabulary 21
   Proficiency Level 23
   Vocabulary Size 35
   Conclusion 38

3 Vocabulary and Writing 40
   Developing Writing Skills 40
   Assessing Writing 51
   Conclusion 67

4 Lexical Errors in SLA 70
   Definitions of 'Lexical Error' 72
   Taxonomies of Lexical Errors 75
   Lexical Errors as Evidence of Vocabulary Acquisition 93
   Lexical Errors in Communication 95
   Lexical Errors in the Educational Context 100
   Conclusion 103

Part 2: Lexical Error Production in Young Spanish Learners' Written Compositions

5 Designing a Study to Explore Lexical Errors in Writing 107
   Research Questions and Hypotheses 108
   Design of the Study. 112
   Participants 113
   Materials. 115
   Procedures 121
   Analysis 125

6 Lexical Error Production: Changes Over Time. 129
   Proficiency-Related Lexical Error Types. 129
   Formal and Semantic Lexical Errors 137
   L1-Oriented and L2-Oriented Lexical Errors 139
   Discussion. 140
   Conclusion 162

7 Lexical Errors in Writing Quality 164
   Lexical Errors as Predictors of the Quality of Written
   Composition 164
   Changes over Time in the Relationship between
   Lexical Errors and Essay Quality. 166
   Discussion. 172
   Conclusion 179

8 Lexical Errors and Receptive Vocabulary Knowledge 181
   Lexical Errors as Negative Indicators of Vocabulary
   Knowledge 181
   Discussion. 188
   Conclusion 192

9 Some Concluding Remarks 193
   Pedagogical Implications. 198
   Limitations of the Study 205
   Further Research. 207

Appendices 210
References 222

Acknowledgements

Many people have made valuable contributions to the process of writing this work. First and foremost, I thank Prof Dr David Singleton for his help and insightful comments on the original proposal of this book and for his keen interest in this research. Without his support this would have never been possible. I also express my thanks to the editorial staff of Multilingual Matters, especially to Anna Roderick for her kind mails and ready help.

I am very much indebted to Dr Diana Carter for her help with the language of an earlier version of this work, and especially to Amanda McCaughren Morris for her proofreading of the manuscript, her suggestions, her comments and her assistance in linguistic matters. I am also very grateful to the mathematician and lecturer at the Universidad De la Rioja, Montserrat San Martin Pérez, for her support and advice with statistics.

I offer my sincere gratitude to the reviewer of the manuscript who provided me with very interesting, perspicacious and intelligent comments and suggestions, which have largely improved the quality of the book.

I am especially and deeply grateful to Prof Dr Francisco José Ruiz de Mendoza Ibañez for his generous help and his support and kind treatment.

At an institutional level my thanks are due to the *Comunidad Autónoma de La Rioja* and the *Universidad de La Rioja* for financial and institutional support through the GLAUR group (glaur.unirioja.es). I also acknowledge my debt to the Department of Modern Languages of the *Universidad de La Rioja* and its academic and administration staff for their help and support. I am also indebted to the *Ministerio de Educacion y Ciencia* for its financial support through the research projects (grant nos. BFF2003-04009-C02-02 and HUM2006-09775-C02-02).

Finally, I most warmly thank Dr Rosa María Jiménez Catalán, who has shown her usual generosity in assisting me all throughout my academic life and has always offered me her clear-sighted and generous guidance.

Every effort has been made to trace and acknowledge all sources, but I apologise to those whom I may have inadvertently missed. I am also aware that despite the help and assistance received from the people and institutions above, the work is far from perfect. Any faults and failings are my sole responsibility.

List of Abbreviations

CPH	Critical period hypothesis
EA	Error analysis
EAP	*English for Academic Purposes*
EFL	English as a foreign language
ESL	English as a second language
FL	Foreign language
IL	Interlanguage
L1	Mother tongue
L2	Second/foreign/target language
NL	Native language
SLA	Second language acquisition
T1	Testing time 1 in fourth grade
T2	Testing time 2 in sixth grade
TL	Target language

Introduction: An Outline

The past decades have seen a noteworthy increase in research about vocabulary and vocabulary-related issues.* The observation that vocabulary is central to language development has promoted this increase in research studies in the lexical field. Several reasons account for this (James, 1998: 143–144). Firstly, the boundaries between grammar and lexis are now seen as more blurred than assumed. Lexis is inextricably intertwined with the other linguistic systems. The study of language from various perspectives, phonology, syntax, morphology, semantics and pragmatics, has the word as its central and definitional element (cf. Singleton, 2000: Chap. 1). Secondly, learners consider vocabulary as the most important aspect of language, thus equating language learning with vocabulary learning. We agree in this sense with Singleton (2000: 12) that 'language is popularly conceived in terms of words'. In addition, lexical errors have been found to be the most numerous in many different research studies. Furthermore, they have been judged as the most serious category of errors. Finally, we have to highlight the functional role of vocabulary as a crucial aspect in communication and language assessment, especially in writing assessment. If knowledge of vocabulary is at hand, then communication is possible even though no grammar knowledge exists. It then becomes significant for language teaching and learning.

Lexical errors have also occupied researchers in second language acquisition (SLA) and teaching in recent years. In all, research on lexical errors as the central issue is not very abundant as compared with research on general vocabulary matters. Especially scarce are studies with primary school graders. Longitudinal studies on the development of the lexicon examined through the light of lexical errors are also almost non-existent. Moreover, most studies that deal with lexical errors have mainly addressed the description and classification of these lexical errors

---

* This study is part of the research projects: FFI2010-19334, BFF2003-04009-C02-02 and HUM2006-09775-C02-02.

and the field is in need of studies that explore the role of lexical errors in writing assessment, lexical knowledge and L2 vocabulary acquisition.

In most teaching situations a frequent appearance of errors is considered as a failure either in the process of learning or in the process of teaching. However, focusing on errors can provide very telling and informative insights regarding the process of SLA. Finding out the what, why and when of lexical errors can be very valuable and useful in determining how to remedy them and get a successful performance (Ellis, 1997b: 15). More specifically, lexical errors can serve to indicate L2 writing ability and vocabulary knowledge. The need to establish objective and reliable measures and criteria to evaluate the writing competence of learners in the L2 calls for the examination of the role of lexical errors in this issue.

Ignorance or imperfect knowledge of lexical items leads to errors. The notion of error has changed from a negative view to a positive one as an inevitable phenomenon in the process of SLA. It helps us to understand how language acquisition proceeds and where it does not proceed smoothly, what stages it goes through, what processes are at stake, and in particular, at which moment of acquisition the learner is. Errors put forward any possible methodological shortcoming and any problematic learning area, so that EA should precede any pedagogical design. Furthermore, lexical errors shed light on the structure of the L2 lexicon, just as L1 errors are indicative of the properties of the L1 lexical store (Laufer, 1991a: 321). Finally, learners can learn from their errors by spotting problematic L2 areas where they need more practice.

There is enough evidence to assume lexical errors to be important predictors of writing quality, relevant measures of lexical knowledge and crucial insights into the vocabulary acquisition process. Writing is a very difficult skill for any language user, particularly for non-native learners; so lexical errors are numerous. Evaluation of the writing process and written products of learners is an arduous task, and objective measures of writing quality are needed that facilitate and quicken this writing evaluation. Vocabulary has proven to be crucial in establishing writing quality. Likewise, lexical errors have been shown to be important composition assessment criteria and quality predictors. The quality of interlanguage performance is generally assessed in terms of communicability, so that if an utterance communicates well, its quality will be assessed positively. Considering this, the more lexical errors a text displays, the less is its communicability and, therefore, the lower is its quality (Engber, 1995).

Introduction: An Outline

Hence, this book focuses primarily on lexical error production of young Spanish learners over two years from fourth to sixth grade. It aims at exploring the development of the participants' written production and vocabulary knowledge through the observation of lexical errors. By examining the mechanisms that explain lexical errors we can start discovering the processes that are activated in lexical acquisition.

Considering the methodology of analysis and the types of objectives pursued by the investigation, the study presented in this book is framed into EA and the field of lexical SLA. The main merit of our research concerns the correlation between lexical error and essay score, which, if finally found, will provide with objective criteria for evaluation and clues about what to concentrate teaching on. For learners the findings are important since they could be shown what they have to pay more attention to when writing.

This investigation claims novelty for its approach to the study of lexical acquisition from lexical errors. Moreover, this study is original and novel, because although it is framed within the traditional EA methodology, its perspective is new. This study uses EA and lexical errors as an instrument to assess, valuate and measure other language constructs such as writing ability and receptive vocabulary knowledge.

This book is divided into two main parts. The first part provides the theoretical background to the second, which is an original empirical study. Chapter 1 looks at the process of L2 vocabulary acquisition, and Chapter 2 examines some of the variables which affect lexical (error) production, concentrating basically on proficiency level and vocabulary size. In Chapter 3, the relationship between writing assessment and vocabulary is examined. Chapter 4 gives a critical review of previous research on lexical errors. The second part of the book reports on an original study, which relates lexical errors, writing assessment and receptive word knowledge. Individual chapters are devoted to explaining the method, the changes in lexical error production over time, the role of lexical errors in writing quality and their relationship with receptive vocabulary size. Finally, implications for practice, limitations and suggestions for further research are discussed.

Part 1
Lexical Competence and Lexical Errors

Chapter 1
Vocabulary Acquisition in the Second Language

The importance of vocabulary in general language acquisition and communication (first and second[1]) cannot be denied (Clark, 1993; Dagut, 1977; Harley, 1995; Laufer, 1990b; Singleton, 1999, 2000; Smith & Locke, 1988; Yoshida, 1978). The process of L2 vocabulary acquisition begins as soon as the L2 is encountered and continues long after other aspects of the L2 have been mastered. Despite being such a central and durative phenomenon, there are still many aspects of the L2 vocabulary acquisition process that remain mysterious, as Schmitt (1998: 281) points out: '[t]he mechanics of vocabulary acquisition is one of the more intriguing puzzles in second language acquisition'. This chapter explores L2 vocabulary learning with a particular focus on young learners' vocabulary acquisition. Accounts of differences in L1 and L2 lexical development processes as well as the relationships between the L1 and L2 lexicons are also dealt with in this chapter.

There has been copious research in lexical development in L1 and L2,[2] but the absence of an overarching psycholinguistic framework to interpret these studies results in a fragmentation of the field, with studies addressing, for example, vocabulary size, different dimensions of word knowledge, passive/active distinctions in respect of vocabulary knowledge, reception and comprehension, vocabulary instruction and vocabulary learning strategies. In 1988, Channell already noted this problem:

> There are now theories of L2 vocabulary acquisition, a wide (and growing) range of teaching techniques available, and a greatly increased awareness on the part of most teachers (and learners) of the importance of vocabulary development. At the same time, understanding of the psychological aspects of L2 vocabulary acquisition and vocabulary use is still rather limited. (Channell, 1988: 83)

Hudson (1990) also recognized this general area of deficit.

> To my knowledge, a systematic model of how *meanings* of words are acquired is absent from the field. Most writers on the subject assume L2 lexical development proceeds in the same way as in a first language (L1), without specifying what this is in formal terms. (Hudson, 1990: 222)

The situation has not changed much in the last decade, although research on L2 vocabulary learning has significantly increased. The most frequently brandished explanation of L2 vocabulary learning extends L1 research findings to the learning of vocabulary in an additional language, on the basis of a view that the L2 lexicon is operationally similar to the L1 lexicon and that L1 and L2 lexical acquisition and processing follow in at least comparable ways. Thus, the findings in respect to L1 lexical processing are also seen as relevant to L2 (Singleton, 1999: Chap. 3; Stoller & Grabe, 1995). The fact, however, that L2 learners have already started developing their L1 lexicon by the time L2 acquisition begins may imply some differences between L1 and L2 lexical development (Singleton, 1999: Chap. 2). We further deal with this issue later. Our focus to begin with is on the different theories that attempt to explain vocabulary acquisition.

Theories of Vocabulary Acquisition in the Second Language

There are a number of disparate stances regarding the nature of L2 vocabulary acquisition, but two main complementary approaches can be distinguished, each emphasising different aspects of the process. The first focuses on the development of vocabulary as a process in stages (cf. Ellis, 1997a: 133ff; Jiang, 2000; Schmitt, 1998). The second represents vocabulary acquisition as the development of associative networks (Meara, 1984, 1996).

Vocabulary acquisition as a process in stages

One possibility is that vocabulary develops in consecutive stages. Researchers have made attempts at discovering some systematicity in how vocabulary items are acquired, trying to isolate predictable stages of acquisition. Thus, Gleitman and Landau (1996: 1) claim that vocabulary learning is not just the result of a mapping procedure, but that there is a systematic process at work comparable to the highly structured innate principles that guide syntactic acquisition.

The study of vocabulary acquisition in this perspective can have a number of dimensions: (1) order of acquisition of different types of knowledge (morphological, syntactic, collocational, semantic, etc.) for each lexical item, (2) order of acquisition of word classes (noun, verb, adverb, adjective, etc.), (3) order of acquisition of particular lexical items and (4) developmental stages of lexical processing.

Concerning the first, Schmitt (1998) advocates the study of the acquisition of individual words diachronically. In his 1998 article, for example, he measured the developmental acquisition of four types of word knowledge: written form, associations, grammatical behaviour and meaning. The study was intended to find out whether there is any hierarchical relationship between these four aspects of word knowledge. None of the measures used yielded positive evidence of a developmental hierarchy of lexical competence components. Other studies that follow the same line have been equally unsuccessful in identifying the stages through which lexical acquisition might develop. However, the existence of some regular patterns of vocabulary development is generally acknowledged (cf. Curtis, 1987: 45; Palmberg, 1987; Schmitt & Meara, 1997; Viberg, 1996; Yoshida, 1978). Naturalistic observations of L1 lexical development support the idea that knowledge of a word is not a yes/no issue. New words and word aspects are acquired in an incremental way. Different aspects of word knowledge, for example morphological knowledge, collocations, appropriate use of lexical items in context or knowledge of polysemous words, seem to be incorporated to the lexical entry at different moments during the L2 acquisition process. Similarly, lexical items belonging to a different word class appear to undergo different rates of acquisition, with nouns being acquired first and verbs second (Ellis & Beaton, 1993; Laufer, 1990b, 1997b; Marsden & David, 2008; Myles, 2005; Singleton, 1999: 141–142).

Research on word class acquisition is not very copious, but some recent studies by Marsden and David (2008) and Myles (2005) have claimed that verb production increases as learners' L2 proficiency develops. Parallel to this increase in verb production, there is, in this view, a decrease in noun production. Low-proficiency learners' productions abound in nouns, but verbs are practically non-existent in such productions. The higher cognitive and linguistic demands made by verbs seem to result in their being acquired after nouns. The same argument applies to adjectives and adverbs, which also appear after nouns in learners' production. In particular reference to verbs, the argument runs as follows: verb acquisition implies not only the development of form–meaning connections but also the acquisition of syntactic constraints, morphological inflections and knowledge of the correspondences between verb and subject and verb complements. According to this view, the cognitive load involved in the acquisition of verbs is higher than that involved in the acquisition of nouns, which explains the former's later appearance.

As learners' L2 competence progresses, they start developing morphosyntactic features of verbs and other word classes. To illustrate this point, I would like to refer to some example essays taken from our data. It can be observed in the sample essays that as the learner's proficiency increases, his or her production of nouns proportionally decreases, but the proportion of verbs (including the modal *can*), adjectives and adverbs rises.

< learner 30, grade 4 >
Monday 29th March
Dear Mr. and Mrs. Edwards:
Hello! My name is XXX. I live in Logroño and I from Spain. I'm nine. I am tall I've got brown eyes and. big ears. My school's name is XXX. I live in a little city. I like football, tennis, basketball, and I like rice, potatoes, cucumbers, spaghettis, salad, ice-cream, chocolate cake, rice and bananas, My English teacher's name is Luis. My favourite subjet is gym. My favourite colour is yellow. I live in a big house with 2 bathrooms, four bedrooms and don't have hall and stairs. My class is small with 27 chairs and desks, a computer, a blackboard and 34 photos. My birthday is 18 of August Isaac

Nouns: *hello, name, eyes, ears, city, school, football, tennis, basketball, rice, potatoes, cucumbers, spaghettis, salad, ice-cream, chocolate, cake, bananas, English teacher, subject, gym, colour, house, bathrooms, bedrooms, hall, stairs, class, chairs, desks, computer, photos, birthday, August*: 33
Verbs: *to be, live, like, have, do*: 5
Adjectives: *tall, brown, big, little, favourite, yellow, small*: 7
Adverbs: 0

< learner 30, grade 6 >
Hello! My name is XXX. i live in Logroño, (La Rioja). I'm an only child. My fathers name are XXX and XXX I go to XXX school, in this place there are camps of basketball and football. Logroño is a small city. But there are lots of houses I like playing football with my friends and eating pizza but I don't like eating fish. I go to my villag. It's name is bezares. It very small village. It has a fronton, a church and a town hall. It has only ten habitants. This habitants live in a very old houses. I am tall and my hair is blond in summer and more dar in

autum. My eyes are brown. My school has three places. A small house. In this house are the young pupils A big house. In this house go the big children. And the last place is a sports centre. In this place I can play football. Oh And I the Preseident of the United States I have got a bird and a dog in north pole and my father win the lotery It's incredible! I have got a clock only of gold. I have got two noses and three arms but one arm is very small. Cristian is a mosquits.

Nouns: *name, child, fathers, place, camps, football, city, houses, friends, pizza, fish, village, church, town hall, habitants, hair, summer, eyes, school, pupils, children, president, bird, sports centre, dog, lottery, clock, gold, noses, arms, mosquits*: 31.

Verbs: *to be, live, go, like, play, eat, can, win, have got, do*: 10

Adjectives: *small, old, tall, blond, dark, brown, young, big, last, incredible, a lot of, only*: 12

Adverbs: *very, more*: 2

Among the factors that affect the rate of acquisition of individual words, researchers distinguish, among others, pronounceability, length, morphological complexity, abstractness, polysemy, semantic opacity, synonymy, word frequency and salience (Ellis, 2004; Ellis & Beaton, 1993; González Álvarez, 2004; Laufer, 1990b, 1997b; Singleton, 1999: 136–147). Apart from these phonological, orthographic and semantic characteristics of the L2 word, the degree to which the L2 and L1 words correspond will determine the 'learnability', that is the degree of ease of learning of L2 items. The more difficult a word is to learn, the more lexical errors can be expected to affect this word. In this vein, a long and formally complex word such as *birthday* gives rise to many lexical errors in our sample. Examples of the different renderings of the word are as follows:

- My *bidray* is in febroary.
- My *birthey* is the third of April.
- My *birday* is in September.
- My *verdey* is day 22 may.
- On friday is my *birdthay*.

Considering the degree of integration of the components of a lexical entry (semantic, syntactic, morphological and formal), Jiang (2000) proposes a theoretical model of tutored L2 lexical development that proceeds in stages. The model draws on the two basic differences between L1 and L2 vocabulary acquisition in a formal instructional setting. L2 vocabulary acquisition is constrained by (1) 'poverty of input in terms of both quantity and quality' and (2) 'presence of an established conceptual/semantic system with an L1 lexical system closely associated with it' (p. 49) (cf. Ellis, 1997a: 133ff).

According to Jiang (2000) L2 vocabulary acquisition proceeds in three phases. Firstly, learners focus on the formal specifications of a particular lexical item, and may even try to relate given L2 forms to their L1 translations. This is called the 'formal stage of lexical development'. Secondly, as experience with the language and its lexicon increases, learners add to L2 lexical entries the semantic and syntactic features of their L1 translation equivalents. This stage of vocabulary learning implies the matching of a new word form with pre-existing (L1) meanings (Ellis, 1997a: 134). Jiang describes this stage as the 'L1 lemma mediation stage'. Lexical transfer is common at this stage (cf. Ellis, 1997a: 134). Finally, when the learner has considerable L2 experience, semantic, syntactic and morphological information relating to the L2 word is incorporated into the corresponding lexical entry, and there is a movement away from any type of L1 mediation; this is the 'L2 integration stage'. The cognitive linguistic interpretation of lexical acquisition follows the same line (Robinson & Ellis, 2008; VanPatten *et al.*, 2004).

The belief that L2 vocabulary acquisition can proceed as a set of hierarchically and systematically ordered stages implies systematicity and regularity in the lexical system. This is a step forward in research in the field of lexical development, since, traditionally, the lexicon has been deemed to be a chaotic mass of words arranged or listed without any predetermined order (cf. among many others, Dušková, 1969; Warren, 1982). Attempts such as the above at explaining the nature of lexical acquisition in L2 illustrate a major change in perspective as well as renewed research interest in the lexical component of language. A similar development can be observed in research in lexical errors, as will be presented below.

Vocabulary as associative networks

The second main trend within lexical studies suggests that vocabulary development occurs through associative networks (Meara, 1984, 1996). The belief that there is some systematic disposition of words in the lexicon led to the proposal of explanations that would account for lexical learning while taking full account of such systematicity (Dagut, 1977; Meara, 1996; Singleton, 1999). In this perspective, a new lexical item is incorporated into the L2 lexicon by establishing relations of various kinds to already existent words.

Meara (1984, 1996) asserts that learning vocabulary involves developing a set of associations, a semantico-formal network that reorganises itself with every new word learned; Beheydt (1987) and Robinson (1989, 1995) support this view, according to which new lexical information relates to old information by means of semantico-formal connections. Thus, lexical learning implies extending and strengthening those associations as the result of the incorporation of new words, or of further semantic and/or formal features of already known words.

At the core of these networks lies the notion of *prototypicality* (cf. Weinreich, 1974). A prototype is seen as the central or best example of a semantic category. In this view, vocabulary acquisition consists in broadening the semantic category by adding new shades of meaning or even new meanings to the prototype and by stretching the category with new lexical items that establish polysemy, synonymy, antonymy or metonymy relations among themselves (Cameron, 1994, 2001; Coady, 1995; Gass, 1988; Laufer, 1991a; Meara, 1996; Nagy & Herman, 1987; Nation, 1990; Schmitt, 1995; Schmitt & Meara, 1997; Wesche & Paribakht, 1996). Imagine, for example, that an EFL learner acquires the word *dog* with its denotative meaning of a 'domestic four-legged animal known for its loyalty to men'. This will constitute the prototype term, and as experience with the L2 increases, new meanings of the term such as figuratively or connotatively derived 'contemptible person', 'ugly person', 'any of various usually simple mechanical devices for holding, gripping or fastening that consist of a spike, bar or hook' or 'uncharacteristic or affected stylishness or dignity' (cf. www.merriam-webster.com) will also be incorporated. Moreover, the learners will also incorporate other words semantically and formally related to the prototype: morphological variations of the word (*doggie, to dog, dog-eared*), synonyms (*canine, hound*), expressions with the word (*put on the dog, lazy dog, going to the dogs, hot dog*), words in opposite or contrastive relationships (*cat, wolf*) and words in hyponymous or superordinate relationships (*mammal, animal, spaniel, German shepherd*).

From this model, it follows that not all L2 words have the same opportunities to be acquired within a certain time span by L2 learners. The fact that our minds are organised into categories and that these categories revolve around a prototypical term determines the possibilities of a word to be learned (González Álvarez, 2004). Basic- level terms are the first to be learned and remembered by L2 learners, because they are conceptually the easiest. Going back to the previous example, the word *dog* will be learned more quickly and more easily than the related words *animal* or *spaniel*, since the first is more neutral and less marked than the latter two (Cameron, 1994, 2001; Singleton, 1999; Weinreich, 1974). If the learned L2 prototypical term does not coincide with the native prototype, the learner will have to restructure the categorisation with the aid of further L2 lexical information until it resembles a native prototype (Beheydt, 1987; Cameron, 1994, 2001). A very conspicuous example here is the notion or concept *bread*. The prototype *bread* does not correspond in exact ways with its Spanish equivalent *pan*. The Spanish EFL learner first attaches the form *bread* to the already existing conceptual image of *pan*. However, as experience with the L2 increases, learners abandon the L1 concept, replacing it with the L2 concept and incorporating L2 meanings and L2 forms that relate to *bread* (*bread and butter, loaf, brown bread, bread roll, bread slice, bun*).

According to this line of thinking, how well a particular lexical item is known may condition the strengthening and consolidation of the relationships between words in the mental lexicon. As the knowledge of a word increases, the connections it maintains with other words in the lexicon vary in nature and intensity (cf. Singleton, 1999: Chap. 4). Thus, the closer a word is to the core vocabulary, the stronger its semantic associations with other core vocabulary items will be (Wolter, 2001).

Formal aspects of lexical items (phonology and orthography) are also seen as playing an important role in structuring and connecting words in the mind. Relationships among lexical items in the mental lexicon of native children and, especially, in that of low-proficiency L2 learners are claimed to be significantly characterised by phonological connections, that is words relate to each other via formal similarities rather than by meaning relations. For instance, a word such as *dog* would relate semantically with *cat* or *bark* (paradigmatic and syntagmatic association, respectively) and phonologically with *bog* (examples taken from Wolter, 2001: 43). Such evidence of both phonological and semantic lexical relationships emphasises the importance of the formal aspects (phonological and graphemic) of a word in L2 vocabulary learning. Lexical errors can, accordingly, not only involve the semantic component of a word, but its form is also liable to be affected, for example spelling errors, coinages, misselections.[3]

Lexicon organisation in L2 and L1

Knowing how lexical items are organised and accessed can provide relevant insights into how vocabulary is acquired, and especially into how it can be best taught. There are three basic perspectives that try to provide an account of the organisation of the lexicon, in the L1 and L2, in terms of the types of links established among the stored lexical items.

The first line of research (Meara, 1983, 1984, 1992, 1996) contends that the L1 and L2 lexicons are qualitatively different in their structure. It claims that while the L1 lexicon is predominantly semantically organised, the words stored in the L2 lexicon are mainly phonologically related. The comparison of data obtained from word association tests performed by L1 and L2 learners has led to this conclusion. To illustrate this point, we can think of the associations of the word *book*. In the native speaker's lexicon, these would probably include the words *read, write, novel, library, edit, publish, hardback, bookshop, one for the book, in one's book,* and so on. In the L2 learner's lexicon, on Meara's view, formal associations such as *bookshop, cook, hook, textbook, foot* may manifest themselves.

The second account of lexicon organisation postulates that even beginner L2 learners store some words in the lexicon via the establishment of semantic associations. In this view, the L1 and L2 lexicons function in essentially the same manner. It is the number of words integrated into the lexicon (i.e. how many words the learner knows) and also the extent of the integration of each particular item (i.e. how well the item in question is known), as well as the nature of the particular word in question, which influence the type of associations established (Ellis & Beaton, 1993; Meara, 1996; Nation, 1990; Ringbom, 1983; Singleton, 1996, 1999: 139; Wolter, 2001).

Still a third model of lexical organisation and access exists that is based on the production/comprehension distinction. Some authors (Channell, 1988; López Morales, 1993; Nattinger, 1988) claim that in production, words are accessed via semantic associations, while in comprehension, it is the formal (phonological/orthographic) relationships between words that account for lexicon organisation and access, both in L1 and in L2. According to this model, for production, words are organised into semantic networks, and for comprehension, lexical items are arranged into formal (phonological/orthographic) networks. For advocates of this model, the L1 and L2 lexicons also function in the same way and share organisational structure.

In comparing L1 and L2 speech errors, Channell (1988) reached the conclusion that the nature of lexical errors produced by both groups was similar, implying that, at some level, the L1 and L2 lexicons resemble each other and are organised in a similar way, with words arranged phonologically and related by semantic links (Coady, 1995; De Groot, 1993; Kroll, 1993; Kroll *et al.*, 2002; Singleton, 1999: Chaps. 4 and 7).[4]

L1 and L2 lexicon relationships

The lexicon is usually defined as the mental store of the set of words or lexical items that a speaker of a language possesses and can recognise and use productively in communication (e.g. Cervero & Pichardo Castro, 2000: 189–193). It seems reasonable to believe that if a person speaks more than two languages, he or she will possess as many lexicons as languages. However, the situation is far from being clear, and discrepancies abound about the existence and the relationships between the lexicons.

There are a number of studies addressing the issues of lexical processing, lexical organisation and lexical access (see, e.g. De Bot & Schreuder, 1993; De Groot, 1993; Ecke, 2001; Hatzidaki & Pothos, 2008; Kroll, 1993; Kroll *et al.*, 2002; Li, 2009; Pérez Basanta, 1999; Singleton, 1999: Chaps. 4 and 7; Sunderman & Kroll, 2006; Wolter, 2001). Weinreich (1974: 9–10) discusses how two language systems relate to each other in the mind of the bilingual learner. According to his account, three conceptualizations can be discerned regarding the relationship between the L1 and L2 lexicons:

(1) coordinate, in which two separate form–meaning links coexist in the mind of the learner;
(2) compound, where bilinguals have a single concept associated with two different words;
(3) subordinative, in which the L1 word form mediates between the L2 concept and the L2 word form.

These are summarised in Figure 1.1. Weinreich (1953, 1974) believes that these different types of relationship between the L1 and L2 lexicons are not static but may depend on the learner's experience with the L2 and that different types of lexical organisation may coexist in the same mind. Subsequent research (De Groot, 1993; Kroll, 1993; Kroll *et al.*, 2002; Li *et al.*, 2008) has come to support this claim associating subordinative relations with low L2 proficiency and compound structure with higher L2 proficiency. Apart from the proficiency level, other factors that can influence the type of relationship established between the L1 and L2 lexicons are thought to be the formal or semantic similarity perceived between the L1 and L2 words; the learning environment, that is how the word has been acquired (Singleton, 1999: 189–190, 2000: 183); and the direction of the access (L1 → L2 or L2 → L1) (see Kroll, 1993).

It may be speculated that the process of L2 vocabulary acquisition by children is broadly similar to the adult process reported above.

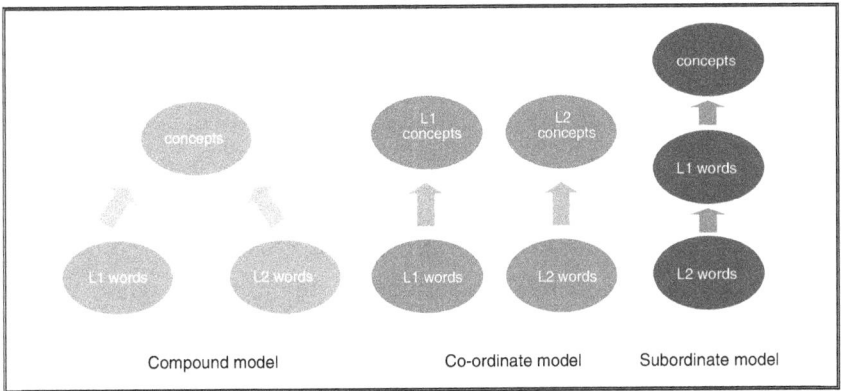

Figure 1.1 Illustration of the three models of L1 and L2 lexicon relationships

Nonetheless, there are clear differences between adults and young learners deriving from differences in cognitive development, linguistic and lexical development, instructional experience and input. Such differences are likely to impact both the route and the rate of vocabulary acquisition. Hence, we need to review in detail the process of L2 vocabulary acquisition in children. The following section is devoted to the analysis of language acquisition by young learners.

Vocabulary Acquisition by Young Learners

This section will explore the processes of lexical development in young learners. Finding out how children acquire vocabulary will be of help in identifying, classifying, analysing and finally explaining their lexical errors. Not only is it relevant for research on lexical errors to investigate L2 vocabulary learning, but, in addition, how the L1 lexical store is acquired offers interesting insights into the strategies underlying the appearance of lexical errors. So far, we have dealt with different explanations that try to account for the process of L2 vocabulary acquisition in general. However, when investigating and discussing the lexical error production of young English learners, it is essential to point out differential particularities of adult and children L2 vocabulary learning, as well as the specifications related to L1 and L2 vocabulary acquisition in young learners. Research on SLA by young learners is, alas, relatively scarce (but see Philp *et al.*, 2008), and especially rare are research studies on L2 vocabulary acquisition by children.

Bearing these considerations in mind, we provide a summary of the research that deals with how infants and children learn their mother tongue vocabulary. After briefly expounding the hypothesis of how lexical development proceeds in the L1, an account will be given of the process of L2 vocabulary acquisition by young learners.

Vocabulary acquisition in the mother tongue

Generally, L1 vocabulary acquisition begins during infancy. It is a usually acknowledged fact that words are the first strictly linguistic production of an infant.[5] Despite being the earliest linguistic system to appear, it is never attained completely. We spend our whole lives expanding our lexical store by adding new words to the list of already known words (lexicon), or by 'building up knowledge about words we already know partially' (Cameron, 2001: 74; Goldsmith, 1995; Harley & King, 1989; Laufer, 1991b). Ard and Gass (1987) support the pre-eminence of vocabulary in language acquisition with their proposal that lexical development is a cause, and not an effect, of syntactic development. This implies not only that lexis comes first before syntax but also that syntax is learned through lexis (Cameron, 2001: xiii; Robinson, 1995: 240; Singleton, 2000).

It is widely assumed that it is the need and the intention to communicate that triggers L1 lexical development and with it L1 vocabulary acquisition (Ninio, 1995; Sánchez Rodríguez, 2002; Singleton, 2000: 166). In this view, infants feel the necessity to interact with their parents, caretakers or peers, and as a consequence, they start incorporating new words in their lexicon quite rapidly. This phenomenon of rapid growth of the infant's lexicon has been termed 'vocabulary spurt[6] (see, e.g., Goldfield & Reznick, 1990). Research findings have revealed that this rapid lexical growth is characterised by the increase in nouns or object names in the lexicon (Goldfield & Reznick, 1990). This is called the 'naming explosion' and seems to originate in the urge of young learners to name the objects around them (see, e.g. Goldfield & Reznick, 1990; Poulin-Dubois, 1995; Singleton, 1999: Chap. 2; Vihman & Miller, 1988: 180).

Children learn words primarily for communicative purposes. They need the names to encode their daily life experiences and the objects and persons surrounding them. In order to do this, children have to learn the conventional linguistic signs that refer to those realities. These words naming the world around them constitute the semantic content and the linguistic form of their communicative utterances.

Clark (1993) terms the essential processes involved in learning words as 'isolating word forms in the input, creating potential meanings and mapping meanings onto forms' (Ellis & Heimbach, 1997: 249). Single words are used to perform a variety of communicative functions, so that with the same word the child orders, questions or expresses surprise. For example, the utterance *daddy?!* pronounced by a small child can mean the following:

(1) *Where is daddy?*, so that it poses a question;
(2) *Tell daddy to come*, so that it orders; or
(3) *Daddy is here!* indicating surprise in this case.

This early stage of lexical acquisition is characterised by two basic general phenomena: *over-* and *underextension* of meaning. The former refers to the process by which the child applies the same term to all surrounding realities that have something in common with the actual referent of the word – for example all men might be called *daddy*. The latter is the opposite phenomenon, so that children use a term to refer to the particular reality they know. For instance, *dog* will be used for the family dog exclusively; for other dogs, the child will use other terms (Anglin, 1985; Goldfield & Reznick, 1990; Sánchez Rodríguez, 2002). Gradually, the infant incorporates more and more words and is able to combine them into chains of lexical items: two-word strings, three-word strings and so on, until syntactic and morphological rules are acquired and complete sentences are formed (Crystal, 1980; Singleton, 1999: Chap. 2).

In sum, L1 vocabulary acquisition is a slow but recurrent process that stretches over the lifespan. It is a dual process that includes lexical and conceptual development, in the sense that new forms are learned in association with new meanings and concepts. This is a basic difference that distinguishes L1 and L2 vocabulary acquisition. L2 vocabulary acquisition implies the incorporation of new L2 forms which are (usually) attached to already existent concepts; that is the L2 learner learns new words to refer to old concepts, although new concepts lacking in the L1 also have to be acquired and existent concepts need to be modified (Singleton, 1999). Imagine, for example, the way in which English and Spanish structure the day. In Spanish, each 24-hour period is conventionally divided into three parts called *mañana* (from dawn until lunch), *tarde* (from lunch until dusk) and *noche* (from dusk until dawn, when it is dark). English on its part considers up to four different day-periods: *morning, afternoon, evening* and *night*. While the first and fourth roughly coincide, the Spanish L1 learner of English has to learn the new concepts imposed on by the new words: *afternoon*, and especially *evening*.

Vocabulary acquisition in the second language

Research on children's acquisition of L2 vocabulary is represented in the literature by two main directions: (1) the simultaneous acquisition of two languages and (2) L2 acquisition after L1 acquisition has already started. Studies on the simultaneous acquisition of two languages – that is studies on simultaneous bilingualism – make up the bulk of studies in early acquisition. These studies deal with individual bilinguals (cf. Burling, 1978; Celce-Murcia, 1978; Itoh & Hatch, 1978; Leopold, 1978) and with community bilingualism (cf. Hancin-Bhatt & Nagy, 1994; Pearson *et al.*, 1995; Umbel & Oller, 1994; Verhallen & Schoonen, 1993, 1998). The other trend in child L2 vocabulary acquisition research is represented by studies of the longitudinal type that follow the lexical development of individual subjects in their process of adding a second language (cf. Moya Guijarro, 2003; Niżegorodcew, 2006; Yoshida, 1978). What both these trends have in common is that they investigate L2 vocabulary acquisition in natural environments.

Unfortunately, studies addressing the acquisition of L2 vocabulary by young learners in a formal context through instruction are sparse (but see Cameron, 2001; Moon & Nikolov, 2000; Moya Guijarro, 2003). Therefore, we have to draw on work from beyond the language classroom from L1 vocabulary acquisition, vocabulary development of bilingual learners and L2 lexical acquisition in contexts where the target language is the language of interaction (Cameron, 2001: 2).

Word association, as well as translations tests, have been used to explore the process of child vocabulary acquisition in L1 as well as in L2 (see, e.g. Cameron, 1994, 2001; Erdmenger, 1985; Li *et al.*, 2009; Meara, 1992, 1996; Singleton, 1999). By tracing the word connections made by young learners, the researcher is able to determine how different lexical items are acquired in relation to other previously known words. In this context, probably, the most important discovery to emerge relates to the field of categorisation and has to do with *prototype effects* (Cameron, 1994: 30).

Several studies (e.g. Cameron, 1994; Erdmenger, 1985) have revealed that children learning L2 vocabulary rely on their L1 categorisations and lexical connections as the basis for further L2 vocabulary development. In short, children tend to build up the same associations among L2 words as they had built among L1 words (Erdmenger, 1985). This finding has important consequences for L2 vocabulary teaching to young learners. Considering that mother tongue categorisation is present through the L2 vocabulary acquisition process, children may not benefit from instruction in native L2 associations, since this may slow down or even hinder L2 lexical development. An alternative approach which seems to have much to recommend it is the exploitation of L1 associative paths in order for lexical growth in the L2 to be promoted (Cameron, 1994, 2001; Erdmenger, 1985).

In this perspective, introducing a foreign language in the first years of primary education should involve a systematic sequencing of L2 vocabulary items based on the already developed L1 lexicon (Cameron, 2001). Moya Guijarro (2003) found that young EFL learners first acquire concrete and abstract words that belong to their everyday immediate context and to their physical reality. Later on they will incorporate less familiar words accompanied by more complex morphological inflections. They will also easily understand the meaning of new words whose referents are concrete, such as *table, tree* and *dog*. In this way, it seems useful to introduce words whose meaning can be easily connected with an action, body language, flashcards, photographs, drawings and other objects. Words whose meaning is abstract and have no concrete referents, such as *love, justice* or *hope*, will be acquired later. This very much echoes what is found in L1 lexical development (see, e.g. Anglin, 1985).

Another important discovery in studies about L1 and early L2 vocabulary acquisition is the production of language chunks. In the same vein as children learning their L1, L2 learners produce chunks or whole expressions at a time before they can analyse them into individual words (cf. Robinson & Ellis, 2008). This prefabricated language refers to ready-made expressions that are used by learners as memorised chunks that remain unanalysed and function as one single lexical item. Research has shown (see, e.g. Ellis, 1997a) that prefabricated language constitutes one important stage in the development of L1 and L2. It is related to creative processes of SLA and socialisation skills. As Palmberg (1987) had already noticed (see also Ellis, 1997a; Wray, 2002), young learners show clear patterns of vocabulary development through which their lexical competence evolves; the use of formulaic language is one of these. We have observed this phenomenon in our data. We find the following examples in the written interlanguage of our informants:

- My *happy birthday* is in February.
- My *whats your name* is Ana.

L1 and L2 Vocabulary Acquisition: Similarities and Differences

The acquisition of a second language after the internalisation of the L1, even if this happens in the context of child L2 lexical development, lacks, patently, a prespeech phase. It seems, as already noted above, that the utterances produced by L2 learners 'are from the outset mostly comprised of combinations of meaningful elements' (Singleton, 2000: 180). Nevertheless, (child) L2 learners have a number of problems in common with L1 developers regarding the 'struggle to isolate meaningful units and connect them with aspects of reality, to internalise and replicate the formal characteristics of these units, and to puzzle out and store their precise meanings' (Singleton, 1999: 82).

The similarities of L1 and L2 lexical acquisition can be observed in all linguistic subsystems. Thus, L1 and L2 learners struggle to acquire new sounds, to distinguish which phonetic differences are phonemic and which are not, to learn the spelling of words and their derivations, and to acquire (partially) new concepts and new distributions of old concepts (Singleton, 2000: 181). Furthermore, L1 and L2 lexical development seem to proceed in similar ways, as attested by the fact that both display common phenomena such as lexical fluidity, change in the type of associations, from syntagmatic to paradigmatic, overextension, underextension and early acquisition of imageable words (Ellis & Beaton, 1993; Moya Guijarro, 2003; Singleton, 2000: 181).

These similarities, notwithstanding the fact that 'L2 lexical development does not happen in a vacuum', but 'against the background of lexical development in at least one other language' (Singleton, 1999: 41), point to some contrast between the processes. Basically, two main differences have been pointed out (see Singleton, 1999: 79–80): (1) the more advanced stage of cognitive and physical development of L2 lexical acquisition and (2) the existence of already lexicalised concepts.

The presence of a previous linguistic system differentiates L2 vocabulary acquisition from L1 vocabulary acquisition. When L2 words are learnt, they are mapped onto L1 concepts and enter already existing (L1) schemas (Ellis, 1997a: 133; Ellis & Heimbach, 1997; Jiang, 2000).

Frequently, the mapping of L2 words onto L1 schemas results in discrepancies and problems, because different languages organise the world in different ways (Cameron, 2001: 80; Robinson & Ellis, 2008). These asymmetries between the L2 lexical item and the L1 concept or schema onto which it is mapped give rise to lexical errors (see also Jiang, 2000). It is precisely the appearance of these particular kinds of lexical errors that distinguishes L1 from L2 vocabulary acquisition. As happens with adults, the child learner of L2 vocabulary also uses the strategy of L1 lexical transfer to cope with the lexical difficulties imposed by the new vocabulary (see, among others, Celaya & Torras, 2001; Erdmenger, 1985; Harley & King, 1989; Selinker *et al.*, 1975; Szulc-Kurpaska, 2000). Generally, although not necessarily, L1 lexical transfer leads to fossilised lexical errors in children's production. Fossilised errors change from learner to learner, but likely candidates for fossilisation are semantic confusions of the type *much* and *many*, in *There weren't much people at the party, or adjective and adverb confusion such as *badly* and *bad* or *funny* and *fun* in **It was a very fun* [in the sense of 'comic'] *movie*.

Furthermore, Niżegorodcew (2006) claims that L2 lexical development by very young children (aged 3–4) in strict FL learning settings is different from L1 vocabulary acquisition, because for the former the L2 is not their usual medium of communication (p. 174). They are aware that L2 and L1 belong to different domains of communication. Moreover, poverty of input in quantitative and qualitative terms also makes a difference between L1 and L2 development in formal contexts.

Conclusion

Vocabulary is seen as a major component in children's language development. In L1 and L2 acquisition, vocabulary represents the onset of language development and plays a central part in it. Therefore, finding out how vocabulary acquisition proceeds is of extreme relevance to the field of SLA. This chapter has reviewed the main theoretical trends that try to explain lexical development, stressing how children acquire L1 lexical abilities and then focusing on the L2 scenario.

It appears that child vocabulary acquisition proceeds from social interaction in a similar way for the L1 and the L2. Nevertheless, the emergent lexical and cognitive systems already present in L2 vocabulary learning influence the later process. L1 lexical transfer is the most important and visible effect of the L1 presence. Even so, L1 and L2 lexical development appear to proceed in fairly similar ways.

Apart from the aforementioned aspects, L2 vocabulary acquisition and written performance may be affected by other variables such as learner, task and context variables. Depending on the particular learning situation and the individual characteristics of the learner and of the task to be performed, the production of the young learner of the foreign language can vary. Age, sex, L1 background, L2 proficiency, intelligence, motivation, language attitudes, topic task and learning environment may be variables affecting the performance of the children. The following chapter will comment on some of the main learner and situation variables that may influence the production of young learners. Special attention will be given to the analysis and explanation of the variables considered in the design of this study.

Notes

1. Here the terms *second* and *foreign language* (FL) will be used indistinctly, except when said otherwise.
2. See Pavičić Takač (2008), Bogaards and Laufer (2004), Read (2000), Singleton (1999), Coady and Huckin (1997), Gleitman and Landau (1996), Sajavaara and Fairweather (1996), Huckin *et al.* (1995), Schmitt and McCarthy (1997), Clark (1993), Schreuder and Weltens (1993), Arnaud and Béjoint (1992), Gass and Schachter (1990) and McKeown and Curtis (1987), among others.
3. The claim that vocabulary acquisition proceeds as associations and that the lexicon is organised into associative networks explains the existence of misselections or confusion of formally similar lexical items (phonetically (orthographically) driven associations), and of semantic confusions (semantically driven associations). In a like manner, this type of lexical errors support the claim that the lexicon is organised into associative networks and points to both semantic and formal (phonological/orthographic) relationships between items in the lexicon.
4. For the contrary view, see Wolter (2001), who contends that although functionally similar, the L1 and L2 mental lexicons differ structurally. That is, they are organised differently, but serve the same purpose in identical manner, that is effective communication.
5. Actually, infants first produce sounds that they later combine to form words. These phonological manifestations (sounds, sound combinations (cooing), babbling, protowords) are considered prelinguistic phases of language acquisition (see, e.g. Berko Gleason, 1997; Singleton, 1999; Smith & Locke, 1988). Linguistic manifestations proper imply the consistent use of words with meaning in appropriate contexts (Goldfield & Reznick, 1990: 172; Singleton, 2000: 166).
6. It must be noted that not all infants undergo such a period of rapid lexical growth. Some young children experience a gradual growth of their vocabularies with the simultaneous incorporation of nouns and other classes of words evenly (see Goldfield & Reznick, 1990). Language input and environmental conditions may have something to do with the absence of a rapid lexical growth phase in these children.

Chapter 2
Variables Affecting Lexical Production

Second language acquisition and use are affected by a series of variables determined by the characteristics of the learner and the learning situation. Unlike L1 acquisition, the process of acquiring and using an L2 is influenced by external factors which combine to result in different levels of attainment. This chapter offers an overview of the variables that affect the production of vocabulary in L2 written tasks. The first section of the chapter presents a general summary of the individual and contextual variables in the literature on L2 learning. The subsequent sections look at the level of proficiency and vocabulary size. These two variables will be examined in light of their influence on the production of L2 vocabulary, and, more specifically, of lexical errors.

Overview of Variables Affecting the Production of Vocabulary

Traditionally, researchers and teachers have observed that in spite of the general inclination of L2 learners to process the TL in similar ways, they show great differences in their proficiency, performance and level of attainment. The variability in their Interlanguage (IL) can be traced back to the influence of some variables that can be either external or internal to the learner. Several authors (Cook, 1991/1996; Ellis, 1997b; Littlewood, 1984; Skehan, 1989) have researched the nature of these variables and the degree and type of their influence on L2 production.

Researchers have been able to identify a series of variables that account for the differences among learners' language by looking at the learners' L2 performance (IL studies) and the particulars of each learning environment. These variables can be grouped into two main categories: individual or learner differences and contextual differences (Cook, 1991/1996; Ellis, 1997b; Littlewood, 1984; Muñoz, 2001).

Individual or learner differences

The first set of variables includes those that are particular to the individual learner such as age, sex, mother tongue, intelligence, cognitive style, personality, motivation and language attitude. Because of the learner's internal nature of these variables, little can be done to modify them in a way that would favour learning. Nonetheless, motivation and language attitudes share a particular status, since they can be influenced by the teacher and modified in ways which benefit the learning process (Littlewood, 1984: 67). Depending on variables such as age, sex, mother tongue, intelligence, degree of extroversion and sociability of the learners, we can expect their vocabulary acquisition and use to develop in different ways. Littlewood (1984: 51) believes that 'individual differences simply reflect how quickly – or how far – specific learners progress along this common path', rather than causing learners to progress along different paths in the L2 acquisition process. For example, take two female learners, say one Spanish and another Chinese, of the same age but different L1 starting to learn EFL at the same time. One may expect them to go through the same stages during their L2 acquisition process, but most probably at different times, with the Spanish L1 learner progressing at a faster rate because of L1 and L2 similarity.

The relationship between these individual variables and L2 acquisition and use is still not clear, and research findings are contradictory in this respect. Regarding age, it is a generally acknowledged fact that the age at which the L2 acquisition process starts is a determining factor in L2 learning and performance. However, results are inconclusive as to stating whether younger learners learn faster and obtain better results than do older ones (García Mayo & García Lecumberri, 2003; Muñoz, 2001). Similarly, research findings point to inconclusive results regarding whether or not girls outperform their male peers in general language acquisition (Al-Othman, 2004; Lin & Wu, 2003; Wen & Johnson, 1997), and more specifically in vocabulary development (Agustín Llach & Terrazas Gallego, 2008; Grace, 2000; Jiménez Catalán & Ojeda Alba, 2007; Scarcella & Zimmermann, 1998). Other studies on the learner variable look at whether natives of a particular L1 can learn English or another L2 faster and more effectively than natives of another L1 (Altenberg & Granger, 2002; VanParys et al., 1997) and whether some vocabulary learning styles and strategies are more effective than others (Pavičić Takač, 2008). However, findings differ widely, and clearly, further studies are needed to explore these and other variables in FL vocabulary acquisition and how they interact.

Contextual differences

The second set of variables includes those that are external to the learner and relative to the learning context. These variables are the following:

- learning environment: natural acquisition and formal classroom L2 learning;
- teaching approach: audiolingual, communicative approach, focus on form approach and content language integrated learning (CLIL);
- topic of the task to be performed;
- nature of the linguistic input;
- the emotional climate of the learning situation;
- teacher variables: personality of the teacher, approach and strictness.

Generally, the teacher can modify these external environment variables in order to enhance learning. The rate of acquisition and the quality and quantity of the L2 production are, to a great extent, dependent on these external variables. For example, if we change the type of the task, we can expect qualitatively and quantitatively different linguistic output, or if we modify the type of instruction, differences in L2 acquisition outcomes can also be expected.

In general terms, L2 acquisition and use vary in the same way as individual and contextual differences vary. But the degree and the type of variation from learner to learner and from one learning environment to another are not clear by any means.

Proficiency Level

In formal L2 acquisition, the level of proficiency corresponds to the grade level, increasing amount of instruction and chronological age. To put it simply, as EFL learners at school get older, they go up grade and usually become more proficient (see Muñoz, 2003; Naves et al., 2005).

As learners grow older and their knowledge of the L2 progresses, they perform better than previously. This leads researchers to believe that different proficiency levels have varying impacts on L2 acquisition. Table 2.1 shows the findings of studies dealing with the impact of proficiency levels on L2 acquisition.

There are several areas of L2 acquisition where the level of proficiency of the learner has proved to play a significant role. Broadly, learners with

Table 2.1 Proficiency differences in general L2 learning

Study	Language aspect studied	Proficiency differences
Andreou et al. (2005)	General language performance	High > low
Brutten et al. (1986)	Phonological development	High > low
Hansen et al. (2002)	Word recovery and new word learning	High > low
Atai and Akbarian (2003)	Idiom learning	High > low
Yang (2001)	Knowledge of colour names	High > low
Mecartty (1998)	Reading skills deployment	High > low
Codina Espurz and Usó Juan (2000)	Reading comprehension	High > low
Victori and Tragant (2003)	Strategy use and complexity	High > low
Wen and Johnson (1997)	Strategy availability	High = low
Wen and Johnson (1997)	Adequate strategy use	High > low
Agustín Llach (2009a), Celaya (2006), González Álvarez (2004)	L1 influence	High > low
MacIntyre et al. (2002), Wen and Jonson (1997)	Motivation	High > low

High = high-proficiency learners; Low = low-proficiency learners

high levels in L2 show superiority in different L2 tasks (Andreou et al., 2005). For example, more proficient learners were found to perform better in productive and receptive phonology (Brutten et al., 1986), in word recovery and new word learning (Hansen et al., 2002), in idiom learning (Atai & Akbarian, 2003) and in production of more colour words (Yang, 2001).

Learners with different proficiency levels also show different abilities in their reading skills. While low-proficiency learners perform quite well with basic inferential skills, more proficient learners are better with more complex reading skills (Mecartty, 1998). In addition, proficiency level is a determining factor in reading comprehension. Codina Espurz and Usó Juan (2000) suggest the need for a threshold level in the L2 in order to be able to make use of previous knowledge to understand written texts.

The higher the proficiency of the learners, the better their reading comprehension skills will be.

As the proficiency level of the learners increases, so does their repertoire of vocabulary learning strategies (Victori & Tragant, 2003). Most proficient learners rely on strategies that require higher levels of elaboration, such as analysis or classification, rather than on social strategies. Wen and Johnson (1997) demonstrate that low achievers use the same strategies as higher-level peers, but fail to apply these strategies adequately. Moreover, as experience with the L2 increases, reliance on the mother tongue decreases, and so high achievers rarely resort to their L1 (Agustín Llach, 2009a; Celaya, 2006; González Álvarez, 2004; Wen & Johnson, 1997). Highly proficient learners also display higher levels of motivation when learning an L2 (MacIntyre *et al.*, 2002; Wen & Johnson, 1997). These studies are summarised in Table 2.1.

Proficiency level and writing skills

Research into writing skills has shown that the greater the linguistic competence of the learners, the better the quality of their L2 written production will be (Lasagabaster & Doiz, 2003; Manchón *et al.*, 2000; Wang, 2003). High-proficiency learners outdo less proficient learners in several measures of written production, such as lexical and syntactic complexities. Lasagabaster and Doiz (2003: 155) note that 'the more competent students produce longer, more complex and more accurate texts than those students with a lower degree of competence'. Similarly, De Haan and van Esch (2005), Cumming (2001), Grant and Ginther (2000) and Fernández (1997: 54–56) suggest that texts get longer and lexically richer as L2 experience increases. The writings of more proficient learners show a move from a rather 'spoken' type of discourse to a more 'written' type, with nominalisations, passive constructions, conjunctions, subordination and devices for lexical cohesion characterising their texts (Cumming, 2001; Grant & Ginther, 2000).

Problems at the lexical level are most recurrent and learners of all proficiency levels solve them recurring to their L1 knowledge. Nevertheless, while less proficient learners resort to the L1 to cover lexical gaps, more proficient learners use the L1 to seek inspiration and elaborate their ideas further (Berg, 1999; González Álvarez, 2004; Manchón *et al.*, 2000; Wang, 2003; Wang & Wen, 2002). Similarly, the time spent on planning the writing increases with proficiency at the expense of actual writing time (Manchón *et al.*, 2000). De Haan and van Esch (2005) found similar results for L1 and L2 writing, with learners devoting less time to planning when they write in their L2. Other writing processes, however, are independent of proficiency, as a recent study by Roca de Larios et al. (2007) suggests. They conclude that *basic components* of writing processes are independent of learners' L2 competence, whereas *developing components* of composing processes are clearly associated with the learners' mastery of the L2.

Manchón et al. (2007) observed that strategic composing processes are transferred from the L1 when writing L2. This transfer has proven to have a close relationship with L2 proficiency level. In fact, the transfer of writing skills acquired for L1 writing is not possible if the learners have not reached a certain L2 proficiency level. This is called the *threshold level* for skill transfer (Cabaleiro González, 2003). As a consequence, the higher the L2 proficiency of learners, the more likely that L1 writing skills are transferred, and thus learners' essays are judged to be better. Codina Espurz and Usó Juan (2000) observed a similar threshold level for transfer of reading skills.

Table 2.2 offers an overview of the studies on L2 proficiency and writing skills dealt with in this section.

Table 2.2 Proficiency differences in L2 writing

Study	Language aspect studied	Proficiency differences
Lasagabaster and Doiz (2003), Wang (2003), Manchón et al. (2000)	Quality of written production	High > low
Berg (1999)	Quality of written production	High = low
De Haan and van Esch (2005), Cumming (2001), Grant and Ginther (2000)	Text length and lexical richness	High > low
González Álvarez (2004), Wang (2003), Wang and Wen (2002), Manchón et al. (2000), Berg (1999)	Recourse to L1	High = inspiration and ideas elaboration Low = cover lexical gaps
Manchón et al. (2000)	Time on planning	High > low

High = high-proficiency learners; Low = low-proficiency learners

Proficiency level and error

Two main claims can be made regarding the relationship between error production and proficiency level: (1) as proficiency increases, error production decreases and (2) as proficiency increases, the type of errors produced changes.

The first claim is not always supported by empirical evidence. The perennial observation that even very advanced learners still continue to make errors when using the L2 has led researchers to conclude that there are some errors that *fossilise* in the IL of the learner and are never remedied (see, e.g. Olsen, 1999; Palapanidi, 2009; Selinker, 1972; Vázquez, 1991). Furthermore, studies of IL reveal high instances of errors in highly proficient learners, thus refuting the claim that advanced learners produce fewer errors than their lower-level counterparts (Ambroso, 2000; Lennon, 1991b, 1996; Vázquez, 1991). Although advanced learners still make a considerable number of errors, some research studies (Bardovi-Harlig & Bofman, 1989; Fernández, 1997; Grant & Ginther, 2000; Lennon, 1991b; Palapanidi, 2009) show a decrease in the production of errors, which points to a positive evolution of learners' IL with error production decreasing and text length increasing.

To explain the fact that advanced learners make a considerable number of errors, some authors allude to the more complex nature of the production of more proficient learners (Fernández, 1997; Lasagabaster & Doiz, 2003; Ruiz de Zarobe, 2002, 2005b). In other words, an infrequent production of errors in a certain structure does not imply a lack of difficulty in the structure or a high command of the said structure, but it rather points to the infrequent presence of that structure in learners' production (cf. avoidance). An increase in errors in the particular structure may hide an increase in the production of this structure, and consequently, it can be a positive sign of development rather than a negative one.

As for the second claim that as proficiency increases, the types of errors produced change, Lasagabaster and Doiz (2003) highlight that the types and frequency of errors observed in written texts depend on the degree of competence of the learner. Several studies have investigated the persistence of certain types of errors in advanced learners and have compared them to the errors made by lower-proficiency learners. Typically, low-proficiency learners are found to produce more L1-influenced errors, whereas high-proficiency learners tend to display more target-oriented errors (Ambroso, 2000; Fernández, 1997; Olsen, 1999; Palapanidi, 2009).

An analysis of research findings reveals conflicting results. In a study conducted by Taylor (1975), transfer errors appeared most frequently in intermediate learners' production. Palapanidi (2009), Naves et al. (2005), Lasagabaster and Doiz (2003), Wang (2003), Celaya and Torras (2001), Olsen (1999), Fernández (1997) and LoCoco (1975) report higher numbers of errors attributed to cross-linguistic influence in less-proficient learners, although they concede that the influence of the L1 is also present at more advanced levels. By contrast, Mukattash (1986) and Sanz (2000) determined that mother tongue influence was more pervasive in advanced learners and that those errors traceable to L1 influence were candidates for fossilisation.

A possible explanation for this contradictory result may be that low-competence learners mainly use L1 words without any modification to cover their lexical gaps (González Álvarez, 2004), while more advanced learners use their L1 knowledge basically for lexical creation purposes (see Ambroso, 2000; Celaya & Torras, 2001; Manchón et al., 2000). However, Roca de Larios et al. (2007) observed that the compensatory and creative processes of lexical search are not dependent on proficiency.

In line with this, Palapanidi (2009) observed that formal lexical errors are very frequent in less-proficient learners, but as they grow more proficient, these reduce, and instead, semantic lexical errors become the most frequent category of errors produced.

By coding errors of various types (González Álvarez, 2004; Grant & Ginther, 2000: 143), it is possible to examine how L2 writers develop as they become more proficient in the TL. This fact is based on the different types of errors found at different stages of L2 development. An example of this would be the number of word choice errors decreasing as the proficiency level increases (Grant & Ginther, 2000: 141; see also Hawkey & Barker, 2004).

Table 2.3 lists the studies that deal with proficiency differences in L2 error production.

Certainly, to increase the level of proficiency, the learner needs to be exposed to the L2. Different amounts of exposure and varying numbers of hours of instruction are liable to generate different levels of L2 competence. Consequently, it is reasonable to believe that participants who have been exposed to different numbers of hours of instruction will show different levels of proficiency, and thus will perform in a different way when using the L2. It is worth noting that to date there are few studies examining and comparing the production of lexical errors made by learners of different proficiency levels (but see Palapanidi, 2009).

Table 2.3 Proficiency differences in L2 error production

Study	Language aspect studied	Proficiency differences
Grant and Ginther (2000), Fernández (1997), Lennon (1991b)	Error production	High < low
Bardovi-Harlig and Bofman (1989)	Lexical error production	High < low
Ruiz de Zarobe (2002, 2005b), Lasagabaster and Doiz (2003), Fernández (1997)	Error production	High similar to low
Bardovi-Harlig and Bofman (1989)	Morphological and syntactical error production	High similar to low
Taylor (1975), LoCoco (1975), Fernández (1997), Olsen (1999), Palapanidi (2009)	L1 transfer errors	High < low
Mukattash (1986), Sanz (2000)	L1 transfer errors	High > low
Naves et al. (2005), Lasagabaster and Doiz (2003), Wang (2003), Celaya and Torras (2001)	L1 transfer lexical errors	High < low

High = high-proficiency learners; Low = low-proficiency learners

Hours of instruction and language development

The issue of amount of exposure to the target language is very much related to the issues of age and proficiency level. The type, length or intensity of the exposure determines, to a varying degree, learners' L2 performance. Furthermore, '[i]t may be worth emphasising that exposure time per se is widely recognised as a crucial factor in differentiating levels of language proficiency' (Singleton, 1989: 237). Consistently, the length of exposure to the target language, which roughly equates to the amount of instruction when L2 learning proceeds in classroom settings, is recognised, beyond all doubt, as a relevant factor in proficiency

Table 2.4 Amount of instruction differences in L2 learning

Study	Language aspect studied	Amount of instruction differences
Muñoz (2001)	Listening comprehension/ auditive perception	More > less
García Mayo (2003)	Grammaticality judgements/ metalinguistic awareness	More > less
Ruiz de Zarobe (2002, 2005b), Muñoz et al. (2005), Naves and Miralpeix (2002), Torras and Celaya, (2001)	Writing proficiency	More > less
Ruiz de Zarobe (2002, 2005), Lasagabaster and Doiz (2003), Torras and Celaya (2001)	Error types	More ≠ less
Naves et al. (2005)	Lexical error production	More < less
Terrazas Gallego and Agustín Llach (2009)	Receptive vocabulary size	More > less
Martínez Arbelaiz (2004)	Fluency	More > less but for advanced learners
Martínez Arbelaiz (2004)	Grammatical accuracy	More > less but for advanced learners
Martínez Arbelaiz (2004)	L1 use	More < less for low intermediates
Martínez Arbelaiz (2004)	Lexical use	More = less

More = learners with more hours of instruction; Less = learners with less hours of instruction

development and as an important predictor of second language learning success (Burstall et al., 1974: 123; Carroll, 1969: 63; Harley, 1986: 21; Muñoz, 2001: 15; Singleton, 1989: 237).

As shown in Table 2.4, empirical research supports this theory. The findings of recent investigations in Catalonia (see Muñoz, 2008; Muñoz et al., 2005) and the Basque Country (see García Mayo & García

Lecumberri, 2003) have positively attested the effect of the amount of exposure or hours of instruction on the development of L2 competence.

Thus, the amount of exposure time to input predicts quite precisely language learning outcomes, especially with regards to listening comprehension and oral perception (Muñoz, 2001: 31). Length of exposure also has positive effects on tests of grammaticality judgement and metalinguistic awareness, and so the higher the amount of input received by learners, the more native-like their performance in grammatical terms will be (García Mayo, 2003). Lexical and syntactical complexities increase in learners who have been largely exposed to the target language (Muñoz et al., 2005; Naves & Miralpeix, 2002; Ruiz de Zarobe, 2005a, 2005b; Torras & Celaya, 2001). This brings about a slight decrease in error production and differences in error types at different proficiency stages (Lasagabaster & Doiz, 2003; Ruiz de Zarobe, 2002, 2005b; Torras & Celaya, 2001). As the amount of instruction increases, the production of lexical errors from cross-linguistic transfer decreases (Naves et al., 2005). A longitudinal study conducted on development of receptive vocabulary size (Terrazas Gallego & Agustín Llach, 2009) shows that as the hours of learner instruction increase, receptive vocabulary knowledge also increases. Moreover, results point to a gradual and constant increase in the number of words incorporated into the lexicon. From the examination of studies that have explored receptive vocabulary size, it can be concluded that the more hours of exposure to the target language, the greater the vocabulary size will be (Laufer, 1998; López-Mezquita Molina, 2005; Milton & Meara, 1998; Pérez Basanta, 2005).

In a very recent study of an immersion situation within the Spanish context (Spanish as an L2), Martínez Arbelaiz (2004) noted progress in several areas after three months of instruction. More specifically, for the low intermediate learners, fluency and grammatical accuracy showed significant improvement. Furthermore, the use of their L1 was also reduced after the period of instruction. For the intermediate learners, fluency and grammatical accuracy also improved considerably. Nevertheless, advanced learners did not experience any significant progress in their written production in fluency, in grammatical accuracy or in lexical use after the period of instruction.

In light of this evidence, we can conclude that for intermediate learners, the amount of instruction will lead to significant improvements, but for more advanced learners, this progress will not be that remarkable, but slower and more difficult to perceive at first sight with nuances and details being learned rather than whole new structures.

Age and language development

A survey of the literature yields a remarkable diversity of stances that have attempted to account for age-related differences in L2 learning: (1) physiological (the CPH), (2) neurological (see Stowe & Sabourin, 2005), (3) cognitive (Cenoz, 2002; Moskovsky, 2001; Muñoz, 2000; Singleton, 2003), (4) affective (Kormos & Csizér, 2008; MacIntyre et al., 2002), (5) linguistic (competition between L1 and the target language; Singleton, 2003), (6) input factors (Cenoz, 2002; Marinova-Todd, 2003; Muñoz, 2000; Scarcella & Higa, 1982; Singleton, 1989, 2003) and (7) input negotiation factors (Marinova-Todd, 2003; Oliver, 2000; Scarcella & Higa, 1982). However, the precise nature of the role of age has not yet been stated clearly (Harley, 1986: xi, 22; Larsen-Freeman & Long, 1991; Singleton, 1989: Chap. 5).

These factors can be arranged in a nature–nurture continuum (Hakuta et al., 2005; Harley, 1986; Muñoz, 2001) to account for age-related differences in L2 acquisition. This continuum includes explanatory hypotheses that ranges from biologically based explanations, such as CPH, lateralisation of the brain, to environmentally based ones, such as classroom interaction, nature of input, input negotiation or time of exposure.

In general measures of English proficiency in instructed learning contexts, late starters perform better than early starters in different tests of oral and written skills (Cenoz, 2002, 2003; Muñoz, 2000, 2001, 2008; Muñoz et al., 2005). However, for low-proficiency learners (after 200 hours of instruction), results in listening comprehension are similar in younger and older learners (Muñoz, 2000, 2001). Considering this result, Muñoz (2000: 174) concludes that 'an early start particularly favours listening comprehension'. Cenoz's (2002) findings reveal that younger learners exceed older students only in pronunciation and present a similar performance in mechanics of writing and listening comprehension. Likewise, Harley (1986) also finds that students enrolled in English–French bilingual late immersion programs obtain similar levels of proficiency as children in early immersion programs.

The advantage for late starters can also be noted in different areas of L2 linguistic development in formal learning contexts, such as acquisition of subject pronouns in English (Ruiz de Zarobe, 2005a, 2005b), lexical production (Cenoz, 2002; Ruiz de Zarobe, 2005a), morphosyntactic development (Marinova-Todd, 2003), grammaticality judgements and metalinguistic awareness (García Mayo, 2003), sound-type (vowel/consonant) perception (García Lecumberri & Gallardo, 2003), pronunciation skills (García Lecumberri & Gallardo, 2003; Muñoz, 2003), auditory receptive skills (Muñoz, 2003), general writing skills (Lasagabaster & Doiz, 2003), communicative ability (Lasagabaster & Doiz, 2003), written fluency (Lasagabaster & Doiz, 2003; Naves & Miralpeix, 2002), lexical, syntactical and discoursal complexities in written texts (Lasagabaster & Doiz, 2003) and lexical complexity but not syntactical complexity (Naves & Miralpeix, 2002).

Contrary to most studies in age-related differences in classroom L2 learning, Yamada et al. (1980) reveal that younger learners exceed their older peers in vocabulary acquisition. Therefore, they conclude that the younger the better for vocabulary acquisition. In addition, they allude to the superior rote memory and the better ability to pronounce and imitate sounds of younger learners to support their claim.

Research into errors shows conflicting results. The studies by Ruiz de Zarobe (2002, 2005b), Lasagabaster and Doiz (2003) and Celaya and Torras (2001) found error production to be lower in older learners than in younger starters with the same amount of instruction. Nonetheless, Torras and Celaya (2001) observe that the age of onset has no impact on accuracy in written performance measured as the number of error-free sentences (p. 112). Celaya and Torras (2001) (see also Lasagabaster & Doiz, 2003) found that learners of different ages make different types of lexical errors as a result of L1 influence. Transfer from the L1, however, is found to be similar for learners of different ages in a study conducted by Cenoz (2001, 2003). García Lecumberri and Gallardo (2003) also stated that L1 influence and use are pervasive in all age groups and the main strategy for all learners independent of age (p. 128).

As regards the issue of strategy use, Victori and Tragant (2003) report that older learners use more strategies, and a wider variety of strategies and also more cognitively complex strategies, such as mnemonic techniques, analysis or classification. By contrast, younger learners prefer to employ social strategies and thus rely more on external resources for their learning, such as asking the teacher for help or learning with parents.

In light of these findings, one can conclude that L2 learners in formal school settings benefit from a late start. Researchers unanimously agree that if L2 exposure is not intensified, an early start in the L2 does not pay off in terms of rate of acquisition and eventual attainment (Muñoz, 2008). Table 2.5 summarises the results of the previously mentioned studies.

The age factor is closely related to the different degrees of cognitive and linguistic development of learners. In most studies examining L2 learning in school settings, age is usually operationalised as grade level.

Table 2.5 Age-related differences in L2 learning

Study	Language aspect studied	Age differences
Muñoz et al. (2005), Cenoz (2002, 2003), Muñoz (2000, 2001)	General proficiency	LS > ES
Harley (1986)	General proficiency	LS = ES
Muñoz (2000, 2001), Cenoz (2002)	Listening comprehension	LS = ES
Ruiz de Zarobe (2005a), Cenoz (2002)	Lexical production	LS > ES
Ruiz de Zarobe (2005a, 2005b)	Acquisition of subject pronouns	LS > ES
Marinova-Todd (2003)	Morphosyntactic development	LS > ES
García Mayo (2003)	Grammaticality judgements and metalinguistic awareness	LS > ES
García Lecumberri and Gallardo (2003)	Sound-type perception	LS > ES
García Lecumberri and Gallardo (2003), Muñoz (2003)	Pronunciation skills	LS > ES
Muñoz (2003)	Auditory receptive skills	LS > ES
Lasagabaster and Doiz (2003)	General writing skills	LS > ES
Lasagabaster and Doiz (2003)	Communicative ability	LS > ES
Lasagabaster and Doiz (2003), Naves and Miralpeix (2002)	Written fluency	LS > ES
Lasagabaster and Doiz (2003), Naves and Miralpeix (2002)	Lexical complexity	LS > ES
Lasagabaster and Doiz (2003)	Syntactical complexity	LS > ES

Table 2.5 (*Continued*)

Study	Language aspect studied	Age differences
Yamada et al. (1980)	Vocabulary acquisition	Older < younger
Ruiz de Zarobe (2002, 2005b), Lasagabaster and Doiz (2003), Celaya and Torras (2001)	Error production	Older < younger
Torras and Celaya (2001)	Error production	Older = younger
Lasagabaster and Doiz (2003), Celaya and Torras (2001)	Error type	Older ≠ younger
Cenoz (2003), García Lecumberri and Gallardo (2003)	L1 transfer	Older = younger
Victori and Tragant (2003)	Strategy use (frequency and range)	Older > younger
Victori and Tragant (2003)	Type of strategy	Older = mnemonics, analysis, classification Younger = social (external resources)

LS = late starters; ES = early starters

Proficiency level and hours of instruction are generally kept constant to investigate differences attributed exclusively to age.

Vocabulary Size

The other learner variable of relevance to this study is L2 vocabulary size. This section explains the notion of vocabulary size and reviews some of the studies that have dealt with this notion and explored its nature. It also addresses the issue of the role of vocabulary size in SLA, pinpointing the reasons why it is crucial in language development and performance. Finally, in order to provide a brief account of how vocabulary size is measured, we look at some of the tests which have been developed to determine how many words learners know.

A frequently made distinction in the field of lexical studies is between the depth and the breadth of vocabulary knowledge. The former refers to the quality of the lexical knowledge; in other words, how well learners know the words they know. The construct *depth of vocabulary knowledge* aims to answer questions such as what is involved in knowing a word, how the lexicon is organised, what aspects affect the quality of lexical knowledge or how to measure it (Laufer, 1991b, 1997a, 1997b; Laufer & Paribakht, 1998; Meara, 1983, 1992, 1996; Nation, 1990, 2001; Qian, 1999, 2002; Read, 1997, 2000, 2004; Schmitt, 1998, 2000; Schmitt & Meara, 1997; Waring, 2002; Wesche & Paribakht, 1996). The breadth of vocabulary knowledge alludes to the size of the lexical store of learners, that is how many words learners know.

Vocabulary is acquired in an incremental fashion (Schmitt, 2000; Schmitt *et al.*, 2001: 79; Terrazas Gallego & Agustín Llach, 2009); therefore, vocabulary size varies as experience with the language increases and new words are incorporated into the mental lexicon. Studies on vocabulary size also deal with the number of words that a native speaker knows. Depending on the definition of what should be considered a word and on the test format used to measure vocabulary knowledge, estimates vary drastically. For English L1, Meara (1996) observes that estimates range from 15,000 words (Seashore & Eckerson, 1940) to 200,000 (Hartman, 1946), and in a more recent estimate, Nation believes that native speakers know 20,000 word families (Nation, 1993a; Nation & Waring, 1997).

Foreign language learners never manage to accumulate such a considerable lexical store as native speakers; however, the size of their vocabularies depends very much on their proficiency level. Likewise, their proficiency level depends largely on their vocabulary size (Morris & Cobb, 2004; Qian, 1999, 2002). Establishing the number of words that a learner needs in order to be functional in the L2 is very important and has consequences in programs of lexical instruction.

Although the number of words needed would vary depending on the particular task to be performed, research has concentrated on investigating the vocabulary size required to read general texts (Laufer, 1992, 1997a). Based on frequency criteria, from most to least frequent, Laufer (1992, 1997a) determined that in order to be able to understand 95% of a text in English, the learner should know around 5000 words, which make up 3000 word families. In short, for every 20 words in a text, just one could be unknown (Cobb & Horst, 2004; Hazenberg & Hulstijn, 1996; Hirsh & Nation, 1992; Nation, 2001, 2006). These 5000 words with a 95% of text coverage belong to the most frequent words of the language. As a corollary, we may say that if a learner knows the 5000 most frequent words in English, he or she will be able to understand 95% of a text written in that language. Researchers have also addressed the issue of the number of words necessary to understand spoken discourse (Adolphs & Schmitt, 2004; Nation, 2001). Estimates suggest that at least 2000 word forms have to be mastered in order to understand around 90%–94% of spoken discourse in different contexts (Adolphs & Schmitt, 2004). Several studies have found important correlations between vocabulary size and reading comprehension (Terrazas Gallego & Agustín Llach, 2009; Cameron, 2002; Laufer, 1992, 1996; Qian, 2002). These studies point to vocabulary as a facilitating factor in reading comprehension. The more words a learner knows, the better his or her reading comprehension is. According to Laufer (1996: 55), 'it has been consistently demonstrated that reading comprehension is strongly related to vocabulary knowledge, more strongly than to the other components of reading'.

Vocabulary size is crucial not only to promote L2 reading (Anderson & Freebody, 1981; Coady *et al.*, 1995; Grabe & Stoller, 1997; Laufer, 1996, 1997a; Nation, 1993a; Qian, 1999, 2002), but also, as Meara (1996: 37) observed, '[a]ll other things being equal, learners with big vocabularies are more proficient in a wide range of language skills than learners with smaller vocabularies'. Written production, as we shall presently see, also benefits from a large vocabulary (Engber, 1995; Grant & Ginther, 2000; Jarvis *et al.*, 2003; Laufer & Nation, 1995; Lee, 2003; Leki & Carson, 1994; Meara & Bell, 2001; Meara & Fitzpatrick, 2000; Meara *et al.*, 2000; Miralpeix & Celaya, 2002; Morris & Cobb, 2004; Muncie, 2002; Nation, 2001). In short, a rich and varied vocabulary and 'an adequate knowledge of words is a prerequisite for effective language use' (Read, 2000: 83).

In contexts of strict SLA, where learners learn the L2 in the country where it is a native language, lack of lexical knowledge causes general academic failure. In other words, a large vocabulary knowledge leads to success not only in L2 learning but also in other school subjects (Hancin-Bhatt & Nagy, 1994; Harley, 1995; Verhallen & Schoonen, 1993, 1998).

When establishing estimates about vocabulary size, it is important to adequately select both the testing instrument and the word sample undergoing testing. Words to be tested have to be randomly selected. There exist two basic instruments for the selection of words to be included in tests: frequency lists and dictionaries (Curtis, 1987: 38–41; Nation & Waring, 1997; Read, 2000: 86–87; Schmitt, 2000: 165; Wesche & Paribakht, 1996: 15–16). There are several methods to test vocabulary size, and these take the form of (1) multiple choice tests, (2) checklists, (3) matching exercises (synonyms and antonyms) and (4) translation exercises (Meara, 1996; Nation, 2001: Chap. 10; Read, 2000: 87ff, 1997; Schmitt, 2000: 174ff; Wesche & Paribakht, 1996: 16ff).

Among the most frequently used vocabulary size testing instruments in the context of EFL are the following:

- *Vocabulary level tests* designed by Nation (1990: 261–272) (test of receptive vocabulary knowledge) and Laufer and Nation (1999) (test of productive vocabulary knowledge);
- *Lexical Frequency Profile*[1] by Laufer and Nation (1995);
- *Eurocentres Vocabulary Size Test* by Meara and Jones (1987);
- Lex_30,[2] a vocabulary size test based on associations designed by Meara and Fitzpatrick (2000);
- P_Lex, an association test designed by Meara and Bell (2001);
- The *DIALANG* test funded by the European Union (Lingua Programma, Consejo de Europa (Council of Europe), 2001: Appendix C), and designed and implemented by about 20 European Universities (scientific coordinator Charles Alderson). It includes vocabulary tests of the bilingual list type and checklist type for 14 European languages, among them Spanish and English. Nowadays it is hosted by Lancaster University.

All these vocabulary size tests are based on frequency lists, and they measure vocabulary size depending on the number of words from each frequency level the learner knows, from the 1000 most frequent word levels, the 2000 most frequent word levels and so on. According to this measurement criterion, learners' knowledge of rare words or less frequent words indicates a larger vocabulary size. Nation (2001) argues that testees' knowledge of less frequent words implies knowledge of more frequent words, but not the other way around.

Despite the frequent attempts at designing reliable testing instruments for the assessment of vocabulary size, some problems related to the selection of the sample and its size, to the generalisation of results or to the type of lexical knowledge the tests are actually measuring keep on cropping up (Meara, 1996; Wesche & Paribakht, 1996). It is crucial to examine the level of vocabulary knowledge of L2 learners, since previous research has identified vocabulary and vocabulary size as one of the most important contributing, and even predicting, factors of quality of composition and reading comprehension.

Conclusion

This chapter has presented research regarding two learner variables that influence the production of language learners: level of proficiency and vocabulary size. These variables are observed to be interrelated and co-occur in development and to contribute positively to language development and language performance. There is a positive correlation between the level of proficiency, the amount of instruction, the size of learner's vocabulary and the learner's performance in several language areas. Nonetheless, it must be noted that in the particular case of errors, the absolute frequency of production does not necessarily decrease as the level of proficiency, amount of instruction or vocabulary size increase, but the type of errors produced changes.

Notes

1. There also exists a French version of this test for French FL (see www.lextutor.ca).
2. There also exists a French version of this test (see www.lextutor.ca).

Chapter 3
Vocabulary and Writing

So far issues of general linguistic nature related to language, and more specifically to vocabulary acquisition and the variables that influence that process have been examined. The development, use and evaluation of writing skills will be addressed in this chapter. The relationship between writing, writing assessment and vocabulary knowledge will be the main focus of this chapter. Writing and writing assessment are determined to a certain extent by the level of learners' L2 lexical competence. And conversely, writing practice also exerts some influence on the development of vocabulary knowledge.

Developing Writing Skills

Writing skills are closely related to speaking and reading. Writing and speaking are both productive skills, but the latter relies on the aural mode, whereas the former materialises through the visual channel. There have been different theories trying to explain the relationship between writing and speech. The traditional belief, strongly supported by the structuralist and behaviourist schools, contended that oral language is the genuine manifestation of language and that writing is merely a rendering of the spoken language. This theoretical trend has more recently been discarded in favour of the view that defends the independence of writing and speaking as two different, but related modes of communicating (see, e.g. Harklau, 2002; Matsuda, 2003: 16; Weigle, 2002: 14). Thus, although drawing on the same linguistic sources, the two skills are carried out by different mental processes, are used in different social contexts and for different purposes. Since they are two distinct language abilities, speaking and writing deserve correspondingly different treatments in the process of language teaching and acquisition (Cassany, 1989: 40–44; Weigle, 2002: 14–16). As regards vocabulary, writing displays a wider variety of words and words of lower frequency than oral texts (Cassany, 1989: 39; Weigle, 2002: 16).

One of the most outstanding differences between the two productive skills is the context and manner in which learners acquire them. While oral language is acquired naturally and unconsciously in the first years of life, written language is developed in a conscious way, most often at school, and when oral skills are already at the learner's disposal (Cameron, 2003; Weigle, 2002: 14).

The process of learning how to write is closely linked to learning to read. The development of literacy is of relevance in language learning, especially in formal-school contexts. Although it may seem common sense that reading and writing are related, researchers have only started to explore the connection between both (Eisterhold, 1990: 89).

There are several theories that try to account for the reading-writing relationship (Cassany, 1989; Eisterhold, 1990; Grabe, 2003). The directional perspective suggests that reading and writing are acquired using the same mechanism or structure and that once this has been acquired for one modality, it can be transferred to the other modality. Transfer, however, proceeds only in one direction, that is either from reading to writing or from writing to reading. The determination of the direction of transfer is crucial for pedagogical concerns, since it will influence the decision of what skill to introduce first in language teaching (Eisterhold, 1990: 89). Although there is considerable evidence for both directional models, typically the relationship is discussed in terms of the impact of reading on the development of writing (Eisterhold, 1990: 89; Grabe, 2003: 243).

Reading is considered to be central to the process of developing writing skills, as well as a valuable source of content information and examples of real language. Reading contributes to writing in several ways by providing (1) the content for writing through source texts (Campbell, 1990; Grabe, 2003: 244; Hyland, 2003: 17; Vandrick, 2003; Weigle, 2002: 27-28); (2) real instances of language use (Hyland, 2003: 17; Vandrick, 2003); (3) rhetoric models of information organisation in the target language (Cassany, 1989: 63-80; Eisterhold, 1990: 88; Grabe, 2003: 246); and (4) skills and strategies for the acquisition of writing (Grabe, 2003: 247; Hyland, 2003: 17; Weigle, 2002: 27).[1]

It seems that (extensive) reading leads to vocabulary expansion, thus providing the means of expression to be used in writing (Grabe, 2003: 249). Krashen (2004) argues for extensive pleasure reading as the most effective way of acquiring vocabulary, especially if this reading is enhanced with vocabulary activities (see also Kweon & Kim, 2008; Lehmann, 2007; Min, 2008; Pigada & Schmitt, 2006; Webb, 2008). Many different authors have also set out to prove the effectiveness of reading tasks as compared to other vocabulary acquisition tasks, for example bilingual lists, sentence writing, matching exercises or enhanced reading. They have found that the latter can also be very effective, even more than extensive reading, but are measured over short periods of time

(Agustín Llach, 2009b; Barcroft, 2004; Cho & Krashen, 1994; Horst *et al.*, 1998; Laufer, 2003, 2006).

First and second language writing seem to reflect quite similar, but not wholly identical, processes. The different and varied situations in need of consideration for L1 and L2 development make it a difficult task to define what writing ability is and how writing skills are acquired.

Theories of writing

Models that account for the learning of L2 writing see it as being a product or a process, a social or a cognitive activity, or a focused-on-form or a focused-on-content activity. Views explaining the acquisition and development of L2 writing skills draw on L1 research, highlighting the main differences between L1 and L2 writings. These concepts of the nature of writing also reflect different pedagogical approaches implemented in L2 writing courses (Cumming, 2003: 74–75; Hyland, 2003: 2; Matsuda, 2003: 19).

The different concepts of writing can be grouped into three main dichotomies, which should not be understood as opposing, but as complementary and overlapping, each focusing on a particular aspect of writing[2] (Cumming, 2003: 74–75; Hyland, 2003; Johns, 1990; Matsuda, 2003; Silva, 1990; Weigle, 2002). Writing is then conceived as

- a product or a process,
- a cognitive or a social activity, and
- a content-oriented or a form-oriented activity.

The product–process distinction has probably been the most recursive in the literature and the one that has generated the most heated debate. The product approach to writing suggests that special attention should be paid to language structures, since the focus is the written texts of learners. Accuracy is crucial, and grammatical and lexical knowledge is indispensable and preconditional to writing. Writing involves making the right choices concerning syntactic patterns, morphological inflections, vocabulary and cohesive devices, and combining them all into coherent pieces of text (Hyland, 2003: 3; Matsuda, 2003: 19–20; Silva, 1990: 13). Consequently, grammatical and lexical errors are considered as signs of 'bad' writing and lack of writing skills on the part of the learner.

According to this view of writing as a product, practising writing and producing extensive quantities of writing is the way in which learners learn to write (Kroll, 2003: 115). The basic purpose of writing in the L2 classroom is to practise grammar and lexis and to reinforce oral habits.

Writing is not practised as an end in itself but as a service activity through which learners can solidify their knowledge of vocabulary and other grammatical structures (Hyland, 2003: 4; Silva, 1990: 13). Conversely, teachers can use writing exercises to evaluate students' progress in language acquisition (Chastain, 1988: 364). Therefore, the goal of writing is twofold: firstly, it practises the vocabulary and grammar of the lesson (see also Hyland, 2003; Weigle, 2002: 12), and secondly, it helps develop writing ability that serves communicative purposes.

More recent research trends in the field of writing skills see writing as a cognitive process consisting of several phases that interact with each other (Grabe, 2001; Hyland, 2003; Kroll, 2003; Matsuda, 2003: 21; Wang & Wen, 2002; Weigle, 2002: 22–35). The main proponents of this theory, Flower and Hayes (1981), point to planning, drafting, revising and editing as the main stages of the composing process. (For specific theories of L2 writing, see, e.g. Wang & Wen, 2002.) These stages are not in linear sequence but occur recursively, whenever deemed necessary (Hyland, 2003: 11). The objectives of the editing phase include not only linguistic correction but also the organisation of ideas and the introduction of new ones.

Learning to write for the process approach involves going through the stages of the composing process: planning and outlining the writing, generating ideas, writing several drafts, re-reading the text, revising, restructuring, editing and being able to call on any of these cognitive subprocesses whenever they are required. The process model conceives writing as a cognitive activity and also recognises that the main purpose of writing is to communicate and express meaning(s) (Silva, 1990: 15; Valero Garcés *et al.*, 2000; Zamel, 1983: 165). Writing is also seen as a social activity, and as such, composing processes must incorporate discourse and contextual factors of language use such as consideration of the content of the particular discipline or culture, the target audience, structural conventions or aims (Hyland, 2003: 18; Weigle, 2002: 20). Different genres need to be considered such as how to write a report, a news article, an academic paper or a verdict. English for Specific Purposes (ESP) and English for Academic Purposes (EAP) have their origin in this approach (Bruce, 2005; Silva & Matsuda, 2001; Zhu, 2004).

Theories of writing that focus on writing as a process, whether they emphasise its cognitive nature or its social nature, highlight the content orientation of the composing process. So the ideas expressed in he writing are at least as important as the accuracy of the discourse (Hyland, 2003: 16; Silva, 1990: 15–16). In contrast, other views of language are form-oriented, in the sense that they pay attention to sentence and paragraph building. From this perspective, writing is a matter of arranging words into sentences and these, in turn, into paragraphs according to rhetorical conventions (Hyland, 2003: 3; Silva, 1990: 14).

The focus on content approach emphasises the importance of source texts to help generate ideas, and thus contribute to the composing process. Therefore, reading is given a relevant role in developing writing skills (Hyland, 2003: 17). Apart from reading, research pinpoints the influence of L1 literacy skills on learning to write in the L2. For L2 contexts, the transfer of L2 reading skills and of L1 literacy skills to L2 writing depends on the degree of mastery of the target language. Most researchers agree that L1 and L2 writings differ to some extent, since their acquisition contexts are very different.

First language literacy and second language proficiency in second language writing

Two main issues deserve special attention when dealing with the acquisition of L2 writing skills: L1 literacy and L2 proficiency (Cabaleiro González, 2003; Eisterhold, 1990; Hyland, 2003; Krapels, 1990; Kubota, 1998; Wang, 2003; Weigle, 2002). Learning to write in the L2 seems to involve the same composing processes as L1 writing. However, there are some differences between both situations.

The first main obvious difference between L1 and L2 writers is that L2 writers already have at their disposal a fully, or in some cases only partially, developed linguistic system and L1 literacy abilities. While toddlers do not say and write their first word on the same day, L2 learners in the classroom do (Harklau, 2002: 334). Nevertheless, L2 learners' command of the L2 is underdeveloped (Eisterhold, 1990: 94), and there are many degrees of variability in L2 proficiency among learners. Individual differences in L2 learners regarding their L1 and other L2s, and their sex, age, motivation or personality influence their proficiency rate, which may account for the wide range of levels of achievement (Hyland, 2003: 33–34; Krapels, 1990: 45). Mother tongue literacy skills and L2 proficiency are crucial factors in L2 writing acquisition.

The fundamental process shaping L2 reading–writing interactions and the relationship between L1 and L2 literacy skills is the phenomenon of transfer (Eisterhold, 1990: 99; Grabe, 2003: 247; Kobayashi & Rinnert, 2002; Wang & Wen, 2002). However, the exact influence of L1 literacy skills on L2 writing is controversial. While researchers disagree as to what the effect of this transfer is, it is generally agreed that prior language and cultural experiences are factors in L2 writing acquisition

(Eisterhold, 1990; Grabe, 2001, 2003: 247; Hyland, 2003: 34; Krapels, 1990; Kroll, 1990; Kubota, 1998; Wang, 2003; Wang & Wen, 2002; Weigle, 2002: 35–39).

Several studies have pointed to the beneficial impact or positive transfer of L1 literacy abilities on L2 writing (Eisterhold, 1990; Freidlander, 1990; Krapels, 1990; Kubota, 1998; Manchón et al., 2000, 2007; Silva et al., 2003). When learning to write in the L2, learners benefit from the skills that they have acquired for reading and writing in their L1. Learners transfer composing skills and processes they apply in L1 writing to L2 writing. While L1 and L2 writing follow the same recursive process of planning, drafting, reviewing and editing (Cabaleiro González, 2003; Krapels, 1990; Kubota, 1998; Manchón et al., 2000; Matsuda, 2003; Weigle, 2002: 35–37; see also De Haan & van Esch, 2005: 102), L2 writers display fewer idea units, and they also spend less time in planning and editing, focusing more on linguistic errors (grammar structures and lexical choices) (Cabaleiro González, 2003: 36; Krapels, 1990; Manchón et al., 2000; Woodall, 2002). This is especially true for low-proficiency learners, because the more proficient the learners are, the more their L2 writing resembles native writing (see Manchón et al., 2000; Wang, 2003; Wang & Wen, 2002). Furthermore, L2 writing shows more variability than L1 writing, which is much more homogeneous. The degree to which L2 learners transfer their L1 literacy abilities varies (Freidlander, 1990; Wang & Wen, 2002; Woodall, 2002).

Apart from drawing on L1 literacy skills to implement L2 writing, learners also use their L1 when composing in the L2 to make up for lexical gaps with L1 vocabulary or to generate new ideas by retrieving L1 content information (Berg, 1999; Freidlander, 1990; Krapels, 1990; Manchón et al., 2000; Roca de Larios et al., 2007; Wang, 2003; Wang & Wen, 2002; Woodall, 2002: 11). Negative transfer of L1 writing conventions has also been the subject of research studies. Research findings show that L1 interference results in poorer L2 writing, because learners directly transfer the rhetorical conventions of their L1, which are often different from those of the L2 (for a review of these, see Hyland, 2003: 34; Kubota, 1998).

The transfer of L2 reading skills to L2 writing can be hampered by limited knowledge of the L2 and more specifically by limited knowledge of target vocabulary (Clark & Ishida, 2005; Pérez Basanta, 2005; Qian, 2002, and many others). As Weigle (2002: 36) notes, insufficient language proficiency may impede source text interpretation, text generation may also be disrupted by grammar and lexical problems and finally, lack of cultural and social knowledge or of audience expectation may result in faulty rhetoric patterns. A limited L2 knowledge results in shorter texts, which contain fewer ideas, are less cohesive and display more errors, as several research studies have indicated (see, e.g., Hyland, 2003: 34; Wang, 2003).

Transfer from L1 is not the whole story for L2 writing development. Grabe (2003: 248) and others ask whether L2 writing is more dependent on L1 literacy skills or on L2 proficiency. Empirical evidence supports both. The belief that if a learner is a poor writer in his or her L1, he or she will also be a poor writer in the L2, and if he or she is a good writer in the L1, he or she will be a good writer in the L2, regardless of his or her L2 proficiency, summarises opinions that highlight the role of L1 literacy (Freidlander, 1990; Krapels, 1990; Medgyes & Ryan, 1996). More recent research points to L2 proficiency as the most important factor in acquiring L2 writing expertise (Grabe, 2003: 248; Kubota, 1998; Wang, 2003). Roca de Larios et al. (2007) note that some formulation processes are independent of proficiency, whereas others develop with L2 proficiency.

As L2 proficiency increases, L2 writings appear to resemble more and more native productions in their use of syntactic patterns, rhetorical conventions and lexical choices (Cumming, 2001; Grant & Ginther, 2000; Manchón et al., 2000; Wang, 2003; Wang & Wen, 2002). The texts of proficient writers display a wider range and specificity of vocabulary (Cumming, 2001: 4; Hawkey & Barker, 2004). In short, writing contributes to vocabulary development, and vocabulary use in writing enhances the quality of the written text (see "Assessing Writing" section), since 'vocabulary knowledge has been shown to co-develop and co-vary significantly with literacy experiences' (Harklau, 2002: 338). Furthermore, Díaz Galán and Fumero Pérez (2004) confirm the importance of vocabulary in teaching writing, as providing students with the appropriate vocabulary facilitates text organisation and general text production (see also Bacha, 2001; De Haan & van Esch, 2005; Wang, 2003).

Overall, research on L2 writing has concentrated on advanced learners. As Krapels (1990: 49) notes, studies of L2 writing by L2 beginner learners and by young L2 learners are scarce. The following section reviews some of the scant literature that deals with the development of children's L2 writing skills.

Writing and young learners

Foreign language teaching to children takes a predominantly oral approach. Primary school language learning proceeds through speaking and listening. Reading and especially writing are relegated to higher levels of education, usually secondary education and even tertiary education. It is likely that all around the world primary school teachers do, in fact, devote some time to teaching L2 literacy skills to their young pupils. As Roca de Larios *et al.* (2007) note, primary and secondary school curricula highlight the necessity of teaching L2 writing. However, actual practices reveal that by the end of secondary education most learners are unable to produce texts in the L2 and their only experience in L2 writing is confined mostly to the completion of grammar and vocabulary exercises.

While some authors (Cameron, 2001; Harklau, 2002; Matera & Gerber, 2008; Torras & Celaya, 2001) explore how children learn to read and write in the L2, most studies dealing with child language acquisition focus on L2 oral communication (see Philp *et al.*, 2008). Despite some research in the area, little is really known about how L2 literacy skills are acquired. Teaching young learners to write and read in the L2 is a particularly complicated task. Children face the challenge of having to learn to write in an L2 with a still developing L1 literacy system and an underdeveloped L2 oral system (Weigle, 2002: 6). In this sense, Matera and Gerber (2008: 29) claim that L2 literacy should follow when learners already know extensive L2 vocabulary, are confident about their new language, and have developed some literacy in their own L1.

Torras and Celaya (2001) examined the writing development of two groups of young Spanish learners who were aged between 8 and 11 at the beginning of the experiment and were between 12 and 14 by the end of it. They observed that learners progressed in the fluency, accuracy and lexical and grammatical complexities of their writings, but fluency developed faster. So, by the end of the study, learners were writing longer compositions. Learners under 12 had used a limited range of syntactic structures in their compositions, which allowed them to be very accurate and fluent. When learners reached 12, a grammatical growth was observed. This growth is attributed to (1) higher cognitive and conceptual development, (2) better linguistic competence in the L2, (3) more developed L1 literacy skills and (4) the explicit grammar instruction received by learners at school up to the age of 11–12.

Overall, two main approaches can be combined in order to contribute to the successful development of literacy skills in the primary school L2 classroom. On the one hand, reliance on L1 skill transfer can have very positive effects on learning how to read and write in the L2. On the other hand, highlighting the communicative nature of reading and writing in the sense that they serve to express and share meanings may be essential in triggering literacy development.

By the time young learners start to read and write in the L2, their literacy skills are only partially developed in the L1. This allows for limited transfer (Singleton, 1999: 48–50). Like other types of knowledge, skills and strategies, literacy skills can also be transferred from the L1 to the L2 (Kobayashi & Rinnert, 2002; Manchón *et al.*, 2007). Researchers observed that the same strategies are used in L1 and L2 composing processes, but these are less frequent in L2 writing. The cognitive load imposed by having to write in a language not yet completely mastered is responsible for differences in the amount of strategy use in L1 and L2 writings (Cabaleiro González, 2003: 36).

Notwithstanding the facilitative nature of L1 skill transfer in the development of L2 literacy, one cannot forget that L1 literacy is only partly developed in young learners, and so only some aspects of that literacy knowledge are available for transfer. Torras and Celaya (2001) claim that young EFL beginner learners cannot benefit from L1 composing skills, since they have not fully developed literacy strategies in their L1. Other aspects of L2 writing will have to be acquired altogether by the young learners themselves, for example those referring to the organisation of ideas into paragraphs and of paragraphs into longer texts (Cameron, 2001: 136–137). Considering that the linguistic resources of young learners in the L2 are very limited, L2 oral skills are a relevant factor in literacy learning. Teaching literacy skills to young learners involves promoting L1 reading and writing, as well as L2 learning through oral skills. Matera and Gerber (2008: 34) claimed that 'explicitly emphasizing awareness of written language produced significant improvement in children's writing outcomes'. In other words, writing practice and instruction in other literacy activities promotes writing and improves the quality of the written production as well.

Developing writing skills in EFL

Learning to read and, especially, write in EFL imposes a particular challenge for users of other native languages, even if these share the same writing system. For Spanish native speakers, two main problematic areas can be identified. The first main difficulty is that grapho-phonemic relations in English are characterised as being quite irregular, which makes 'English a complicated alphabetic written language' (Cameron, 2001: 138), where sound and grapheme do not usually coincide. Nevertheless, Spanish writing offers a faithful rendering of sounds. This large gap between what is pronounced and how it is represented in writing makes the task of writing in English quite an arduous one. Mute letters, such as in *through, climb* or *talk,* different pronunciations of the same letters, such as the different pronunciations of the letter 'a' in *hand, cat* and *walk,* or several different letters to represent the same sound, such as the caret sound /ʌ/ in *but, son* and *none,* are some examples that illustrate these difficulties. Mastering spelling conventions in English involves learning a great deal of irregularities, spelling rules and quite a number of isolated examples.

The second main difficulty that young Spanish learners have to face when learning to write in English is the distribution of letters in the syllable. Double consonants, consonant clusters, repeated vowels or vowels arranged in arrays, for example *beautiful, doors* and *intelligent,* are very challenging for L1 Spanish learners, which generates many writing problems.

Further challenges that the learners face when writing in EFL are related to rhetoric conventions. Contrastive rhetoric studies and compares discourse patterns across languages in order to find differences and then isolate possible sources of difficulty (Connor, 2003). Different cultures and languages have different preferences regarding how to organise their ideas into coherent discourse, and this may cause problems and result in poor L2 writing (Connor, 2003: 218; Weigle, 2002: 20–22).

In the particular case of English, research has shown that text structure is linear, whereby the main idea is introduced and then developed along the rest of the essay, which is also known as deductive argument (Connor, 2003: 226; Hyland, 2003: 45–47; Kubota, 1998; Weigle, 2002: 20–22). English prose is defined as being writer-responsible, which means that the responsibility of creating meaningful and effective communication falls exclusively on the writer, while the reader plays a more passive role by being fed with meaning (Connor, 2003: 226; Johns, 1990). A writer-responsible text includes signposts concerning how the discourse is structured: what comes first, and last; numerous cohesive devices; clear, direct and straightforward statements; and reader-friendly explanations (Hyland, 2003: 48; Johns, 1990: 27; Weigle, 2002: 21). Moreover, L1 English writing places emphasis on critical thinking, originality, creativity, logic, insight and individual voice (Grabe, 2001: 44). Neff (2006) maintains that studies dealing with Spanish rhetorical conventions are scarce. Nevertheless, she found that Spanish EFL learners transfer L1 rhetorical conventions as regards the construction of authorial voice through the use of *we.* Neff (2006) suggests the use of topic introducers, such as *Es preciso admitir que* ... ('It is necessary to admit that ...'), *Es conveniente apuntar que* ... ('It is convenient to point out that ...') and *Es necesario señalar que* ... ('It is necessary to indicate that ...') (p. 66), as another feature present in Spanish writing. In their comparison of Spanish and English, López Guix and Wilkinson (2001) found that English favours parataxis while Spanish favours hypotaxis.

Writing skills and vocabulary

The interactions between vocabulary and writing skills are twofold. On the one hand, writing practice contributes to the development of vocabulary. On the other hand, vocabulary knowledge is central for the writing activity, and moreover, vocabulary is considered a criterion for assessing writing.

By writing, learners practise language, syntactic structures, morphology and, especially, vocabulary. Vocabulary has been observed to benefit from writing practice, and, conversely, as a result of a writing course lexical competence improves considerably (Cameron, 2001; Harklau, 2002; Katznelson et al., 2001; cf. also Lee & Muncie, 2006). L2 learners are reported to acquire much of their lexical competence via the written language (see Urquhart & Weir, 1998; Nippold, 1998; and Fitzgerald, 1995, in Harklau, 2002: 338–339).

Further evidence for the role of writing practice in the development of lexical competence is provided by Muncie (2002), who found that vocabulary development correlates highly with writing practice. In his experiment with Japanese university students, he found that process-writing helped students enlarge their vocabularies, and from the data analysed he concluded that if explicit concentration on vocabulary follows from the prewriting phase, then even greater vocabulary development was attested.

Similarly, a further study by Lee (2003) also found that writing tasks maximise vocabulary learning opportunities and help learners develop L2 vocabulary by retaining new learned words, and especially by activating receptive vocabulary, and using already known words. These research findings are indicative of the positive effect that writing has on vocabulary development and point to the benefits of using written texts in L2 classrooms as instruments to practise and develop vocabulary skills (Bruton, 2007; Hulstijn & Laufer, 2001; Raimes, 1985: 248; San Mateo Valdehíta, 2003/2004).

Teachers, researchers and learners all acknowledge the importance of lexical knowledge in the development of writing. In research conducted by Polio and Glew (1996), students mentioned the importance of knowing the appropriate vocabulary to write an essay and commented on the difficulties they ran into when writing about a topic for which they lacked adequate and sufficient vocabulary (pp. 43–44). In an examination of learners' views concerning their EAP courses, Leki and Carson (1994) found that learners ranked vocabulary as the most important factor in academic writing and claimed that vocabulary expansion was the key element needed to improve their writing performance. Tercanlioglu's (2004: 152) subjects also considered vocabulary as the most crucial aspect in writing. Recently, Matera and Gerber (2008) discovered that young learners with higher L2 vocabulary produced significantly better writings than did their peers with poorer vocabularies. Moreover, learners with larger vocabularies responded better to writing instruction activities.

In summary, as revealed by students' perceptions and research studies, vocabulary knowledge is a factor that contributes to determining writing ability. However, vocabulary is not the only factor that contributes to writing quality as other aspects also come into consideration when assessing writing.

Assessing Writing

Writing ability is considered to be an indicator of language proficiency, especially in academic contexts. Placement tests as well as entrance and exit examinations of many universities all over the world consist of writing tests, either exclusively or as part of a larger battery of tests (Hamp-Lyons, 2001, 2003; Hyland, 2003; Weigle, 2002). Similarly, in institutional language tests (Test of English as a Foreign Language [TOEFL] and Cambridge Exams for English as a foreign language, or the *Deutsche Sprachdiplom* for German FL, Diploma de Español como Lengua Extranjera for Spanish FL or Diplôme d'études en langue française/Diplôme approfondi de langue française for French FL), writing skill accounts for a considerable part of the final score. Because of this, assessing writing competency becomes an important task, which must be carried out with accuracy and fairness.

Reliability and validity issues are a prominent concern of research in the field of writing assessment (Bacha, 2001; Cherry & Meyer, 1993; Crusan, 2002; Hamp-Lyons, 1990, 2003; Hyland, 2003: 215–220; Janopoulos, 1993; Penny *et al.*, 2000; Polio, 2001; Smith, 1993; White, 1993). Firstly, reliability refers to the consistency with which a test measures what it is supposed to measure. A test will be said to be highly reliable if a rater obtains similar results at two or more different measuring times (intrarater reliability), if two or more raters obtain similar results using the same assessing instrument (interrater reliability) or if a subject displays similar performance on different writing tasks (instrument reliability) (Cherry & Meyer, 1993: 114–118).

Secondly, a test is considered to be valid if it actually tests what it claims to be testing (see Hamp-Lyons, 1990, 1992, 2003).[3] In order to search for validity, the particular writing test is examined using other testing instruments known to measure the same construct (Hamp-Lyons, 2003: 165). Reliability and validity are related issues. Cherry and Meyer (1993: 115) note that reliability is a necessary but insufficient condition for validity. Attempts at obtaining highly reliable and valid measures have led to varied assessment procedures of writing competency regarding (1) measuring instruments, (2) scoring procedures and (3) scoring criteria. The following sections explore these aspects in detail.

Assessing instruments of writing ability

Writing ability is evaluated using a variety of testing formats. The three main approaches to assessing writing are multiple-choice testing, timed impromptu writing tests and portfolio assessment. Figure 3.1 shows a summary of the three testing formats in diagrammatic form, and Table 3.1 lists the main features of these three methods of writing assessment.

The multiple-choice test, often referred to as an 'indirect' test of writing (Crusan, 2002; Hamp-Lyons, 2001, 2003; Hyland, 2003; Weigle, 2002; Williamson, 1993), claims to assess writing through indirect measures of grammar and vocabulary proficiency. It produces judgements of writing ability, by inference, from the grammatical and lexical competence of the learners. Because of its multiple-choice format, indirect testing provides an objective measurement of writing ability. Although the design is quite time-consuming, it is easy and quick to administer and mark, with raters requiring little or no training (Hyland, 2003: 217). However, indirect testing lacks validity, since it evaluates the writing indirectly through other linguistic measures. Of all the advantages of multiple-choice

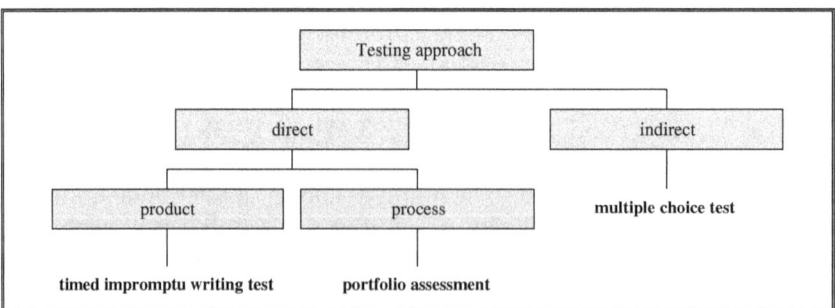

Figure 3.1 Writing testing methods

Table 3.1 Main features of writing testing methods

Multiple-choice test	Timed impromptu writing test	Portfolio assessment
Objective	Subjective	Subjective
Easy to administer	Easy to administer	Time-consuming
Easy to mark	Requires rater training	Requires rater training
High statistical reliability	Lower reliability	Lower reliability
Low validity	High validity	Highest validity

writing testing, its high statistical reliability[4] stands out (Hyland, 2003: 217). In fact, objective indirect testing arose as a response to fulfill standardisation and reliability requirements for entrance and placement examinations in US universities. It replaced the former so-called 'direct testing' approach (Camp, 1993; Hamp-Lyons, 2001: 118; Hyland, 2003: 216; Williamson, 1993).

Two main approaches to direct testing can be distinguished: timed essay tests and portfolio assessment. Direct measures of writing competency are based on the production of written texts – they assess actual writing (Weigle, 2002: 46). Any writing test that involves composition is considered to have high validity, since writing competence is measured directly through writing performance. Despite its high validity and integration of all elements of writing, direct testing displays lower reliability values than indirect assessment. Raters do not always coincide in the scores that they give to the writings, in spite of their previous training (Hyland, 2003: 217). This fact notwithstanding, Jacobs *et al.* (1981: 3) contend that direct assessment can reach high levels of reliability if carried out adequately.[5]

The approach to writing that predominates in writing courses as well as in writing theory is the writing-as-a-process approach. However, in writing assessment, product assessment prevails over process-oriented assessment (Cho, 2003: 166; White, 1993: 91). By far, the most used method of writing testing is the essay test. Nevertheless, recent practices in writing assessment have brought to light a new trend: the portfolio assessment (*Council of Europe,* 2001 [CEFR]; Hamp-Lyons, 2001; Hirvela & Sweetland, 2005; Hyland, 2003; Weigle, 2002).

The portfolio assessment reflects an idea of writing as a recursive process consisting of planning, drafting, revising and editing stages. In short, it emphasises the notion of writing as a process, 'writing as it is taught and practiced in the classroom' (Weigle, 2002: 197; see also Halden-Sullivan, 1996). Many authors believe that assessing writing as a process rather than as a product can be a more effective and fair way of judging writing ability (Cho, 2003; Halden-Sullivan, 1996).

A portfolio is a collection of students' texts that shows the progress from first drafts early in the course to final versions (Hirvela & Sweetland, 2005; Hyland, 2003: 233; Weigle, 2002: Chap. 9). By analysing the multiple writing samples of learners, and the changes made from one draft to the next, the teacher can see how their writing skill develops over the course (Halden-Sullivan, 1996; Weigle, 2002: 217). Portfolio assessment seems to share with essay tests the judgements of writing quality that serve to measure writing ability, such as accuracy, vocabulary richness or error-free units (Hyland, 2003: 238; Weigle, 2002: 217–227).

The timed impromptu writing test, characteristic of the direct approach, regards writing as a product, and consequently assesses a single text. Performed under time constraints and initiated by a previous reading or a writing prompt, the essay test is the most common writing assessment instrument even in the present days of the process approach (Hyland, 2003; Weigle, 2002; White, 1993: 91).

The essay test is easy to administer, although its evaluation and scoring is much more problematic. The necessity to enhance test reliability has brought about a number of different scoring procedures. The next section reviews the main assessment methods in the literature within the direct testing approach.

Scoring procedures of direct assessment of writing quality

Judgements of quality are approached from a number of different perspectives. Researchers, in their attempts to obtain highly reliable testing instruments, have devised a set of evaluation methods with claimed testing consistency. The most relevant of these assessment methods are holistic scoring, analytic scoring, scoring based on primary traits and scoring based on multiple traits (Argüelles Álvarez, 2004; Hamp-Lyons, 2001, 2003; Hyland, 2003; Weigle, 2002). The four rating scales differ on two grounds: (1) whether they give a single score or a multiple score for essay quality and (2) whether they are general instruments or specifically designed for particular tasks. Table 3.2, adapted from Weigle (2002: 109), summarises the four types of rating scales.

Holistic scoring has generated much research in terms of its reliability (see, e.g. the collection of studies in Williamson & Hout, 1993; see also

Table 3.2 Types of rating scales (adapted from Weigle, 2002: 109)

	Specific to a particular task	*Generalisable to a class of writing tasks*
Single score	Primary trait	Holistic scoring
Multiple score	Multiple trait	Analytic scoring

Penny et al., 2000). Assessing writing ability with holistic scoring implies giving an overall impression of the text and assigning a single global judgement to the writing. Judgements of writing competency are made against the background of a rating scale or scoring rubric that outlines the main scoring criteria, that is criteria of what makes a good piece of writing (Hyland, 2003: 227; Weigle, 2002: 112-114). Furthermore, raters also have benchmark texts at their disposal that represent the model text for each level (Smith, 1993: 148-149).

Communicative effectiveness can be said to lie at the heart of quality judgements, and so the writing ability of learners will be assessed according to whether their writings get their meaning across. Assessments of writing competency should be based on the author's ability to communicate (Cumming et al., 2005; Engber, 1995; Janopoulus, 1993: 320). Janopoulus (1993: 318) put forward that holistic scoring of L2 writing proficiency possesses construct validity when the construct being measured is communicative competence.

In order to perform holistic scorings, raters are trained in the scoring criteria and they are told the characteristics of good writing. This training is aimed at enhancing interrater reliability and, with that, instrument reliability. Apart from the training, which is a time-consuming activity, the implementation of a holistic rating is quite fast because it requires only a single reading from the raters (Hyland, 2003: 227; Weigle, 2002: 112-114). Additional advantages of the holistic method are its focus on the strengths of the writing, its capacity to emphasise different aspects of the text and thus provide important information about these concrete aspects (Hyland, 2003: 227; Weigle, 2002: 112-114; White, 1993). Similar to White (e.g. 1993), Weigle (2002: 114) supports the high validity of holistic scoring over other types of writing assessment forms, such as analytic scoring. The way holistic scoring requires raters to read and assess the text as a whole resembles the way readers approach writing in reality.

Weigle (2002: 114) lists a set of drawbacks of holistic scoring which allude mainly to the fact that it provides a single score (also Hyland,

2003: 227). Especially in L2 contexts, the single score tells us little about what aspects are predominantly responsible for the real writing ability of learners, be it good rhetorical organisation skills, accurate use of syntactic structures, appropriate lexical choices or adequate content development. The single holistic score is also difficult to interpret in terms of what each particular rater is emphasising in giving the score. In short, the score of a holistic rating is not transparent nor informative (Bacha, 2001).

There are numerous examples of holistic rating scales (Weigle, 2002: 112; Williamson, 1993: 2). Among the most cited examples is the scoring rubric used in the TOEFL writing test, the scale formerly known as Test of Written English (TWE), and the Michigan English Language Assessment Battery (MELAB) (Polio, 2001: 92; Weigle, 2002: 112–114). Further examples of holistic rating scales can be found in Weigle (2002: Chap. 7) and Hyland (2003: 228). The main distinguishing feature of these holistic scales is the way in which they define the descriptors in the scoring rubric and the number of mastery levels they consider, with the most common scales distinguishing between four and six mastery levels (Hyland, 2003: 227).

Analytic scoring solves the main disadvantages associated with holistic scoring, where a single score is provided. In analytic scoring, judgements of writing quality are made on several features of the text. In this sense, analytic scoring is claimed to view writing as multifaceted and complex (Hamp-Lyons, 2003: 176). Rather than giving a single score, analytic scoring provides assessment ratings of the different text components separately (Argüelles Álvarez, 2004: 85). Examples of these components include content, organisation, cohesion, vocabulary, register, grammar and mechanics (Hyland, 2003: 229). Thus, analytic scoring gives more detailed information about the characteristics of the writing (Bacha, 2001; Hamp-Lyons, 2003: 176; Hyland, 2003: 229; Weigle, 2002: 114–115). This is particularly useful for L2 learners who may display different competency levels in different aspects of writing ability (Hyland, 2003: 230; Weigle, 2002: 120).

For each rating scale, for example content, organisation or vocabulary, analytic scoring distinguishes several levels of mastery such as very good, good, average, poor or very poor. Every subscale is clearly defined with a set of descriptors and every mastery level is well defined (Weigle, 2002: 119–120). Defining the descriptors for each level of each subscale involves stating how good a writing looks at each level with respect to each particular feature of the writing. It is a rather arduous task, but crucial for a reliable assessment.

One of the main disadvantages of analytic scoring is the difficulty in providing clear-cut and unambiguous definitions for each descriptor. Assessment with an analytic scoring scale may render unreliable results if the descriptors for each mastery level at each scale are not clearly defined (Weigle, 2002: 120). Further drawbacks of analytic scoring (see Weigle, 2002: 120) are (1) the amount of time it takes to design the scale and establish the scoring criteria, (2) the time-consuming nature of having to read every essay twice and (3) its higher cognitive demands, that is raters have to pay attention to a number of features simultaneously, and this involves a heavy cognitive load (Hyland, 2003: 230). Thus, although more time-consuming, analytic scoring is more reliable than holistic scoring (Penny *et al.*, 2000: 146).

Some analytic rating scales provide a single composite score resulting from the combination of the particular scale scores. This represents an additional problem, since while giving this overall quality score, some of the information provided by the analytic scale is lost (Weigle, 2002: 120). One of the best known and most widely used analytic scales, the ESL Composition Profile, also provides a composite score (Weigle, 2002: 115; Wolfe-Quintero *et al.*, 1998). Designed by Jacobs *et al.* (1981), the Profile, as the scale is commonly known, has five rating scales, each of which, in turn, distinguishes four levels of mastery: excellent to very good, good to average, fair to poor and very poor.

The five rating scales are content, organisation, vocabulary, language use and mechanics. Each of them scores differently, with content scoring up to 30 points, organisation and vocabulary scoring up to 20 points, language use scoring up to 25 points and mechanics scoring up to 5 points. The maximum score is 100 points, and the minimum is 34 points. The Profile usually reports a composite score, but it may also provide the scores for each scale. Appendix 1 reproduces the scoring rubric of the Profile with the descriptors for each rating scale and mastery level.

Other examples of analytic rating scales are the Test in English for Educational Purposes (TEEP) and the Michigan Writing Assessment Scoring Guide (see, e.g. Hamp-Lyons, 1992; Weigle, 2002: 115–119).

When the rating scale used for the assessment of writing has been designed for a specific writing assignment, it is called primary-trait or multiple-trait scoring (Hamp-Lyons, 1992, 2003: 175–176; Hyland, 2003: 229–230; Weigle, 2002: 110–112). Trait-based scoring methods highlight the features of good writing for each particular task. In primary-trait scoring, a particular aspect of the writing task, for example *appropriate text staging, creative response, effective argument, reference to sources* and *audience design* (Hyland, 2003: 230), is made prominent, and a detailed scoring rubric or a set of descriptors for that trait is designed against which writing performance is assessed (Hamp-Lyons, 2003: 175; Weigle, 2002: 110). Primary-trait scoring resembles holistic scoring in this regard, with the difference that the former depends on the particular writing task being performed at the moment, and does not necessarily rely on communicative effectiveness as the main quality indicator, but on how successfully the learner accomplishes the writing assignment.

In contrast, in multiple-trait scoring several salient features of the writing task are selected on which to base writing quality and ability judgements. Separate scores for different writing features are given in this case, one score for each of the traits or features chosen for assessment in each specific context. Examples include *ability to 'summarize a course text'*, *'consider both sides of an argument'* or *'develop the move structure of an abstract'* (Hyland, 2003: 230). Multiple-trait scoring, which was developed by Hamp-Lyons (1992, 2003) herself, is in fact a type of analytic scoring designed for a particular task. Examples of a primary-trait and a multiple-trait scoring rubric are offered in Weigle (2002: 111) and Hyland (2003: 231), respectively.

Scoring procedures developed for particular writing tasks have high validity and reliability values (Hamp-Lyons, 1991: 253, in Argüelles Álvarez, 2004: 88), whether they report a single score or multiple scores. This is because their rubrics reflect and assess the real performance of learners in terms of what they are asked to do; in other words, they are context-sensitive (Hamp-Lyons, 2003: 176; Hyland, 2003: 229). Nevertheless, their design is very costly and time-consuming, since it can be used only for a single writing task/topic. Because primary-trait scoring is too labour-intensive, it is not widely used (Hamp-Lyons, 2003: 176; Weigle, 2002: 110).

Table 3.3 shows a summary of the main characteristics of scoring procedures.

Although different examination formats and scoring procedures have been reviewed, the criteria against which the assessment of writing ability is implemented have not been examined in detail. The following section will look at the main features of a written text which are considered by raters for assessment.

Scoring criteria in direct assessment of writing quality

Writing ability is a skill usually evaluated through the examination of the quality of written texts produced by learners. Several features of the writing contribute to the quality of the essay, and consequently, scoring

Table 3.3 Summary of the main characteristics of scoring procedures

	Holistic	Analytic	Primary trait	Multiple trait
Fundamentals	- overall impression - scoring rubric, benchmark - communicative effectiveness	- several rating scales (sometimes composite score) - scoring rubric - different writing features	- single assessment on a single feature	- different writing features - scoring rubric - context-sensitive
Role of vocabulary	- contributor to communicability - not explicitly looked at	- one aspect of writing quality - explicitly looked at	- may be a primary trait or not (depending on context)	- may be a trait looked at or not (depending on context)
Examples	TOEFL, TWE	Profile, TEEP, MWASG[1]	NAEP[2] Scoring Guides	Those in particular studies
Studies	Cumming et al. (2005), Woodall (2002), Berg (1999), Engber (1995), Janopoulus (1993)	Cabaleiro González (2003; Profile), Helms-Park and Stapleton (2003; Profile), Fathman and Whalley (1990; Profile), Campbell (1990; Profile)	See Weigle (2002: 110–111)	See Hyland (2003: 231), Gearhart et al. (1995)

[1]This abbreviation stands for the Michigan Writing Assessment Scoring Guide (Hamp-Lyons, 1992; Weigle, 2002: 115)
[2]This abbreviation stands for the National Assessment of Educational Progress (Weigle, 2002: 115)

scales or scoring rubrics focus on one or several of those aspects (Cho, 2003; Hyland, 2003: 220–226; Polio, 2001; Weigle, 2002: 122–127).

A good piece of writing is not the result of the presence of a single aspect, for example whether the text is linguistically accurate or whether it is very well organised, but rather it derives from a composite of features such as cohesion; cohesiveness; linguistic, grammatical, lexical and syntactic accuracy; appropriate and relevant content; and an adequate organisation of sentences and paragraphs (Council of Europe, 2001: 64–68; Jarvis et al., 2003; Polio, 2001; Reid, 1990). In fact, Wolfe-Quintero et al. (1998) identify three main components of writing ability: fluency, complexity and accuracy.

By way of illustration, Jarvis et al. (2003) state that 'the quality of a written text may depend less on the use of individual linguistic features than on how these features are used in tandem' (p. 399). They base their experiment on the written production of a group of learners from different L1 backgrounds. The authors suggest that the quality of composition is dependent on the presence of certain linguistic features; some other may appear or not in highly rated texts (p. 401).

A summary of the main writing assessment criteria and the descriptors that define them is provided in Table 3.4.

One of the most prominent and widely used criteria for the assessment of writing quality is communicability or effectiveness of communication (Cumming et al., 2005; Hawkey & Barker, 2004; Hyland, 2003; Weigle, 2002). Many highly prestigious scoring scales are explicitly based on communicative effectiveness, for instance the writing sections of the Test of English as a Foreign Language (TOEFL), the Cambridge First Certificate in English (FCE), the International English Language Testing System (IELTS) and the Basic English Skills Test (BEST) (Weigle, 2002: Chap. 7). Judgements of writing ability are made on the basis of the learners' ability to communicate in the L2 (Janopoulus, 1993). The higher the communicative effectiveness of a message, the higher the quality will be. In fact, the notion of communicative effectiveness seems to underlie the assessment of writing quality. Linguistic accuracy, grammar and vocabulary are not an issue in writing assessment, unless they obscure communication (Weigle, 2002: 164–165).

Other aspects regarding how the message is transmitted also play an important role in judgements of essay quality: rhetorical conventions. In addition, a writing that displays an adequate range of vocabulary, appropriate syntactic structures, coherence and cohesive devices, register features and few errors (spelling,[6] punctuation, lexical or grammatical) will be judged as a high-quality writing (CEFL, 2001: 64–68; Polio, 2001).

Table 3.4 Exemplary summary of the main qualitative writing assessment criteria

Scoring criteria	Descriptor
Communicability	Does the text communicate well? Can it be understood?
Content	Is the text relevant to the task and to the prompt? Does the text successfully and effectively respond to the writing task?
Rhetorical organisation (discourse features)	Is the text organised according to the rhetorical conventions of the genre? Is it coherent and cohesive? Do main ideas stand out? Are they correctly developed?
Vocabulary	Does the text use adequate vocabulary? – a wide range of vocabulary? Is the lexical choice appropriate? Are there any errors of word choice? Do they interfere with communication? Is meaning obscured?
Syntactic accuracy	Does the text use appropriate structures? Are there any errors of morphology or syntax? Do they interfere with communication? Is meaning obscured?
Mechanics	Does the text comply with the spelling, punctuation and capitalisation conventions? Are there many errors? Do they interfere with communication? Is meaning obscured?

Qualitative judgements of writing ability are based either on communicative effectiveness or on the accomplishment of certain textual requirements that refer to content, rhetorical organisation, linguistic accuracy, lexical choices or text mechanics. These qualitative judgements of writing ability derive from overall impressionistic observations concerning writing features.

But quantitative measures are also used to assess writing ability. These consist of counting textual features that are known to correlate with language development and essay score (Helms-Park & Stapleton, 2003; Polio, 2001; Reynolds, 2001: 442). So, as the presence of these features increases, the quality of the essays also increases. Among these features are the total number of words per composition, which is 'often indicative of development within paragraphs, structural completeness, and fluency' (Reid, 1990: 195), average word length, number of lexical words, lexical specificity or diversity, lexical sophistication (use of less frequent words), lexical originality or individuality, number of T-units, number of clauses per T-unit, number of words per T-unit, number of error-free T-units, number of errors and number of lexical errors.[7]

These quantitative features can usually be grouped into measures of fluency (number of words per essay and number of T-units), complexity (number of subordinated sentences, and lexical density and specificity) and accuracy, for example number of error-free sentences and error density (see, among others, Grant & Ginther, 2000; Martínez Arbelaiz, 2004; Torras & Celaya, 2001; Wolfe-Quintero *et al.*, 1998).

The use of quantitative measures of writing quality has benefitted from the implementation of a fourth generation of writing assessment: computer-based writing assessment[8] (Hamp-Lyons, 2001, 2003; Weigle, 2002: 236). The computer scoring of essays allows for the identification and quantification of quality-defining features of the writing, such as the essay length, lexical density, lexical diversity and average sentence length, at different levels of proficiency (Hamp-Lyons, 2003: 120–121; Weigle, 2002: 234). The essay is given a score on the basis of the salient surface features (e.g. essay length, number of T-units or lexical density) present in the text considering their frequency and their relative contribution to overall writing quality. The degree to which each feature contributes to the quality of the composition must be decided on beforehand. Many studies have investigated the predictive power of different textual features (Cumming *et al.*, 2005; De Haan & van Esch, 2005; Engber, 1995; Grant & Ginther, 2000; Jarvis *et al.*, 2003; Lee, 2003).

The most important advantages of the computer scoring method are the following: (1) it is a very quick scoring procedure and (2) it is highly dependable, since the computer program can reliably spot and count every textual aspect it is commanded to (Hamp-Lyons, 2001: 121; Weigle, 2002: 234–236). Nonetheless, computer-geared scoring also has some drawbacks. The first drawback is that it does not consider meaning, since only surface features are taken into account. Nonetheless, Weigle (2002: 235) mentions Latent Semantic Analysis (LSA), a computer essay-scoring program designed to extract semantic similarity of words and passages from texts. The second drawback is that designing programs for writing assessment purposes is an expensive and time-consuming activity (Weigle, 2002: 234; see also Valero Garcés *et al.*, 2000: 1852).

Polio (2001: 95–107) notes that apart from measuring writing quality, counts of textual features serve other purposes. These include assessment of the effects of a specific teaching approach (Berg, 1999; Frantzen, 1995; Kepner, 1991), comparison of different tasks or topics (Kobayashi & Rinnert, 1992; Reid, 1990; Zhang, 1987), comparison of different types of writers (Bardovi-Harlig & Bofman, 1989; Berg, 1999; De Haan & van Esch, 2005; Hawkey & Barker, 2004), examination of the validity and reliability of a language test (Fisher, 1984) or examination of learners' progress in writing and change in accuracy over time (De Haan & van Esch, 2005; Fernández, 1997; Grant & Ginther, 2000; Laufer, 1991b).

The number of textual features that have been found to correlate with writing quality, or, with essay score, is incommensurable. However, not all writing features contribute the same to essay score (Chiang, 2003; Reid, 1990). Vocabulary and lexical features are frequently considered as important indicators of writing quality. Most scoring scales, whether holistic or analytic, include a vocabulary component. The choice of the appropriate lexical items, the use of a wide range of vocabulary and the confusion of semantically or formally related words are often found as criteria descriptors when dealing with vocabulary use in compositions. The following sections will describe the role of vocabulary and errors in assessments of essay quality. Examination of vocabulary as a writing-quality indicator followed by a discussion of the role of errors as indicators of quality of composition will be the focus of the section. Special emphasis will be placed on the relationship between lexical errors and essay score.

Vocabulary as a scoring criterion in direct assessment of writing quality

A well-developed lexical competence or 'a large and varied vocabulary' (Laufer & Nation, 1995: 307) is indispensable for good writing. Vocabulary also plays a prominent role in judgements of writing quality. Vocabulary knowledge is preconditional, especially to reading, and also to writing and listening, and so vocabulary knowledge may even predict performance in these skills (Qian, 2002; Staehr, 2008). Lexical richness is frequently taken as a reliable measure to assess the quality of a written text, because lexical competence is perhaps the strongest indicator of the quality of composition (see, e.g. Santos, 1988; see also Bacha, 2001; Staehr, 2008; Weigle, 2002: 69). Jarvis *et al.* (2003) found that together with essay length, conjuncts, hedges, amplifiers, emphatics, demonstratives, downtoners, definite articles, passives and relative clauses, lexical diversity is consistently found in highly rated compositions.

In writing assessment, vocabulary is found as a qualitative scoring criterion in nearly every rating scale. Likewise, different measures of lexical richness are found to correlate strongly with essay score, thus becoming quantitative criteria of writing quality.

As a further component of rating scales, vocabulary is claimed to contribute to the quality of the essay to some extent. Thus, although every scoring rubric uses different descriptors for vocabulary, in general terms, a text will score highly if it displays a wide and sophisticated range of vocabulary, if it makes adequate lexical choices, if it has few errors and if it shows mastery of formal and semantic properties of L2 words (Hawkey & Barker, 2004; Victori, 1999). In particular, the descriptors for the vocabulary component include word choice, range of vocabulary and no errors of word choice or rare lapses into the L1 (Weigle, 2002: Chap. 7).

Some research studies have revealed strong interactions between essay score and different measures of vocabulary knowledge such as the following:

- lexical specificity (type/token ratio) (Cumming *et al.*, 2005; De Haan & van Esch, 2005; Engber, 1995; Fernández, 1997; Grant & Ginther, 2000; Jarvis *et al.*, 2003; Lee, 2003; Mutta, 1999);
- lexical diversity (Jarvis *et al.*, 2003; Lee 2003);
- lexical sophistication (Lee, 2003; Morris & Cobb 2004; Mutta, 1999);
- lexical originality or use of words not present in other learners' compositions (Mutta, 1999);
- lexical variation, including and excluding errors (Engber, 1995); and
- number of lexical words (Fernández, 1997; Laufer & Nation, 1995; Mutta, 1999; Reid, 1990).

Vocabulary size affects lexical richness. Laufer and Nation (1995), by means of their Lexical Frequency Profile (LFP), demonstrated that vocabulary size was reflected in the learners' productive use of vocabulary. A relationship could be established between vocabulary knowledge and vocabulary use. By this token, learners with a large vocabulary size used fewer high-frequency words and more low-frequency words. Writing quality benefitted from this. The LFP was found to reliably reflect vocabulary knowledge and thus was thought to serve as a useful tool to determine influencing factors in assessing writing quality (Laufer & Nation, 1995). The relationship between vocabulary size, either active or passive, and composition quality has not been widely researched.

Reynolds' (2001) study highlights the importance of lexical repetition as a device for cohesion and the underpinning of meaning. Considering that cohesion is a recognised feature of quality writing (for Chiang, 2003: 476, cohesion is the 'best predictor of an essay's overall quality'), lexical repetition, that is appropriate use of vocabulary to mark semantic relationships in the text, is an index of good writing. Liu and Braine's (2005) findings are similar, with lexical cohesive devices having the highest correlations with composition scores. So that the more lexical devices a composition displays, the higher it will be rated. In relation to this, it is worth noting that as vocabulary is central to communication, it may explain the important role it plays in assessing writing, a communicative activity.

Engber's (1995) study is one of the most relevant to date which examines the degree to which specific text features are related to essay scores. It looks at the relationship with lexical proficiency, measured through lexical variation, number of lexical errors and reader's judgements of the overall quality of compositions. The holistic rating scale of the TWE, which distinguishes six levels of mastery and is based on communicative effectiveness, was used to score learners' compositions. Furthermore, compositions were scrutinised for lexical diversity, lexical diversity without errors, lexical density and lexical errors, and the totals were correlated to essay scores. The results of the analysis revealed that lexical proficiency and lexical variation play a significant role in the assessment of the quality of written work (cf. also Nation, 2001: 177–178).

A 1999 study by Mutta reveals findings similar to Engber's (1995). Compositions that made use of a higher number of words, those that used low-frequency words and those that included original words scored highest. The study concluded by pointing out the importance of using a rich and large vocabulary in writing to improve the quality of the essay. Similarly, studies by Cumming *et al.* (2005), De Haan and van Esch (2005), Morris and Cobb (2004), Jarvis *et al.* (2003), Lee (2003) and Grant and Ginther (2000) have revealed a strong relationship between vocabulary knowledge and writing quality, suggesting that vocabulary measures predict essay score and are indicators of essay quality. More specifically, Staehr (2008) found significant correlations between receptive vocabulary size and quality of written composition. Furthermore, learners' mastery of the 2000 most frequent words accounts for above-average writing performance. However, Chiang (2003: 477) notes that in rating essays raters pay attention to objective features of text quality, as well as to more subjective features, including those aspects of the writing that irritate raters.

In addition to vocabulary, linguistic accuracy also appears as a main criterion for assessing writing, either in holistic or in analytic rating scales, and either with qualitative or with quantitative measures (Glenwright, 2002; Hamp-Lyons, 2003; Hawkey & Barker, 2004; Hyland, 2003; Polio, 1997, 2001; Weigle, 2002). Various measures of linguistic accuracy, which can include morphological, syntactical and lexical accuracy, have been used in the literature (see Wolfe-Quintero *et al.*, 1998). By far, the most common measure of linguistic accuracy is error counts, with or without classification of those errors (Polio, 1997). In the following section, the role of lexical errors as indicators of writing quality will be discussed.

Lexical errors as a scoring criterion in direct assessment of writing quality

Writing assessment is often based on error production. Errors have served traditionally as indexes of writing quality in assessing compositions in formal contexts such as school, academia or general language courses. Even nowadays, in the era of the communicative approach and the writing-as-a-process-strand with recognition that many factors other than the number of linguistic errors determine good writing, linguistic accuracy is a relevant construct for L2 writing assessment (see, e.g. Council of Europe, 2001; Hawkey & Barker, 2004; Lee, 2003; Polio, 1997). This is evident in the amount of research devoted to the examination of linguistic accuracy (e.g. Kroll, 1990; Polio, 1997) and to the investigation of different pedagogical techniques to improve linguistic accuracy and reduce error production (Berg, 1999; Fathman & Whalley, 1990; Frantzen, 1995; Kepner, 1991; Lee, 2003; Polio *et al.*, 1998).

The role of errors as indicators of essay quality seems quite straightforward, considering that errors are landmarks of the acquisition process and in particular of the learning stage of L2 writers (e.g. Carson, 2001; Grant & Ginther, 2000). Errors provide teachers with information about the features of the learners' IL, indicating the areas where this differs from the TL system, thus giving insights into how learners currently make sense of the TL and how they develop as they become more proficient. Furthermore, errors cause communication disturbance or breakdown and this derives in poorer writing quality (Cumming *et al.*, 2005; Kobayashi & Rinnert, 1992: 190, see Chap. 4). The severity of errors is judged either on the basis of the degree of communication distortion or on the basis of the irritation the error produces to the reader/rater. On both occasions, the error will have a negative effect on quality ratings (Chiang, 2003: 477; Santos, 1988).

Numerous research studies have investigated the interactions between essay score and error production. These studies reveal a strong negative correlation between quality writing and linguistic errors in general[9] and lexical errors in particular.[10] Grant and Ginther's (2000: 142) statement that 'The better essays had fewer lexical errors' summarises the results of studies examining the relationship between errors and essay score.

Two major problems can be identified when using errors to judge writing quality. First and foremost, the definition of what constitutes an error presents serious difficulties. Researchers working with error measures must provide a definition of error (Polio, 1997: 113–114). The second main problem is the question of classifying errors and deciding to which particular category an error belongs. Distinguishing between certain error types may be difficult on some occasions (Hawkey & Barker, 2004: 147–148; Polio, 1997: 120). It should be noted that not all studies that use error counts as criteria for writing quality classify errors into individual categories (Polio, 1997).

Among the most common lexical error categories identified in the literature are word choice errors, omissions, unusual word forms, word order, borrowings, lexical creations and spelling.[11] The individual categories do not predict quality to the same extent; thus, researchers have found word choice errors to be the most problematic in that they affect essay quality the most (Grant & Ginther, 2000; Hawkey & Barker, 2004).

In summary, it seems safe to conclude that errors in general, and lexical errors in particular, are important criteria of writing quality, and in this sense, they serve to predict essay score, although some other factors will also influence the final rating of the writing. However, none of the studies reviewed are devoted to the examination of how lexical errors affect the quality of compositions produced by young Spanish EFL learners in primary school contexts, which will be the aim of the study presented here.

Conclusion

This chapter has focused on exploring the development of writing skills with special emphasis on how vocabulary contributes to the development and assessment of these writing skills. The process of writing development is seen to be multifaceted, and writing is conceived as (1) a product or a process, (2) a cognitive or a social activity and (3) a content-oriented or a form-oriented activity. Two highly relevant factors in learning how to write in an L2 are L1 literacy and L2 proficiency. In the particular case of children learning the L2, difficulties arise from an underdeveloped L1 literacy skill. Promoting L1 reading and writing, L2 oral learning as well as L2 writing practice and highlighting the role of writing as a means of communication will help overcome difficulties in learning how to write in the L2.

The first part of the chapter ends with an account of the relationship of mutual influence between vocabulary and writing skills. The second part of the chapter included a review of the main methods for assessing writing ability – direct and indirect – of the main scoring procedures in direct writing assessment and of the main scoring criteria of essay quality. Communicative effectiveness, content, rhetorical organisation, vocabulary, syntactic accuracy and mechanics are among the qualitative criteria. Quantitative measures of essay quality include word counts, number of independent units, mean word and utterance length, density of grammar and lexical errors, and different measures of lexical richness, such as lexical diversity, sophistication and originality. There is evidence in the literature to suggest that vocabulary measures, and especially lexical errors, are important indicators of writing quality.

Notes

1. Most of these authors draw on the work of Krashen, who repeatedly stated the importance of extensive and pleasure reading in the acquisition of the second language, in general, and in the development of L2 writing skills, in particular (Krashen, 1993).
2. Grabe (2001: 53) expresses the nature of writing as a list of conditions to bear in mind for writing to develop. The list goes as follows: (1) knowing the language, (2) knowing how to use the language (communicative competence), (3) the human learner, (4) individual abilities and preferences, (5) the social context, (6) attitudes and motivation, (7) opportunities for learning and practice, (8) formal instructional contexts, (9) processing factors, (10) cultural variability, (11) content and topical knowledge and (12) discourse, genre and register knowledge.
3. Researchers (Hamp-Lyons, 1990, 2003; Hyland, 2003: 217–219; Weigle, 2002) distinguish among several types of validity: face validity, construct validity, content validity and criterion validity, and within this last one, concurrent validity and predictive validity. Explanation of these different types of validity would go well far beyond the scope of this study; therefore, we advise readers to go to the original sources for further information.
4. The reliability of indirect tests of writing derives from the multiple-choice format of the tests. Only a single answer can be correct for each question; therefore, scoring is quite straightforward, and intra- and interrater reliability reaches 1.

5. Further comparison of advantages and disadvantages of direct and indirect assessment methods would go beyond the scope of this chapter; but see Argüelles Álvarez (2004: 84), Hyland (2003: 217) and Weigle (2002: 58–59).
6. In some studies (Hamp-Lyons, 1990; Martínez Arbelaiz, 2004; Valero Garcés *et al.*, 2000; Wolfe *et al.*, 1996), spelling errors are considered errors in mechanics. Nonetheless, in some other studies, including the present one, spelling errors are considered a type of lexical error, and therefore belong to the vocabulary section (Arnaud, 1992; Bouvy, 2000; Celaya & Torras, 2001; Dušková, 1969; Fernández, 1997; Lindell, 1973; Mutta, 1999).
7. See, among others, Cumming *et al.* (2005), De Haan and van Esch (2005), Hawkey and Barker (2004), Martínez Arbelaiz (2004), Morris and Cobb (2004), Jarvis *et al.* (2003), Lee (2003), Reynolds (2001), Torras and Celaya (2001), Grant and Ginther (2000), Mutta (1999), Polio *et al.* (1998), Fernández (1997), Engber (1995), Laufer and Nation (1995) and Reid (1990).
8. The other three generations being essay test, multiple-choice testing (indirect assessment and objective testing) and portfolio-based assessment, respectively (Hamp-Lyons, 2001).
9. See Frantzen (1995), Kepner (1991), Kroll (1990), Carlisle (1989), Zhang (1987) and Fisher (1984).
10. See Agustín Llach (2007), Martínez Arbelaiz (2004), Hawkey and Barker (2004), Grant and Ginther (2000), Mutta (1999), Engber (1995), Kobayashi and Rinnert (1992), Bardovi-Harlig and Bofman (1989) and Santos (1988).
11. See Hawkey and Barker (2004), Martínez Arbelaiz (2004), Grant and Ginther (2000), Mutta (1999), Kobayashi and Rinnert (1992), Kroll (1990), Carlisle (1989) and Zhang (1987).

Chapter 4
Lexical Errors in SLA

Lexical errors are a particular type of error which, despite being more numerous than grammar errors, have received little attention (Bouvy, 2000; Jiménez Catalán, 1992; Kroll, 1990: 144; Lennon, 1996: 24; Meara, 1984; Vázquez, 1992: 92; cf. also Tschihold, 2003). The following pages will examine lexical errors in detail. Firstly, a review of the definitions of the term will be provided and a working definition will be proposed. Secondly, the different classification of lexical errors, limitations arising and pedagogical implications will be examined. Finally, the importance of lexical errors as vocabulary acquisition benchmarks, as well as their role in communication and in general educational success, will be looked at.

Researchers allude to the unstable and unsystematic nature of the lexicon to justify their grammatical approach (James, 1998; Warren, 1982). Morphology and syntax have been traditionally considered to be more systematic and rule-governed than lexis, and hence, the lack of research in the area of lexical error (cf. Corder, 1973; Tschihold, 2003). Similarly, Warren (1982) agrees that traditionally lexical items 'represent the idiosyncratic, non-generalizable features of language' (p. 209; see also Meara, 1984: 231), yet she found that it is possible to distinguish clearly between a small number of different types of lexical errors. More recently, Ambroso (2000) also points to the complex, and sometimes irregular, relationships among elements in the lexicon and believes that the context and the communicative situation are necessary in order to determine the correct use of the lexical system (cf. Lennon, 1991a). Dušková (1969), in the light of her analysis, stated that 'errors in lexis presented a much less homogeneous material for study than errors in grammar' (p. 24). This results in a failure to arrive at any satisfactory system of classification because of the wide variety of causes to which these lexical errors may be attributable and the corresponding wide number of categories of lexical error types. Furthermore, the line between lexical and grammar errors is blurred, and distinguishing among both types is not always an easy task (Hemchua & Schmitt, 2006; Morrissey, 1983).

In addition to considerations about the idiosyncrasy of lexical items, the lack of systematicity of the lexicon and complexities in lexicon organisation, a further reason may account for the scant research specifically devoted to lexical errors. On the one hand, the flourishing years of the Error Analysis (EA) methodology coincide with a neglect of research into lexical issues. Research in SLA focused on grammatical development and, as a consequence, more attention was paid to grammar errors in learners' performance. On the other hand, an abundance of lexical studies and the interest in the vocabulary acquisition process (from Meara, 1984, onwards) appear at a time when EA as a methodology of research in SLA is in decline.

The controversy and ambiguity in distinguishing lexical from grammatical errors derive from the difficulties in defining the 'word' or 'lexical item' under scrutiny (cf. James, 1998: 143; Tschihold, 2003). Generally, the term lexical error is used to refer to the deviations in the learner's production of the L2 norm with regards to the use in production and reception of lexical items.

Intuitively everyone knows what a word is, but the formal definition of 'word' is not easy. In general, the terms 'word', 'lexical unit' and 'lexical item' are used interchangeably to allude to the smallest semantic unit or meaning unit (see, e.g. Council of Europe [CEFL], 2001; Clark, 1993: 3; Read, 2000). Consequently, a lexical unit can be made up of a single word or morpheme (e.g. *table*) or of several words (e.g. *take up, rush hour* and *to kick the bucket*). Phrasal verbs, adverbial phrases or idioms are also considered to be words or lexical items (see also Hemchua & Schmitt, 2006; James, 1998: 143). A further distinction is usually made in the literature between lexical and grammatical words. The former group is made up of words belonging to the class of nouns, verbs, adjectives and adverbs, whereas prepositions, articles and conjunctions make up the latter group. Lexical errors will affect lexical words, while errors that affect grammatical words will be studied as grammar errors (Celaya & Torras, 2001; Hemchua & Schmitt, 2006).

Presumably, although in no way necessarily, morphological and inflectional derivations will not count as independent words; so *dance, danced, dancer* or *happy, happiness, happily* make up two-word families and not six independent words (Laufer, 1992; Laufer & Nation, 1995; Nagy & Herman, 1987: 20–21; Nation, 1990, 1993a, 2004; Nation & Waring, 1997). Likewise, polysemous words such as *bank* will count as two different words when they mean either *seat* or *financial entity*. Similarly, idioms or fixed expressions such as *rely on* or *kick the bucket* will also be considered as a single lexical unit, since they are independent semantic units irrespective of the number of formal elements they are made up of (Council of Europe [CEFL], 2001; Hemchua & Schmitt, 2006; Meara, 1996; Nation, 1990, 2001).

The field is thus in need of a more precise definition of the term 'lexical error'. The following section presents the definition of 'lexical error', the controversies found in the literature in that respect and the ways in which researchers solve these inconsistencies.

Definitions of 'Lexical Error'

Once the terms 'lexical item', 'word' and 'lexical unit' have been defined, a formulation of the definition of 'lexical error' is possible. Many of the studies on lexical errors are directed at defining the term 'lexical error' and developing taxonomies that could be used to classify them. As it turns out, neither of these tasks has been easy. Let us consider the issue of defining 'lexical error' first.

The purpose of this section is to identify and analyse the inconsistencies observed in the use of the term 'lexical error' and determine the possible reasons for these inconsistencies. The definition of the term 'lexical error' is based on the notion of lexical competence. Depending on what is understood of what 'knowing a word' implies, and on what counts as a word, the lexical error can be defined. The review of the literature on lexical errors reveals the existence of disparate positions with regards to the definition and treatment of the object of study (see, e.g. Ambroso, 2000; Dušková, 1969; Warren, 1982).

Identifying and isolating lexical errors is not always an easy task. Lexical competence refers not only to semantic knowledge but also to morphological, syntactic and pragmatic knowledge. Thus, 'knowing a word' means knowing how to use it appropriately in context, in combination with other words (collocation) and in particular communicative situations and texts (i.e. style and pragmatic force) (Ambroso, 2000: 58). Therefore, in order to spot a lexical error, the communicative and situational context (interlocutor, mode and style) must also be taken into account.

There is a lack of clear, unambiguous definitions of 'lexical errors' in the research. Most studies are concerned with the identification, description, interpretation and classification of lexical errors, and not with providing an explicit definition. A few provide clear definitions within the framework of their research (Carrió Pastor, 2004; Celaya & Torras, 2001; Fernández, 1997; Hemchua & Schmitt, 2006; James, 1998; Meara & English, 1987; Palapanidi, 2009). Corder (1973) claims that, in fact, a definition of error is more a convention in language teaching to refer to those utterances that somehow differ from those of a native speaker of the L2 than a clear, indisputable reality. Nevertheless, any serious systematic research into lexical errors demands that we have a clear-cut definition of lexical errors to begin with (cf. Zydatiss, 1974).

Two types of inconsistencies in the literature are (1) a polysemy of meanings attached to the term 'lexical error' and (2) a polysemy of terms referring to the phenomenon of deviating from the lexical norm in form or meaning (see Figure 4.1).

In the use of the term 'lexical error' a polysemy of meanings and terms can be observed. Polysemy of meanings refers to the fact that different researchers understand different things under the term 'lexical error'. For some (Laufer, 1990a, 1990b, 1991a; Lennon, 1991a, 1991b; Dagut, 1977), it is the ragbag category consisting of all errors that are not grammatically fit (spelling, phonology, semantic errors, errors of word choice and pragmatic errors). They do not use a differentiating criterion, but provide overall classification of the type: grammar versus lexis errors. They treat the term as an undifferentiated category (cf. Zimmermann, 1986a).

Another group of researchers, the most numerous in fact,[1] allude to 'lexical error' as a superordinate term that serves as a heading for several other classes of errors, such as word formation (spelling in writing and malapropisms in speech; cf. Channell, 1988), field errors, collocation, confusion due to formal or semantic similarity, and relatedness, equivalence or wrong word choice. The term 'lexical error' thus includes several subcategories that group lexical errors according to different criteria which can be descriptive, etiologic and also semantic, epistemic

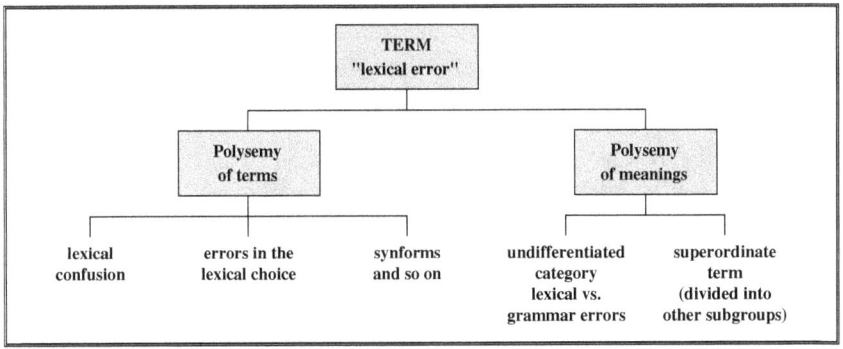

Figure 4.1 Summary of the tendencies observed in the treatment of the term 'lexical error'

(lack of knowledge), or psycholinguistic or process-oriented. This understanding of the term necessarily implies the design of taxonomies of lexical errors. The former view, however, sees lexical errors as an undifferentiated category; so no lexical error taxonomy is called for in this case.

Under polysemy of terms, we understand the use of different terms to refer to the same object. There is frequent avoidance of the phrase 'lexical error' when referring to errors that have to do with lexis. Instead, we find a number of different terms such as 'wrong lexical choice', 'errors in the lexical choice', 'lexical deviancies', 'vocabulary errors', 'incongruencies in lexical "gridding"', 'semantic deviation', 'lexical confusions', 'synforms', 'lexical deficiencies', 'lexical disruptions', 'lexical approximations' and 'lexical simplification'.[2] While they deal with the same phenomenon, they give it a different name depending on the aspects emphasised.

All authors who deal with lexical errors, nonetheless, admit systematicity as a definitional characteristic of errors (cf., e.g. Taylor, 1986: 147). Lexical errors are not accidental or random, but respond to systematic causes that can be accounted for in the analysis of the language sample. In fact, most authors attempt at finding these causes and, thus, at better explaining the lexical errors encountered. Lexical errors are liable to be explained, and therefore, classified, and these explanations are claimed to be generalisable to a greater or a lesser extent (Hemchua & Schmitt, 2006). If this were not so, taxonomies of lexical errors and attempts at defining, explaining, interpreting and classifying them would not make any sense. Nevertheless, these attempts are common in the field.

The inconsistencies in the use of the term 'lexical error' may be due to two factors: (1) the general discarding of the term 'error' in recent years and (2) the perspective taken by the author (Ellis, 1994; Valero Garcés et al., 2000). The term 'lexical error' is used as the reference frame for the analysis, but particular lexical error types are named depending on the dimension of the lexical error that prevails in the research. For instance, Laufer (1990a, 1991a) refers to lexical errors as 'lexical confusions' or 'synforms' (self-coined term), because her investigation is limited to the study of wrong word choice due to formal similarity. Likewise, Zimmermann (1986a, 1986b, 1987) talks about 'semantic deviation', because he deals with confusion of semantically related words (cf. Dagut, 1977; Lennon, 1991a, 1991b). The differentiation of the category of lexical errors (collocation, lexical confusion, semantic equivalence, spelling, relexification, language shift and overgeneralisation) is positive, especially from the pedagogical point of view, since it provides material for a better, richer and more complete explanation of the phenomenon, and more adequate correction and evaluation criteria. At the same time, such differentiation brings order and clarity to the field, for the benefit of researchers, practitioners (teachers of ESL), learners and students of applied linguistics.

In the light of evidence found in the literature, both explanations are closely related, since the latter can explain the former. That is, in their effort to avoid the term '(lexical) error', and in view of the impossibility of doing this, since 'lexical deficiencies' or 'approximations' are, after all, lexical errors, researchers developed a kind of 'roundabout strategy' that allows them to avoid the term. A clear definition of lexical error is needed: a definition that comprises all aspects pointed out by different authors and that serves all perspectives and analyses of errors in vocabulary.

From the review of studies presented above, we can propose a broad definition of the term 'lexical error' that would need to be refined and constrained for each particular research purpose. A 'lexical error' is a deviation in form and/or meaning of a target-language lexical word. Form deviations include orthographic or phonological deviations within the limits of single words, and also ignorance of syntactical restrictions which result in false collocations, for example. Meaning deviations appear when lexical items are used in contexts where they are attributed another meaning or where they violate semantic restrictions; in Berkoff's words (1981: 10), when there is the 'incorrect choice of lexical items', or also when some semantic feature is not considered.

To sum up, a working definition of 'lexical error' allows for delimitation of the topic of study. Similarly, classifying lexical errors into a taxonomy is of high importance in their systematisation. Furthermore, this systematisation into types may reveal much about how the process of L2 vocabulary acquisition proceeds. The following section offers a review of several taxonomies found in the literature on lexical errors.

Taxonomies of Lexical Errors

Heretofore, we have been engaged in defining the terms 'lexical item' and 'lexical error' without further insight into how these errors are classified. Many of the studies on lexical errors set up taxonomies of the errors collected to describe the data in a reasonably coherent, systematic and concise way. The perspectives of the different authors regarding the definition and treatment of the term 'lexical error' give rise to a great number of lexical error taxonomies. The following quotation is illustrative of the variety of typologies of lexical errors:

> No two previous studies on lexical errors have adopted the same error typology, and categorizing lexical errors is far from a straightforward exercise. (Källkvist, 1998: 82)

The criteria that determine the different lexical error categories have their bases, as mentioned earlier, on the notion of lexical competence and on the definition of lexical error. This includes information as to what counts as a word or lexical item liable to be involved in a lexical error and as to what may be the nature of the deviation. The disparity of classification criteria and, as a consequence, of taxonomies makes it very difficult to find common traits in the taxonomies and thus to systematise and group authors. Here, not only papers devoted exclusively to lexical errors will be considered, but the most representative lexical error taxonomies found in the literature will also be examined, including lexical error studies framed within wider error analysis.

Now we present the main classification criteria considered in lexical error taxonomies. Systematising taxonomies into these criteria is not always an easy task, since some of them follow more than one categorisation criterion.[3] The main classification criteria are the following:

(1) Distinction between *form-oriented and content-oriented lexical errors* (Carrió Pastor, 2004; Fernández, 1997; Hemchua & Schmitt, 2006; James, 1998; Mutta, 1999; Palapanidi, 2009; Zimmermann, 1987): This formal/semantic distinction has its justification in the observation that the mental lexicon is organised following both formal and semantic principles. In this sense, words are stored and accessed either via formal or semantic associations (see Chapter 1, Meara, 1996). This distinction is very frequent and quite a number of recent taxonomies categorise lexical errors according to this criterion.

Palapanidi (2009) distinguishes among interlingual and intralingual semantic and formal errors. Among interlingual formal errors, she distinguishes between wrong choice concerning gender and number, code switching, and foreignising and semantic confusion, literal translation, false friends, inadequate register and use of redundancy among semantic interlingual errors. Formal intralingual lexical errors include wrong choice concerning gender and number, confusion of formally similar words and word coinage from TL words. Finally, errors that are classified under semantic intralingual errors include those such as paraphrase, derivational errors, confusion of semantically similar words, inadequate register, collocations and verb confusion. This classification is exhaustive and allows the author to explain all the errors that she encounters in the written production of learners at different proficiency levels.

The classification of lexical errors proposed by Hemchua and Schmitt (2006) is based on James (1998). They distinguish 24 categories of lexical errors divided into the major types of misselection, misformation and distortion among formal errors, and confusion of sense relations, collocation errors, errors in connotative meaning and stylistic errors. Theirs is an exhaustive classification that allows for fine-grained analysis of the different lexical errors found.

Carrió Pastor (2004), following James (1998: 142–154), distinguishes six different types of lexical errors:

(a) formal errors which derive from the confusion of two similar words;
(b) wrong word formation, which includes the following:
   (i) word invention,
   (ii) borrowing from the L1,
   (iii) relexification or adaptation of an L1 word into the grammatical conventions (orthographic, phonetic and morphologic) of the L2, and
   (iv) linguistic calque;
(c) lexical distortions because of the following:
   (i) omission,
   (ii) addition,
   (iii) wrong ordering of letters within the word, and
   (iv) wrong choice of two similar words;
(d) use of base words (hyponym) instead of superonym (more specific word);
(e) collocational errors;
(f) wrong lexical choice because of semantic relatedness.

James (1998: 142–154) devotes some pages to the discussion of lexical errors and offers a taxonomy which rests on the distinction between form- and content-oriented lexical errors. Among the formal errors of lexis, James distinguishes the following:

(a) formal misselection in which two existing target language words are confused because of formal similarity;
(b) misformations which involve the creation of a non-existing L2 word. Three main types of misformations are considered: borrowing, coinage and calque;

(c) distortions originating from letter omission, overinclusion (addition), misselection, misordering and blending.

The semantic error types that James distinguishes are as follows:

(a) confusion of sense relations which imply the confusion of semantically related words, and
(b) collocational errors which result from the association of two words which in native usage do not go together.

This work has been an important source for the present research, and therefore, we provide in Figure 4.2 a summary of the main lexical error types considered by James (1998) to aid in the total understanding and clarification of the issue.

In a study concerned with the vocabulary in entrance compositions, Mutta (1999) examined the lexical errors produced by learners dividing them into form- and meaning-oriented errors. Form lexical errors included, for instance, the use of a wrong verb form (e.g. singular instead of plural), incorrectly used prepositional constructions or syntactic structures (e.g. *open for the world to laugh and criticise at*) or sometimes blends of words (e.g. *high-blooded* from *warm-blooded* and *high pressure* or *describtion* from *describe* and *description*). Errors in meaning were mostly the wrong choice of words (e.g. *The book is full with short-cuts of the chats with people ... for glimpses*).

Fernández (1997) bases her taxonomy of the lexical errors on the already mentioned distinction of form- and meaning-derived lexical errors. She believes that there are form-oriented lexical errors such as

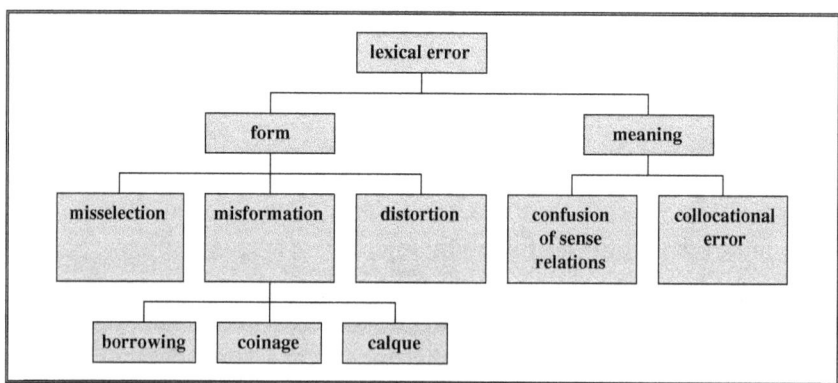

Figure 4.2 Lexical error types in James (1998: 142–154)

distortions (spelling errors), morphology (errors in gender and number morphemes), word formation, confusion of similar forms and language shift. Content-oriented lexical errors are from five different types: word families (derivatives), semantic relatedness, *ser–estar* distinction, register errors and paraphrase errors.[4] Fernandez' subtypes are useful for any research in the area of lexical error analysis. It is obvious that some types dealt with here are language-exclusive (Spanish in this case), but the bulk of the categories can serve other research purposes. This taxonomy is the combination of several classification criteria, basically descriptive on the surface (form/content) and psycholinguistic at a deeper level, for example semantic relatedness, formal similarity, language shift and distortions. In fact, most descriptive taxonomies combine description and explanation, since the description of the lexical approximations often contains hypotheses of the sources.

In his 1987 study, Zimmermann propounds a very interesting typology with two different classes of lexical errors: form-oriented and content-oriented. This taxonomy distinguishes among errors that result from a confusion of a target and an error word due to formal similarity (form-oriented error) or due to semantic relatedness (content-oriented error). The language of origin of the deviation, L1 or L2, also plays a secondary role, thus leaving a four-way lexical error taxonomy as follows: L1 form-oriented, L2 form-oriented, L1 content-oriented and L2 content-oriented. The main pitfall of this valuable contribution is the frequent lack of clear definitions, the abundance of vague explanations and the mixing of classification criteria (psycholinguistic cause of the error, linguistic source of the error [L1 or L2] and product orientation).

(2) *Descriptive criterion* led by purely descriptive considerations that focus on the surface form of the error without alluding to causes or sources of the lexical errors. Thus, we talk of erroneous selection of items (e.g. wrong lexical choice), omission, addition and wrong ordering (Ambroso, 2000: 54; Corder, 1973). Djokic (1999), Hyltenstam (1988) and Zimmermann (1986a) belong to this group of authors who offer descriptive taxonomies (see also Ambroso, 2000, and Lennon, 1991b).

Djokic (1999) establishes three main types of lexical errors: substitution, omissions and additions. He also subclassifies lexical errors depending on the strategies applied: codeswitching, transfer, intercode switching and word-coining. The communicative load of the lexical error is also considered for classification; thus, errors that lead to temporary confusion, to misunderstanding or to breakdown of communication are distinguished. This classification is particularly useful in determining the communicative effectiveness of the lexical error.

For Hyltenstam (1988), the lexical errors of his learners of Swedish L2 can be reduced to two types: approximations and contaminations. The first are errors with clearly identifiable targets that arise from similarity in form or meaning. The latter result from the mixture of two words which are non-existent in Swedish, and are called blends or hybrids in Ringbom's terminology (1981, 1983). This taxonomy has little practical value for other studies, since it is too narrow and may leave out a large number of lexical errors that do not comply with the characteristics of either group pointed out by Hyltenstam. Furthermore, this taxonomy arises from the necessities of the author at that particular moment and for that particular data. It is very improbable that this taxonomy would successfully and felicitously suit another set of data. Notwithstanding, this taxonomy very well serves the purposes of the author, who simply wants to compare quantitatively (total number of lexical errors/ frequency) and qualitatively (types of lexical errors) the lexical error production of Swedish monolinguals and two groups of bilinguals (advanced learners of Swedish in a natural environment).

Zimmermann's descriptive taxonomy (1986a) is a linguistic description of lexical errors based mainly on the semantic relations (hyponymy, part-whole, process-result and synonymy) between the error and the target word. It also considers the semantic features of the words involved in the lexical error, and the syntagmatic relations between error and target. Among the types of lexical errors that Zimmermann distinguishes are sense relation errors, field errors, feature errors, collocation errors, word-formation errors, stylistic errors and connotative errors. The best feature of this taxonomy is its comprehensiveness as well as its sound theoretical and practical basis. In practice, (nearly) all instances of lexical errors seem to find acceptance in this taxonomy. Albeit exhaustive, the taxonomy presents the problem of delimitation and overlapping of categories. Quite a number of lexical errors could be assigned to two or more categories simultaneously; the decision where to ascribe it depends on the perspective of the author.

In general, the main drawback of descriptive classifications is that they offer partial accounts of the phenomenon, since they do not search for the causes of the lexical errors. They are inevitably post hoc, what makes them specific to the research data for which they were designed.

(3) *Etiologic or psycholinguistic criterion*: This refers to the source of the lexical error. In this sense, this criterion classifies lexical errors

relative to their cause, that is to the mental processes underlying the lexical error, by which the lexical error originates, and which reflect the nature of the deviation, for example overgeneralisation, semantic transfer and confusion of related words (Dušková, 1969; Engber, 1995; Santos Gargallo, 1993; Warren, 1982; Zimmermann, 1986b). These authors base their taxonomy of lexical errors on the mental process that leads to the error. According to this, they search for the psycholinguistic causes of the deficiency and this classificatory criterion is based on the belief that lexical errors are the result of a faulty application of vocabulary learning and communication strategies[5] (cf. González Álvarez, 2004; Jiménez Catalán, 1992: 128–135). All these studies are implemented following a similar methodology.[6]

Although Engber's study (1995) was not particularly devoted to the design of a lexical error taxonomy, the typology of lexical errors that she devises is worth mentioning, since it departs from the premise that knowing a word (lexical competence) implies knowledge about different word features such as its derivations, its morphology or its syntagmatic and paradigmatic relations. Thus, she distinguishes between errors in the lexical choice and those in the lexical form. The first category includes a wrong choice of individual words, and of combinations; the second can be subsumed under the more frequent heading of collocation error. Within the group of errors in the lexical form, Engber includes the following: derivational, verb forms, phonetically related and spelling errors. In principle, this taxonomy has a sound theoretical and practical basis, since it rests on the notion of lexical competence and on a wide range of examples. Nevertheless, it is rather confusing since it mixes descriptive categories (spelling errors) and interpretative ones (confusion due to phonological similarity). It is a very limited taxonomy, because it may leave out many lexical errors.

A further taxonomy that classifies lexical errors related to the underlying mental process is that of Santos Gargallo (1993). Her investigation does not centre exclusively on lexical errors, but they are a small part of her account of the errors of Serbo-Croatian learners of SFL. On the basis of Kumaravadivelu's study of lexical simplification (1988), Santos Gargallo (1993) uses four types of lexical errors in her taxonomy: semantic infelicity, transfer, borrowing and wrong derivation.[7] This author attempts to find out the processes and strategies that lead to the production of errors in vocabulary.

For Zimmermann (1986b), semantic transfer is responsible for the lexical error. In his account of the lexical errors of his German students, Zimmermann tries to go one step further and complements the description of the categories of semantic deviation (see Zimmermann, 1986a) with an overview of the genesis of these lexical errors. Thus, he provides a descriptive classification of lexical errors and accounts for the psycholinguistic processes that generate them against the framework of the organisation of the lexicon. In this framework, lexical errors are classified depending on (a) the stage of the speech production process at which they originate, (b) whether they are form- or content-oriented (see Zimmermann, 1987), (c) whether they are a paraphrase of an appropriate form or a complex word as a condensed paraphrase or (d) whether these lexical approximations are traces of L1 and L2 associations simultaneously. In spite of the practical validity of this taxonomy, it has little a priori predictive power, because Zimmermann provides few explanations and bases his taxonomy exclusively on examples.

Warren (1982), for example, distinguishes in the writings of her Swedish learners of English four main types of lexical errors: (a) equivalence errors (transfer of semantic and/or syntactic features), (b) conceptional confusion (confusion due to similarity of meaning), (c) derivational errors (confusion due to wrong derivational processes) and (d) phonetic confusion (confusion due to similarity of sound). These types of lexical error derive from a wrong word choice which originates either from the wrong assumption that the L2 word functions in the same way as the L1 word (interference error) or from a confusion due to various causes (intralingual errors).

After claiming that lexical errors are the least homogeneous material, Dušková (1969) distinguishes four types of lexical errors depending on the psycholinguistic causes that give rise to them. These types are confusion of words due to formal similarity, due to relatedness of meaning, assumed equivalence and distortions (spelling errors). Her 1969 taxonomy of lexical errors has appeared in a number of subsequent studies on student lexical errors (e.g. Zughoul, 1991: 46). It is, nevertheless, quite a limited taxonomy with too narrow lexical error types and no explicit specification of what is considered to be a lexical error. The definition provided of error in general is also too broad; for example, she talks about 'deviation from the normal form' (p. 12). It is, in short, a large study of error analysis, where the treatment of errors in the lexicon receives limited attention. The best and most important contribution of this study to the field of SLA is the comparison that it makes between errors in production and those in comprehension. In the case of lexical errors, it turns out that they are basically the same type of errors, mainly because of confusion over formal and/or semantic similarity. This finding is significant, since it indicates, on the one hand, that vocabulary production and comprehension processes develop in a similar manner, and on the other hand, that learner's language strategies for vocabulary production and comprehension are comparable, if not the same.

(4) *Origin of influence criterion*: Traditionally, within this group three origins of error have been distinguished, that is mother tongue influence (interlingual or interference errors), target language difficulty (intralingual or developmental errors) and teaching-induced errors (cf. James, 1998: 188–190). This tripartite distinction has somehow fallen into disuse and has been overridden in the literature by other classificatory criteria, basically, by psycholinguistic criteria (transfer, overgeneralisation and simplification) (cf. Blum & Levenston, 1978; Richards, 1971; Taylor, 1975). Ambroso (2000: 54) argues that stating that the lexical error is provoked by L1 or L2 influence, although helpful, does not explain the phenomenon satisfactorily. The fact that recent interest has changed from the study of the role of the L1 in SLA to the investigation into the processes of L2 development might be responsible for the decline in lexical error taxonomies using this criterion as their classificatory basis. See Palapanidi (2009), Ringbom (1981, 1983) and Lennon (1996).

Palapanidi (2009) distinguishes between lexical errors which originate from L1 influence and those that derive from L2 confusion. Her intention with this division is finding out which is the most relevant source of learners' lexical errors as they progress in L2 proficiency.

Ringbom, however (1981, 1983), concentrates on interference errors, that is on lexical errors that derive from previous linguistic knowledge, usually L1 influence, but also influence from other previously learned languages (L3 and L4). The main limitation of his taxonomy is the fact that he considers only a set of lexical errors generated by interference with previous linguistic knowledge, ignoring other sources of lexical errors, for example L2-induced lexical errors. However, Ringbom consciously limits his investigations to the study of L1/L3 interference on lexical errors with no claim to exhaustiveness. He works with Swedish- and Finnish-speaking Finns learning English. The taxonomy is not the end in itself, but Ringbom uses it as a tool to unveil the relationships between the different languages at stake. Within these L1-/L3-influenced lexical errors he establishes a dual categorisation of lexical errors, due to borrowing and lexical transfer. The basic difference between the two groups is that although borrowing implies the introduction of an L1/L3 lexical item into the L2 flow, in lexical transfer the semantic features of an L1 word are transferred into an L2 word; that is the L2 word is made to function like an L1/L3 word. Borrowing refers to formal transfer, and lexical transfer is meaning-based. Again within these two types of lexical errors, Ringbom distinguishes other subtypes depending on how the borrowing and the semantic transfer takes place (items involved, formal relation between items involved, process dealing with error and existence of the lexical item in English). In this case, as can be deduced from the instances given, the subtypes are defined according to the psycholinguistic criterion.

Lennon (1996) does not develop a taxonomy of lexical errors as such. In this paper, the author is concerned with the sources of a particular type of lexical error: verb-choice error. The most frequently alluded source of the lexical error is L1 influence, although overextension (L2-oriented error) and a gap in the lexical knowledge are commonly cited sources. Lennon also refers to a hazy lexical knowledge concerning polysemy (semantics), contextual and collocational restrictions (pragmatics), phrasal verb combinations and grammatical environment (syntax) as the responsible factors for errors in verb choice. When the learner notices this gap in the lexical knowledge, reversion to previous linguistic knowledge or to L2 knowledge is the solution most frequently chosen. Resorting to L1 results in complete language shift, blends, hybrids, relexifications, literal translation and transfer of semantic features, among others. Similarly, resorting to L2 knowledge to overcome a gap in lexical knowledge results in an overgeneralisation and spelling or formal/semantic confusion error, among others. This paper is a mere account of the possible reasons that cause errors in the verbal choice in English by German learners. Therefore, it has little value as a working taxonomy of lexical errors.

(5) *Grammatical or linguistic criterion*: Taxonomies following this criterion classify lexical errors depending on the linguistic level at which the error occurs. Consequently, we find lexical errors originating from deviations in phonology, orthography, morphology, syntax, semantics and pragmatics. Such linguistic classification serves as a landmark to establish the limits of each lexical error type, for example semantic confusion, phonetic deviation and pragmatic confusion (cf. Ambroso, 2000; Corder, 1973; Lennon, 1991b).

Ambroso's paper (2000) is a thorough account of lexical errors. She provides the reader with a broad and carefully presented framework of lexical errors and their types. She also includes a very clear definition of lexical error, stating the problems and difficulties in the clear-cut delimitation of the object of study. All the lexical errors that she considers are errors in the lexical choice. These are classified according to the linguistic level at which they occur, that is stylistic errors (pragmatics), syntactic errors, order errors (collocations), semantic errors and system errors or idiosyncratic errors.[8] All types, except this last one, are part of the so-called interlingual errors; that is, they have their origin in mother tongue interference. Ambroso's is a tight working taxonomy of the lexical errors produced by advanced Spanish-speaking learners of Italian. Nonetheless, it can be questioned whether or not this taxonomy can be of any use when analysing the production of younger learners' language and when the languages at stake are typologically, fundamentally lexically, at a larger distance than Italian and Spanish. Furthermore, at times the examples provided are rather vague and the classification of the particular instances is ambiguous.

Ambroso's findings point in two directions. On the one hand, they contradict the general assumption that the further the learner gets, the lower the L1 influence will be, proving that advanced learners are also at the risk of interference from L1. De Groot (1993) and Kroll (1993) believe that for some abstract nouns and words in other grammatical categories, lexical mediation of the L1 is mandatory when trying to retrieve an L2 word. On the other hand, they show that lexical errors behave in a somewhat different way from other types of errors, basically, grammatical. Clearly, further research is needed in the field of lexical errors to find out more about them, the processes that determine them and their patterns of behaviour. These implications are supported by Zughoul's findings (1991).

(6) *Word-class criterion*: This taxonomy distinguishes between lexical error types depending on which class of content word, noun, verb, adjective or adverb, is affected by the error (Lennon, 1991b).

The descriptive classification criterion that Lennon (1991b) follows is the class of content word affected by the error. Thus, he distinguishes the following: noun choice, verb choice, adjective choice, adverb choice and collocational error. He also implicitly includes into his types omission, substitution and addition of any lexical words, and reordering errors. Lennon offers a classification system that is descriptive rather than interpretative: 'Its underlying principle is to classify errors in terms of distributional occurrence rather than to seek to assign psycholinguistic causes to error, which would be to make inferences as to learner "competence"' (Lennon, 1991: 33). This is an exhaustive taxonomy with mutually exclusive categories, and a very small percentage of occurrences where classification is not unambiguous. Thus, this is a very appropriate taxonomy with great explanatory power and may be helpful in other research.

(7) *Product-/process-oriented taxonomies*: Taxonomies of lexical errors can also be classified according to their focus. Therefore, we distinguish process- oriented taxonomies from product-oriented taxonomies. The only difference between these two types is whether they take the psycholinguistic processes that generate the lexical error as the centre of their typology, for example transfer and overgeneralisation, or whether they prefer to depart from the product of that process, the lexical error itself, to establish the taxonomy. According to this differentiation, the following groups can be mentioned:
  (a) product-centred lexical error taxonomies (e.g. Ambroso, 2000; Engber, 1995; Fernández, 1997; Hyltenstam, 1988; Lennon, 1991b; Zimmermann, 1986a, 1986b, 1987);
  (b) lexical error taxonomies that focus on the process (e.g. Dušková, 1969; Lennon, 1996; Ringbom, 1981, 1983; Santos Gargallo, 1993; Warren, 1982).
  (c) Zughoul' (1991) taxonomy is a special case, since in the establishment of the thorough categories, this author combines product- and process-oriented types. He classifies lexical errors after a detailed analysis of the mental processes underlying them, for example literal translation and overuse of lexical items, and also depending on the surface characteristics of the error, for example collocations and circumlocutions.

In general, taxonomies that base their classification on the linguistic description of the lexical errors are all product-oriented, since they do not seek the mental processes that lead to the error, nor do they try to assign a psycholinguistic cause to the error; that is they do not attempt an explanation or interpretation of the error. Similarly, taxonomies whose aim is to determine the causes and sources of lexical errors essentially are of the process-oriented type. Nevertheless, there are some remarkable exceptions: Zughoul (1991), who combines both criteria, and Zimmermann (1987), who, in spite of offering an interpretative taxonomy of lexical errors, concentrates on the product of the processes that he investigates.

(8) *Miscellaneous*: Within this category, we find taxonomies that combine several classification criteria in an endeavour to establish a complete taxonomy that collects as many lexical error types as possible. Some examples of this category are Celaya and Torras (2001), Valero Garcés *et al.* (2000), Lennon (1991b), Zughoul (1991) and Meara and English (1987).

The lexical error taxonomy proposed by Celaya and Torras (2001) is relevant to our research, since we will follow a very similar classification adapted to our objectives. After an analysis of their data, the authors decided to consider interlingual errors exclusively, that is errors deriving from the 'use of words which do not exist in English and which are based on their L1 vocabulary knowledge' (p. 6), since they were by far the most numerous in their findings in a 9-to-1 relation. The interlingual errors that they identify are classified into the following four categories: misspellings, borrowing, coinage and calque. Celaya and Torras' taxonomy (2001) has proven to be very effective for the classification of lexical errors made by young Spanish learners with low proficiency levels in English.

Lexical errors are just one of the error categories that Valero Garcés *et al.* (2000) identify in their subjects' written production. At the lexico-semantic level, they distinguish transfer errors, false friends errors, errors in idioms or fixed phrases and wrong lexical use.[9]

Lennon (1991a) applies his concepts of domain and extent to the classification of lexical errors. Domain refers to the context where the erroneous unit appears and which has to be taken into account in order to recognise the error. Extent or the rank of the linguistic unit affected by the error refers to the erroneous unit (morpheme, word, phrase, sentence and text). Therefore, he distinguishes between three types of errors: (a) collocational restriction violation, where the extent is a word of the collocation and the domain is the sentence; (b) lexical error revealed only by extra-sentential discourse; here the extent is the word and the domain the larger discourse; and (c) lexical error revealed by extra-linguistic context where the extent is the word again, but the domain is the real world.

Zughoul's (1991) taxonomy of lexical errors is by far the most exhaustive and complete of all the taxonomies analysed so far. He divides the lexical errors of his Arabic-speaking students into 13 categories or causes: assumed synonymity, literal translation, derivativeness, influence of Arabic style, collocations, similar forms, message translation, idiomacity, circumlocutions, analogy, overuse of some lexical and other, even new, terms in the literature, for example verbosity and binary terms. As he himself recognises, lexical errors are caused by the strategies that language learners employ for lexical choice. It seems that he implicitly reduces lexical errors to errors in the lexical choice. Zughoul's taxonomy is exhaustive and complete in its classification of lexical errors, and identification of the psychological processes that underlie the error.

Taking this exhaustiveness into account, it seems reasonable to think of the a priori explanatory power of this taxonomy, which would make it very valuable and reliable in the field of SLA and more specifically in EA. Such a taxonomy would allow researchers and teachers to improve the existing instructional approach to vocabulary learning/teaching, for instance by developing word difficulty lists, effective preventive and remedial exercises and explanations, or by implementing an integral teaching program with a vocabulary- and lexical-error-based syllabus.

Meara and English (1987) offer a systematic classification which distinguishes among the following: totally wrong word, phonologically related word, wrong word right semantic area, formal derivational errors, usage and spelling error. This classification is elaborated on the basis of the dictionary information provided to prevent the lexical error.

Table 4.1 offers a summary of the different taxonomies of lexical errors and the classificatory criteria that give rise to them.

General limitations of lexical error taxonomies

Although particular limitations and shortcomings of the individual taxonomies have already been pointed out, some general characteristics and pitfalls of the taxonomies of lexical errors will be addressed here. Meara (1984) observed that concern with lexical errors is rather fruitless, for being too restricted, since many aspects of the lexical behaviour of L2 learners cannot be revealed through lexical error analysis, because this lexical behaviour does not always result in an error. Although he acknowledges the helpful role of lexical error taxonomies to describe and interpret the data in a clear and coherent way, he believes that they are of little value, for 'they are essentially post hoc analysis, and have little predictive or explanatory power' (p. 226). This basically means that the potential of a taxonomy of lexical errors is rather limited.

Lexical error taxonomies can be developed to support some new claim or theory of the author, for example L1 influence on SLA and on transfer errors (Dušková, 1969; Ringbom, 1981, 1983), or to illustrate newly coined concepts (Lennon, 1991a; Zimmermann, 1987). Still, there are few

Table 4.1 Summary of lexical error taxonomies

Criteria	Examples of lexical error types	Authors
Form- vs. content-oriented	Confusion of two formally similar words Wrong word formation Word invention Borrowing from the L1 Adaptation of an L1 to the L2 Linguistic calque Omission Addition Wrong ordering of letters within the word Wrong choice of two similar words Hyponyms instead of supernyms Collocational errors Confusion of two semantically similar words	Palapanidi (2009) Hemchua and Schmitt (2006) Carrió Pastor (2004) James (1998) Mutta (1999) Fernández (1997) Zimmermann (1987)
Descriptive	Approximations Hybrids or blends Field errors Sense relation errors Stylistic errors Connotative errors	Djokic (1999) Hyltenstam (1988) Zimmermann (1986a)
Etiologic	Wrong choice of individual words Wrong choice of combinations Spelling errors Derivational errors Semantic infelicity Transfer Borrowing Wrong derivation Conceptional confusions	Engber (1995) Santos Gargallo (1993) Zimmermann (1986b) Warren (1982) Dušková (1969)
Origin of influence	L1 derived (transfer, borrowing) L2 derived (overgeneralisation, confusion)	Palapanidi (2009) Lennon (1996) Ringbom (1981, 1983)
Linguistic	Stylistic errors Syntactic errors Order errors Semantic errors System errors Idiosyncratic errors	Ambroso (2000)

Table 4.1 (*Continued*)

Criteria	Examples of lexical error types	Authors
Word-class	Noun errors Verb errors Adjective errors Adverbs errors	Lennon (1991b)
Product-oriented	Focus on the product, the lexical error	Zimmermann (1986a, 1986b, 1987) Hyltenstam (1988) Lennon (1991b) Engber (1995) Fernández (1997) Ambroso (2000)
Process-oriented	Focus on the process that leads to the lexical error	Dušková (1969) Ringbom (1981, 1983) Warren (1982) Lennon (1996) Santos Gargallo (1993)

classifications that have practical application in the classroom (see, e.g. Hemchua & Schmitt, 2006; Meara & English, 1987; Warren, 1982; Zughoul, 1991).

Meara believes that taxonomies

do not in themselves predict which types of errors will occur, or explain why certain types of error should occur in preference to other possible error types. It does not even suggest any obvious way of providing instruction which could eliminate the more dramatic errors. Nor, unlike some of the best interlanguage work, does it manage to suggest that such errors as do occur form part of a coherent developmental pattern. Clearly, then, though these error analysis may provide us with some useful preliminary data, they do not on the whole take us very far. (Meara, 1984: 226)

We agree with Meara that while taxonomies on their own have little predictive and explanatory power, and offer no explicit instructional solutions to solve lexical problems in the L2, the importance of the preliminary data that they provide us with cannot be undervalued as an instrument to find out more about L2 acquisition and teaching processes. In the light of results obtained from a taxonomy, it is the task of the researcher to deduce and extract the behavioural and developmental patterns of lexical errors, design pedagogical solutions to the lexical problems evidenced by the analysis of lexical errors, explain the types of lexical errors occurred and predict the ones that will occur subsequently. This prediction can follow only from a coherent interpretation, systematisation and generalisation of results to other similar target groups.

Each EA project and taxonomy development requires a set of procedures, decisions and criteria, and a degree of accuracy which correspond to its goals and needs. The fact that lexical error taxonomies are post hoc, that is designed after the lexical errors have been analysed, makes it very difficult to use them for other sample of data different from that for which they were devised. Unfortunately, these classifications are of little help to researchers who may want to apply one of them to their sample of lexical errors. Typologies are designed according to the needs of each researcher once they have collected, identified and even analysed lexical errors. The classifications are developed to fit the concrete lexical error sample; therefore, one can argue that they are specific. They seem to work for particular cases of lexical errors, but it is unlikely that they can be adapted for other data sets, for instance learners with different L1s than the one considered in the particular study. It is desirable that a working taxonomy of lexical errors be designed that can include the greatest number of instances and types of lexical errors, and can thus be employed as an a priori tool to analyse a wide range of data sets.

In addition, all taxonomies, even the most exhaustive and comprehensive ones, present some problems of overlapping of categories. This implies that there is a changing percentage of lexical errors that could be classified into different types depending on the perspective taken by the classifier as to its source, its cause, its surface structure or the context. Lennon (1991b), when accounting for his very exhaustive lexical error categories, acknowledges:

> For a small number of error occurrences in the corpus (1–2%) classification is not unambiguous in terms of the above categories. This probably is in the nature of things, since any system of error classification represents an attempt to impose order on disparity by means of grouping unique phenomena in terms of their similarities with one another. The above is an attempt to dissect the corpus without murdering it. (Lennon, 1991b: 40)

Most papers on lexical errors deal with the vocabulary production of advanced adult second language learners. There is little research investigating the lexical errors produced by either children or by early ESL beginners.

Pedagogical implications of lexical error taxonomies

Most researchers do not consider the pedagogical implications and applications of the taxonomies of lexical errors that they work with. They merely describe lexical errors as to their form and their sources, neglecting the further step of applying their findings to instruction. Teachers try to prevent and eliminate grammatical errors by means of explaining the rules and applying them to practical cases, whereas lexical errors are ignored in the classroom and teachers expect learners to learn each lexical item in isolation, and hope that vocabulary errors will disappear with time. Some exceptions to this are Hemchua and Schmitt (2006), Zughoul (1991), Meara and English (1987) or Warren (1982), who, in addition to the identification of certain specific problems of vocabulary acquisition, provide a systematic approach to their solution.

A thorough interpretation of the taxonomy of lexical errors can account, for example, for difficulty scales of lexical items, reveal how lexical learning happens, for example what stages the learners go through, determine the lexical competence of learners at each particular stage of their language acquisition process or establish some evaluation criteria as regards, for example, the writing of learners in their L2.

There are several ways in which lexical errors and their taxonomies can be used to improve the teaching of L2 vocabulary. For instance, Warren (1982) suggests that in the same manner that teachers try to eliminate grammar errors of their students' production by informing them about the appropriate rule, vocabulary errors can also be ruled out by providing learners with an explanation of the causes. For her, the best pedagogical approach to dealing with lexical errors is the explanation of the reasons that led to the error, by establishing comparisons between L1 and L2 lexical systems (see also Hemchua & Schmitt, 2006). The most important implication and application of the findings of Zughoul's study (1991) is the development of problematic word lists, which may prove very helpful for the L2 learner in adopting practical strategies for improving his or her semantic competence. Meara and English (1987) suggest that dictionaries should be enhanced to prevent some types of lexical errors and give clues as to how this enhancement should proceed by providing examples of usage, or by contrasting different word meanings or words from the same semantic field.

A dual system of instruction that consists of preventive and remedial sets of exercises and explanations that should proceed after the lexical problems have been encountered is another pedagogical application of the findings on lexical errors. Lexical errors serve as the reference point to spot the difficult lexical items and the words liable to cause problems to L2 learners. This instructional approach can be applied in two modalities, with the teacher structuring the lessons according to a lexical-error-based syllabus, and more immediately, where right after the lexical error has been produced, the teacher uses the taxonomy to explain it and to apply this explanation to a practical case.

Lexical Errors as Evidence of Vocabulary Acquisition

Lexical errors are of extreme significance in the field of SLA, because as observable IL phenomena they serve as insights into the process of L2 vocabulary acquisition, revealing the problematic areas in acquisition and the different learning phases. In other words, lexical errors help learners identify the gaps in their lexical repertoire. They also help the teacher spot the problematic areas in L2 vocabulary acquisition. They also help the researcher find out about the underlying processes in L2 vocabulary acquisition, since they provide insights into these processes (cf. Corder, 1967: 167).

Lexical errors are a reliable instrument to investigate the organisation of the mental lexicon in L2 and to find out more about vocabulary development (Laufer, 1991a). Ecke (2001: 90) claims that non-target lexical items are relevant to determining patterns of lexical organisation, storage and retrieval. More specifically, lexical errors reveal the patterns of associative and synonymy relationships. Depending on whether the lexical error is formal or semantic, the researcher can learn more about the lexicon. Form-oriented lexical errors are evidence of an organisation of the lexicon that reveals that words which are formally similar are stored together. On the contrary, meaning-oriented lexical errors point to an organisation of the lexicon based on semantic links between words; that is, semantically related words are stored together. (Gu, 2003: 14).

Laufer (1991a) suggests ways of determining the properties of the lexicon from the evidence of lexical errors. She examined the structural nature of the learners' mental lexicon on the basis of lexical inconsistencies she calls *synforms* (similar lexical forms). She claims that lexical errors are indicative of the structure and organisation of the foreign lexicon, and she goes on to list some properties of this lexicon:

(1) L2 learners seem to fail in identifying the number of syllables of the words they learn.
(2) L2 learners do generally record stress patterns correctly, since they commit few lexical errors where this salient lexical feature is confused.
(3) It seems that learners store words by paying attention to their beginning letters, but not necessarily their ending letters.
(4) Consonants are more prominent and salient features of lexical items, since they are rarely affected by confusions.
(5) Learners tend to store words according to their grammatical category, so that when they confuse two words, these mostly belong to the same word class.

The source of the lexical error, that is L1 transfer or L2 influence, and the different forms of these phenomena, for example overgeneralisation, confusion, borrowing and lexical creation, provide useful information in examining the nature of the relationships between the L1 and L2 lexicons. Moreover, research on lexical errors evidences the process of vocabulary learning and SLA as a whole. Traditionally, errors have been considered to be an important and reliable source of information about SLA in general, because

> ... they demonstrate conclusively that learners do not simply memorize target language rules, and then reproduce them in their own utterances. They indicate that learners construct their own rules on the basis of input data, and that in some instances at least these rules differ from those of the target language. (Ellis, 1985: 9)

By analysing lexical errors, researchers can find out the underlying mechanisms of the SLA process (Ecke, 2001: 91). Corder (1967) highlighted the importance of errors as evidence of the language system being used in the acquisition process and as reflection of the transitional competence, that is IL of the learner. Some years later, Ellis (1994) claimed that lexical errors are the window that provides researchers with an insight into the learners' lexical competence and how it develops. The lexical errors committed by the learner allow the researcher to find out the problematic lexical items, and the nature of this problem, for example a problem related to collocations, syntactic restrictions and meaning confusion, or a formal problem related to spelling.

Similarly, the study of lexical errors can reveal the different stages that the learners go through in the process of lexical acquisition. The different types of lexical errors are characteristic of a particular stage of vocabulary acquisition (Celaya & Torras, 2001; Hemchua & Schmitt, 2006; James, 1998; Laufer, 1991a; Meara, 1984; Naves et al., 2005; Palapanidi, 2009) except for fossilised errors that pervade over time and over different learning stages. As experience with the language and linguistic proficiency increases, the learner displays different types of lexical errors. In general terms, learners with low proficiency have more problems with the form of the lexical item, whereas at more advanced stages learners make more semantically related errors (Celaya & Torras, 2001; Hemchua & Schmitt, 2006; Meara, 1984; Palapanidi, 2009). In addition, low-proficiency learners tend to rely more on L1 in using borrowings, whereas high-proficiency learners show more instances of L2 influence (Celaya & Torras, 2001; Hemchua & Schmitt, 2006; Naves et al., 2005). The analysis of lexical errors shows the process of lexical acquisition revealing the strategies used by learners in the construction of the language that they are learning. Lexical errors reveal an active process of learning with some constants that show the stage of the process in which learners are and possible pedagogical implications (Fernández, 1995: 203–204; Palapanidi, 2009).

Lexical errors are dealt with in a different way in L2 classrooms where structural teaching methods have been substituted by the communicative approach (cf. Council of Europe, 2001), which has the development of communicative competence as its final aim. The way in which the erroneous utterance differs from the correct one and the causes or psycholinguistic processes that lead to the production of errors are not the only points of interest. The crucial issue now is the examination of lexical errors in light of their influence on successful L2 communication (Skjær, 2004).

Lexical Errors in Communication

Interaction contributes to a better and faster L2 development, and the research stresses its importance in successful SLA (Ellis & Heimbach, 1997; Meara, 1996). Conceivably, vocabulary range or rather lack of vocabulary knowledge has a considerable impact on how this process develops. If vocabulary is relevant for communication, then a deficient lexical competence and lack of lexical knowledge will also influence interaction. Words are the means to express meanings and, accordingly, they are the basic element of verbal communication. If one interlocutor does not know a word or interprets or produces it wrongly, communication (production and reception) will suffer. The role of lexical errors in non-native communication, therefore, cannot be ignored. Lexical errors are important communication distracters. The negative role of lexical errors in communication is significant in the examination of the production of lexical errors in writing, since writing is one way of communication (Djokic, 1999).

In general terms, errors have a negative impact on communication. Errors are relevant not only in terms of accuracy but also as to what misinformation or breakdown in communication they may bring about (Djokic, 1999). Three main consequences of errors in communication can be highlighted. Firstly, errors may cause incomprehension, because due to their presence the reader or the hearer fails to understand the message. Secondly, errors may be the source of misunderstandings, since they give rise to ambiguous messages. And finally, errors may irritate the reader/hearer, or may also cause laughter and hilarity, or even ridicule the learner and consequently hinder communication. This has harmful consequences on the image of the learner (cf. Skjær, 2004).

Contrary to what may be a general assumption derived probably more from the FL classroom than from real-life experience, linguistic correctness is not an essential prerequisite for communicative success. The following example illustrates this matter. Compare the following utterances produced by an L2 learner when addressing his foreign language teacher:

(1) *Give me the result of my exam.*
(2) **Could you to tell me the result of my exam?*
(3) *Could you tell me the finding of my exam?*

Looking carefully at these three example sentences,[10] we realise that although the first one is linguistically correct, that is grammatically perfect, we doubt that it is communicatively effective. Students do not address their teachers with such bold requests, and in this sense, the student might not succeed in the communication of the message and might not obtain the result expected. The second utterance has a typical grammatical error originating in the addition of *to* accompanying the auxiliary *can*, which is always followed by an infinitive. This sentence, although grammatically wrong, will not impose any constraints for communication, and the teacher will know what the learner means. Nevertheless, the last of the examples is a bit more complex. The student seems to have confused two words which in English have similar meanings: *results* and *finding*. This message may give rise to confusion, and the student may fail to convey the intended message, thus generating a communication breakdown (cf. James, 1998: 212).

Faerch and Kasper (1983) show that the elimination of certain formal elements does not interfere with the transmission of meaning. Fernández (1997: 32) also found that grammatical errors with inflections, prepositions and articles do not have important effects on the intelligibility of the message, and, therefore, on communication. Albrechtsen *et al.* (1980) also found that correctness and intelligibility of the message or communicative success do not correlate significantly. Nevertheless, they agree that correct IL is easy to comprehend (see also Khalil, 1985; Picó, 1987). However, communication strategies of lexical simplification turn out to be counterproductive on some occasions if they give rise to a lexical error (Blum & Levenston, 1978; Blum-Kulka & Levenston, 1983). Although grammar errors do not seem to be significant in communicative terms, lexical errors affect the transmission and understanding of the message to different extents, depending on the type of the lexical error.

Inappropriate lexical use often results in an inability on the part of the hearer/reader to decode the intended message of the producer. This leads to a communication breakdown or communication disruption. Haastrup and Phillipson (1983) define the notion of communication breakdown as 'occurring when mutual comprehension is impaired by one of the speakers misunderstanding the other or when the learner is manifestly in trouble in putting across what he/she wants to say' (p. 143). Different studies have yielded clear results that emphasise the notion of lexical errors as communication disturbers (cf. Djokic, 1999). Although the study by Haastrup and Phillipson (1983) was essentially aimed at finding out the type of communication strategies used by language learners in different school types when there is a communication breakdown, their data also revealed that

> so far as the causes [of communication disruptions] are concerned, there is no evidence of either pronunciation or grammar causing communication disruptions: the origin of these lies almost entirely in the learner's lexical limitations, both in reception and in production. (Haastrup & Phillipson, 1983: 145)

These results support the findings of other researchers who claim that gaps in the learners' vocabulary, productive and receptive, account for important communication breakdowns; that is communication is not fluent, and the speaker and the hearer fail to interact and understand each other (e.g. Djokic, 1999; James, 1998: 212; Olsson, 1973; Skjær, 2004).

Lexical knowledge and an adequate vocabulary in size and depth are essential for communication to proceed successfully.

In a recent study, Skjær (2004) found that lexical errors have a negative impact on communication, more so than grammatical errors. More specifically, L1-influenced lexical errors were very damaging. When the strategy of transfer is applied, a lexical error appears which 'may transfer the message more or less correctly, cause momentary confusion, bring about misunderstanding, even result in break of communication. The reader's knowledge of the student's L1 and the context play an important role in the transfer of message' (Djokic, 1999:128).

Lexical errors hinder effective communication. These findings mirror those of Olsson's on semantic errors, which are those that affect the meaning of the utterance, being more disruptive for communication rather than syntactic errors, or those that affect the form of the utterance (see also, among others, Fernández, 1997: 31–32; James, 1977; Lindell, 1973).

The image of the speaker/writer who commits a lexical error can be seriously damaged by it, since the receiver of the message may consider him or her as impolite and rather odd (Gass, 1988: 93). Lexical errors may also greatly irritate and disturb the interlocutor. Misunderstandings coming from misleading utterances, communication impairment caused by unintelligible information and irritation on part of the hearer, be it a native speaker or a non-native speaker, are the worst consequences of lexical errors (Djokic, 1999). Consequently, if language is regarded primarily as a means of communication, and if these errors result in a breakdown in communication, the importance and necessity of their eradication follow (Dagut, 1977: 225). For this to happen, a proper understanding of the source of these lexical errors is important for teachers and researchers (Dagut, 1977: 225), and hence, the relevance of lexical error taxonomies.

Lexical errors are considered to be of the most serious type. The judgement of the gravity of a particular error rests on several criteria. Fernández (1997: 30–32) echoing previous research mentions acceptability, grammaticality, appropriateness, frequency, ambiguity (of the message), intelligibility or communicability, irritability (of the hearer/reader) and stigmatisation (of the speaker/writer) as the main criteria. From a communicative perspective, the most important criterion will be that of intelligibility or communicability. In this sense, the seriousness of an error is assessed in light of the communication disruption that it brings about (Djokic, 1999; James, 1998; Santos Gargallo, 1993; Skjær, 2004; Vázquez, 1987).

The judgement of error gravity is not an objective measure nor are the criteria mentioned above (Fernández, 1997: 30; Vázquez, 1987: 69-72); rather,

> Error gravity is a measure of reaction by native speakers (or sometimes non-native teachers) to language learner errors. The aim of error gravity studies is to find out which type of errors hinder communication most or irritate native speakers most. (Tschihold, 2003: 295)

Several studies on error gravity have shown that lexical errors are judged to be the most severe and damaging by different native and non-native judges, because they constitute the greatest hindrance to successful communication (Ellis, 1994: 63; James, 1998; Santos, 1988). Even students believe that of all error types, those having to do with vocabulary are the most serious (Gass, 1988: 93). Lexical error gravity lies on communicative effect and on comprehensibility; the more an error interferes with communication, the more serious it is from the point of view of the L2 learner (Djokic, 1999; Hughes & Lascaratou, 1982; Johansson, 1978: 41; Khalil, 1985; Picó, 1987; Politzer, 1978; Santos, 1988; Vázquez, 1987).

The studies on error gravity and on the communicative effect of errors on linguistic production have revealed very interesting results, suggesting the importance of communicability as a judging criterion and pointing to the nature of lexical errors as communication distracters. Politzer (1978) found that English-speaking American learners of German L2 and German L1 speakers point to vocabulary errors as the most serious. Subjects reacted most strongly against vocabulary errors, which were definitely considered as the most serious over verb morphology, word order, gender confusion, case ending (grammatical errors) and phonology errors.

In an examination of the judgement of seriousness of an error made by L1 English speakers, by native speaker teachers of English and by Greek teachers of English, Hughes and Lascaratou (1982) found that the categories of errors that were judged to be the most serious because they created the greatest difficulties for comprehension were vocabulary and spelling errors. Likewise, James (1998: 211) reporting on a study by Zola (1984) noticed that 'even minor spelling errors, provided they were of high incidence, often disrupted reading, even when the misspelled words were highly predictable'.

Khalil (1985) asked over 200 native speakers to judge the intelligibility and naturalness of two different types of errors: semantic and grammar errors. The results found that semantically deviant utterances are less intelligible than grammatically deviant ones, since judges considered semantic errors more severe than grammatical ones. Likewise, Olsson (1973) and Picó (1987) found that vocabulary errors were considered to be most serious and of the highest importance, and they concluded that semantic content is more important for successful communication than grammatical accuracy.

One of the most relevant studies on error judgement was conducted by Santos (1988). The reactions of professors to the errors of non-native speakers in academic writing were analysed. The results revealed that lexical errors were judged to be the most serious, because they obscured the meaning of the message and consequently interrupted the normal flow of communication. Similarly, Singleton (1989: 204) mentions a study by Delisle (1982), who observed that 13- to 17-year-old native speakers were most irritated by vocabulary errors. Dordick (1996) performed a gravity analysis of learners' errors framed by communicative success, and found that lexical errors and errors in verb usage were the most serious in the sense that they interfered most with communication. In other words, the texts containing either lexical errors or errors in verb usage involved the greatest comprehension difficulties.

Lexical errors also serve a very important purpose in research about second language (vocabulary) acquisition. Lexical errors have proved to be objective setters of quality criteria, and as such they have been repeatedly used as measures of overall language proficiency, in general, and as indicators of lexical progress, in particular, as we shall see in the following section.

Lexical Errors in the Educational Context

Lexical errors become conspicuous in the pedagogical or instructional context, because they turn out to be useful as quality indicators of learners' written work and as predictors of lexical progress, lexical proficiency level and general academic achievement. Lexical errors as evidence of lack of lexical competence have repeatedly been found to indicate and negatively predict the linguistic competence of learners in several language areas and are indicative of poor school performance.

Vocabulary is widely recognised as an important predictor of linguistic competence. Furthermore, there is common agreement now that vocabulary is central and even preconditional to different areas of language proficiency such as reading and writing. Some studies have even demonstrated that vocabulary may predict performance in these skills to some extent (Cobb, 2000). Likewise, we can safely assume that lexical errors will, by contrast, serve as negative predictors of performance in the different language skills.

Several studies have put forward the importance of a rich and varied vocabulary in developing skills in different language areas. Reading comprehension, for example, is said to benefit largely from both extensive and deep vocabulary knowledge. Qian (1999, 2002) showed that vocabulary measures served to predict performance in reading comprehension, thus confirming the importance of the vocabulary factor in assessing reading (see also Anderson & Freebody, 1981; Clark & Ishida, 2005; Grabe & Stoller, 1997; Laufer, 1997a).

Similarly, writing production also improves as the range of vocabulary employed in composition increases, as we have already seen in previous chapters (Engber, 1995; Grant & Ginther, 2000; Jarvis *et al.*, 2003; Laufer & Nation, 1995). Similarly, oral language skills, listening and speaking are performed better if the learner can depend on a well-developed lexical competence. In this sense, oral discourse is considered to be more fluent when it displays a wide, appropriate and accurate vocabulary (McCarthy, 2006).

Not only is vocabulary central to language development and performance in linguistic skills, general academic performance is also influenced by vocabulary knowledge and lexical competence. Especially in the L1 use, lexical competence has been proven to significantly influence academic performance and school success (Álvarez Castrillo & Diez-Itzá, 2000). Therefore, the better the lexical competence of the learners in L1 is, the higher the school grades will be.

The series of studies conducted by Verhallen and Schoonen (1993, 1998) in the Netherlands provide further evidence and support for the arguments related to the importance of lexical competence in the development of general L2 linguistic abilities and performance. These studies also point out that L2 vocabulary not only is essential for L2 development but also influences general school performance. The more words learners know and the better they know these words, the better they will fare in general school achievement. Educational development and school success are closely linked to, predicted by and dependent on lexical knowledge (see also Hancin-Bhatt & Nagy, 1994; Harley, 1995).

More recent research by Morris and Cobb (2004) shows similar results, suggesting that vocabulary profiles can serve as predictors of academic performance. In their study, learners were required to write an essay in English from which their lexical knowledge was extracted. By analysing learners' knowledge of words belonging to different frequency levels and word classes (function vs. open-class words), the authors were able to establish correlations with grades obtained in grammar courses. These correlations allowed them to conclude that the vocabulary profile they used may serve as a valid assessment instrument of general academic performance.

Consideration of the importance of lexical knowledge in the development of the different language areas, and in school success in general, implies that lexical errors can be reasonably thought to have a negative impact on general educational and academic achievement.

Lexical errors serve to evaluate proficiency, lexical and general, in the different language skills and to measure the quality of their written and oral production. For example, scores of written compositions are based on the percentage of lexical errors (vs. effectively and well-used vocabulary) contained in the writing, among other lexical measures (frequency, originality and variation) (Engber, 1995; Laufer & Nation, 1995; see also Chapter 3). The role of lexical errors as proficiency predictors can be traced back to vocabulary being the basic element in linguistic and academic development. Although the relationship between lexical errors and quality of composition has been just dimly proven (Agustín Llach, 2007; Engber, 1995), there is agreement to consider lexical errors as quality predictors and as evidence of lack of lexical knowledge and of low general language proficiency. Usually, the quality of IL performance is assessed in terms of its communicative effectiveness, so that if the learner's production is communicatively successful, it will be positively evaluated as far as quality is concerned. In order to be communicatively effective, discourse cannot contain many lexical errors, since they clearly obscure meaning.

For L2 oral texts, density of errors, especially of lexical errors, also proves to be highly linked to evaluation of general linguistic performance. In their experiment, Albrechtsen *et al.* (1980) determined that ESL conversation extracts with a high density of lexical errors, that is with many lexical errors (objective measure), obtained negative evaluations (subjective measure given by native speaker judges) with regards to their linguistic deployment. This statement provides further evidence of the correlation between lexical errors and discourse quality (see also Valero Garcés *et al.*, 2003: 14).

In our opinion, the relationship is meaningful enough to allow us to make predictions concerning the quality of compositions. This has important consequences for planning writing courses. These findings are also relevant for evaluation, since they allow teachers to rely on objective evaluation criteria based on the percentage of lexical errors. Teaching can also benefit from the results of this study by providing learners with word lists of problematic lexical items and the lexical errors that affect them. Doing exercises will help reduce the number of lexical errors, and thus improve the quality of students' written tasks.

Conclusion

This chapter has attempted a systematisation of research findings regarding lexical errors. We have examined the definition of the term 'lexical error' and have accounted for several of the most important lexical error taxonomies. Defining and classifying lexical errors allows the researcher to find out what types of lexical errors are the most frequent, and draw conclusions about the pedagogical implications of these lexical errors in L2 vocabulary teaching. It is of interest to determine the ways in which learners learn and use English vocabulary in the performance of written tasks. The mental processes and the compensatory strategies employed to make up for lexical gaps are revealed by the analysis of the lexical errors encountered in the written production of these learners. Grant and Ginther (2000: 143) also highlight the relevance of examining writing errors, basically word-form errors, for a better understanding of L2 writing development and of the real nature of L2 writers' IL.

Lexical errors are a valuable window into the lexical acquisition process. From the evidence provided by the identification, classification and interpretation of lexical errors, researchers are able to establish the main lexical acquisition stages and lexical acquisition processes, and to find out what areas of lexis are more problematic to learners at different stages. Lexical errors have a relevant role in interaction, and they have long been recognised as the most likely cause of unintelligibility (Hughes & Lascaratou, 1982: 179; see also Lindell, 1973; Olsson, 1973). Because of their negative impact on communication, lexical errors are judged to be the most serious and severe of all types of errors among different types of judges. Lexical errors are considered to be very damaging to communication, because they affect the meaning of the message.

In the sense that lexical errors imply a lack of lexical knowledge and an inadequate use of vocabulary, they contribute negatively to language assessment. The quality of written and oral production is influenced by the presence of lexical errors in the composition or discourse. In sum, a piece of language with many lexical errors will obtain a bad score. The following chapters look at this issue.

Notes

1. See Ambroso (2000), Djokic (1999), Fernández (1997), Engber (1995), Jiménez Catalán (1992), Channell (1988), Hyltenstam (1988), Zimmermann (1986b, 1987), Vázquez (1987), Ringbom (1983), Warren (1982) and Dušková (1969).
2. See Laufer (1990a, 1990b, 1991a), Lennon (1991a), Zughoul (1991), Hyltenstam (1988), Zimmermann (1986b), Warren (1982), Blum and Levenston (1978) and Dagut (1977).
3. In those cases where taxonomies follow more than one single classificatory criterion, we ascribe them to one or the other group depending on what we consider to be the main classificatory criterion that prevails over the other.
4. In Spanish in the original: *reconocimiento de los rasgos de género y número de los nombres, formaciones no atestiguadas en español, uso de significantes próximos, deformaciones, barbarismos, lexemas con semas comunes pero no intercambiables en el contexto, 'ser'–'estar', perífrasis, cambios entre lexemas de la misma raíz* and *cambios de registro*.
5. We do not intend to equate lexical errors to learning and communication strategies. Obviously, the application of a vocabulary learning and/or communication strategy does not necessarily result in a lexical error, but they give rise to perfectly correct utterances in some cases.
6. One aspect in which these studies differ though is their product–process orientation. This may seem contradictory, since focus on the mental processes leading to lexical errors is characteristic of this group of authors. However, it is legitimate that they use the very lexical error, the product of the psycholinguistic process that they are analysing as the reference point for their taxonomy. A process-oriented taxonomy seems more reasonable, though. In Point 7 of this section, a classification of the taxonomies depending on their product/process orientation is provided.
7. In Spanish in the original: *impropiedad semántica, transferencia, préstamos lingüísticos* and *derivación errónea*.
8. In Spanish in the original: *errores de estilo, de sintaxis, de orden dentro de la frase, de semántica errores del sistema o idiosincrásicos*.
9. In Spanish in the original: *errores de transferencia, errores en el uso de falsos amigos, de frases hechas o de modismos* and *uso inadecuado de vocablos*.
10. The examples have been invented for illustrative purposes.

Part 2
Lexical Error Production in Young Spanish Learners' Written Compositions

Chapter 5
Designing a Study to Explore Lexical Errors in Writing

The amount of research on lexical errors is considerable, as has been shown in preceding chapters, but few studies deal with the production of lexical errors in young learners (for an example of these, see Celaya & Torras, 2001). Moreover, despite the wide interest in identifying the lexical features that contribute to the assessment of writing quality, the relationship between lexical errors and essay quality has been scarcely investigated (but see Agustín Llach, 2007; Engber, 1995). There is a dearth of studies that explore the role of lexical errors as writing-quality predictors and as measures of receptive vocabulary knowledge (see Agustín Llach & Jiménez Catalán, 2007). There is also a notable lack of longitudinal studies within the field of lexical error analysis (see Palapanidi, 2009). Learners' proficiency level and amount of TL instruction are relevant for determining how lexical learning proceeds. This chapter examines a research study that was devised to explore the production of lexical errors at different testing times and proficiency levels. The effect of lexical error production on the development of receptive vocabulary knowledge and on the global assessment of writing quality was also examined. The participants in the study, the instruments for data collection, the procedures followed and analyses conducted will be explained in the text that follows.

The main purpose of this study was to identify the kinds of lexical errors that appear in the written productions of a sample of young Spanish learners learning English at two different moments in time. Furthermore, the impact of these lexical errors on the quality of the written compositions of learners will also be the object of examination in this study.

The purposes of this research are relevant from the applied linguistic, pedagogical and social perspectives. In this study, we intend to find out more about the processes of lexical acquisition by young learners of EFL in primary education and to improve FL teaching through a better understanding of how FL learning proceeds. This research has important pedagogical implications, especially in regards to the teaching of English vocabulary and other FLs in primary schools. This study provides teachers with objective instruments to measure vocabulary knowledge, with information about some of the strategies used by learners that lead to the production of lexical errors and with data about how lexical competence progresses.

Nowadays, learning and mastering English is a basic academic and even social requirement. English is the *lingua franca* of international communication. Vocabulary is, in turn, a crucial aspect of communication. Lexical errors are important factors leading to communication breakdown. Through the identification and analysis of these lexical errors, we can learn more about the process of lexical acquisition and the strategies used by primary school learners. On the basis of this, we can select the most suitable models and methods of language instruction in order to help our students become communicatively competent and effective within and without the national and regional borders.

Research Questions and Hypotheses

This study was designed to identify the lexical errors produced by young learners of EFL, to investigate the relationship of these lexical errors with measures of essay quality and thus to fulfill a series of objectives.

Specifically, this study pursued the following general and specific objectives:

General objective:

(1) Identify the frequency of lexical errors and the different lexical error types produced at two different measuring times (T1 and T2).

Specific objectives:

Once the main general objective has been accomplished, this study intended to:

(2) find out whether the absolute number of lexical errors decreases as experience with the language increases;
(3) establish a hierarchy of the different types of lexical errors according to their frequency at T1 and T2, and ascertain whether this order of frequency changes;
(4) explore the relationship between lexical errors and lexical error types and quality of composition as measured by the final score obtained in the Profile at T1 and T2 and

(5) explore the relationship between lexical errors and lexical error types and vocabulary level at T1 and T2.

On the basis of these objectives and the theoretical and empirical findings of research analysed in earlier chapters, we formulated a series of research questions and hypotheses that represent the starting point of our study. Our research questions read as follows:

(1) Will lexical error production decrease as experience with the language and age increases?
(2) Will there be any differences in lexical error types produced as experience with the language and age increases?
(3) Will there be any relationship between lexical errors and essay quality?
(4) Will the different lexical error types relate to essay quality in similar ways?
(5) Will the different lexical error types relate to receptive vocabulary knowledge in similar ways?

The null hypotheses and the predictions based on the literature are as follows:

(1) Absolute frequency of lexical errors will stay the same as experience with the language and age increases: There will be no difference in the absolute frequency of lexical errors at both testing times T1 and T2, although the types of lexical errors produced may change. Research has proved that error production does not necessarily decrease with language experience. The higher cognitive demands of tasks at more advanced levels of proficiency cause errors to continue appearing (e.g. Ambroso, 2000; Lasagabaster & Doiz, 2003; Olsen, 1999; Ruiz de Zarobe, 2002, 2005b). In other words, the discourse of learners simply gets more complex, and this leads to lexical errors, some of which are new and some of which have fossilised (Olsen, 1999; Vázquez, 1991). The use of new, more and cognitively more complex lexical items (Cenoz, 2002; Lasagabaster & Doiz, 2003; Naves & Miralpeix, 2002; Ruiz de Zarobe, 2005a) can be held responsible for the production of lexical errors and lack of decrease in these as experience with the language and age increase (Cenoz, 2002; Fernández, 1997; Lasagabaster & Doiz, 2003; Naves & Miralpeix, 2002; Ruiz de Zarobe, 2005a; Torras & Celaya, 2001; also cf. Muñoz *et al.*, 2005). For contradictory results, see Naves *et al.* (2005), Hawkey and Barker (2004), Grant and Ginther

(2000), Fernández (1997), Lennon (1991b) and Bardovi-Harlig and Bofman (1989).

(2) Learners will produce different types of lexical errors as experience with the language and age increases: Beginners and more advanced learners were shown to produce different types of errors. Meara (1984) observed that formal errors were more common at the beginning stages of lexical acquisition, gradually being overcome or substituted by semantic errors or errors caused by confusion of meaning. Several other studies (Carrió Pastor, 2004: 179; Celaya & Torras, 2001; Fernández, 1997; Lasagabaster & Doiz, 2003; LoCoco, 1975; Naves et al., 2005; Olsen, 1999; Palapanidi, 2009; Taylor, 1975; Wang, 2003) put forward that low-proficiency learners commit more errors caused by L1 transfer than do their more proficient counterparts. Nevertheless, these researchers also concede that the influence of the L1 is still present at more advanced levels. On the contrary, Mukattash (1986) found that it was the more advanced learners who displayed higher degrees of L1 influence leading to errors in L2 production. Likewise, Cenoz (2001, 2003) and Sanz (2000) showed that older and more proficient learners transfer more from their L1. L1 interference has been found to be especially prevalent in the writing production of beginner learners (Celaya & Torras, 2001; Djokic, 1999; Olsen, 1999). As proficiency and experience with the language increase, intralingual errors start to be less apparent than interlingual errors.

Hawkey and Barker (2004) and Grant and Ginther (2000) noted that as proficiency increased, production of word choice errors (lexical errors) decreased considerably, concluding that for advanced stages the appearance of this type of lexical error was surprising. At any rate, regardless of the particular type of (lexical) errors at each stage, it is a generally acknowledged fact that for every different phase of language and vocabulary acquisition, different types of errors can be observed. The degree of linguistic and lexical competence of the learner may account for these differences in error type and frequency (Ambroso, 2000; Celaya & Torras, 2001; Lasagabaster & Doiz, 2003).

(3) Lexical errors will correlate negatively with essay quality: Echoing previous findings, lexical errors, as a measure of lexical richness, will predict to a considerable extent the quality of written text in a negative sense. Accuracy in lexis is considered to be one of the most relevant criteria to assess the quality of learners' written production together with communicative effectiveness (Agustín Llach & Jiménez

Catalán, 2007; Grant & Ginther, 2000; Hawkey & Barker, 2004; Hyland, 2003; Jarvis et al., 2003; Kuiken & Vedder, 2007; Polio, 2001; Weigle, 2002). The number of lexical errors, that is lexical error density, serves to evaluate the quality of the written composition (Agustín Llach, 2007; Bardovi-Harlig & Bofman, 1989; Engber, 1995; Grant & Ginther, 2000; Hawkey & Barker, 2004; Kobayashi & Rinnert, 1992; Martínez Arbelaiz, 2004; Mutta, 1999; Santos, 1988).

(4) Different types of lexical errors will have different degrees of impact on essay score: Content-oriented errors affect the meaning of the message more than do form-related errors and, therefore, they will have a stronger influence on quality judgements. As already pointed out by Hawkey and Barker (2004: 148), the negative impact of certain categories of errors may be greater than that of others (cf. Djokic, 1999). There is evidence to believe that content-oriented errors obscure meaning more than do form-oriented errors, because their impact on communication is greater, since they influence the transmission of meaning. In addition to their disturbance of the communication process, errors deriving from semantic confusion are generally judged to be more serious, because they affect the meaning of the message the most (Olsson, 1973; see also, among others, Fernández, 1997; James, 1977, 1998; Lindell, 1973; Santos Gargallo, 1993; Skjær, 2004; Vázquez, 1987).

Further evidence pointing to content-oriented lexical errors as more negatively important in judgements of essay quality is provided by Khalil (1985), who found that semantic errors are considered to be more serious, because they are less intelligible than form-oriented errors. By the same token, the findings of Olsson (1973) and Picó (1987) suggest that semantic content is more important than grammatical accuracy for successful communication. By contrast, James (1998: 214) criticises the contention of the existence of semantic errors as opposed to formal errors, and challenges the dichotomy by claiming that some formal or grammatical errors may affect intelligibility more than others, particularly in specific contexts. This implies that some form-related errors may affect communicative success more than some content-oriented ones in some contexts, and, therefore, will have a higher negative contribution to the judgements of essay quality.

(5) Lexical error types correlate to a similar extent with vocabulary level: As a measure of lack of lexical competence, lexical errors and vocabulary level must correlate negatively, so that learners with high density of lexical errors in their compositions will display low

levels of vocabulary knowledge (Agustín Llach & Jiménez Catalán, 2007). Lexical errors have been repeatedly used to measure lexical knowledge in several ways. For example, studies have used lexical errors to (a) investigate the organisation of the mental lexicon (Channel, 1988; Ecke, 2001; Herwig, 2001; Laufer, 1991a; Ringbom, 2001), (b) establish the stages that learners go through in the process of lexical acquisition (Celaya & Torras, 2001; James, 1998; Naves et al., 2005; Palapanidi, 2009) or (c) explore lexical knowledge (Agustín Llach & Jiménez Catalán, 2007).

If the implicit assumption in the literature that productive knowledge increases in an incremental fashion as receptive knowledge also increases is true (Fan, 2000; Laufer, 1998; Laufer & Paribakht, 1998; Meara & Fitzpatrick, 2000), then there has to be a significant relationship between receptive word knowledge and lexical errors as measures of lack of vocabulary knowledge.

Furthermore, we concede that the different types of lexical errors considered at both testing moments will correlate to a similar extent with vocabulary level. There is no evidence to believe otherwise. All lexical error types are evidence of a lack of lexical competence; therefore, they will contribute equally to vocabulary level or lack thereof. If the converse is true, then we could establish a hierarchy of importance regarding the different dimensions of lexical competence and how they contribute to the construct(ion) of lexical knowledge and use. This could have interesting implications for pedagogy and vocabulary instruction.

One of the few studies that address the relationship between general vocabulary knowledge and different types of word knowledge is by Schmitt and Meara (1997). It looks at how different types of word knowledge, specifically word associations and verbal suffixes, relate to general word knowledge. The findings of this study point to a significant relationship among the two types of word knowledge and between these and vocabulary size. However, they also showed that there is great individual variation in how well the different aspects of lexical knowledge are known.

Design of the Study

This research presents a study of the quasi-experimental type which has as its main objective the identification of the lexical errors and lexical error types produced by learners of English at two different testing moments and the examination of the role of these lexical errors as a whole and of the different types of lexical errors, in particular, as

Table 5.1 Overview of the independent and dependent variables of the study

Variables	
Independent	*Dependent*
Testing time	
Vocabulary level	Lexical errors
Writing quality	

predictors of the quality of learners' written production and vocabulary level. This study examines lexical error production after 419 and 629 hours of uncontrolled input[1] when participants were attending the fourth and sixth grades of a primary school, respectively.

In this investigation, we considered three independent variables and one dependent variable. The three independent variables were (1) testing time, with two levels, 419 hours of instruction and 629 hours of instruction, (2) vocabulary level, with as many levels as values of the variable, and finally (3) writing quality or quality of written composition, with again as many levels as values of the variable. All independent variables were between-groups, that is participants could either belong to one or to the other level of the variable, but not to several. In this study, testing time involved the amount of instruction, which co-occured in this case with proficiency level in the target language and with increasing age.

As for the dependent variable, we observed how the production of lexical errors evolves on the basis of the independent variables and how these influence the production of lexical errors by learners. The dependent variable had a total of six levels: (1) misspelling, (2) borrowing, (3) coinage, (4) calque, (5) misselection or formal confusion and (6) semantic confusion. Each of these levels represents one category of lexical error.

Table 5.1 presents the independent and dependent variables, and the different variables with their levels are presented in Table 5.2.

Participants

A total of 283 young Spanish learners of EFL served as participants in this study. At the time of the first data collection session, learners were enrolled in fourth-grade classes of four schools in Spain. By that time, participants had received a total of approximately 419 hours of instruction in their first FL, English. Two years later, when these same learners were

Table 5.2 Overview of the design of the study with the variables and their levels

Variables	Type of variable	Levels	Within–between groups
Testing time	Independent	• Fourth grade (419 hours) • Sixth grade (629 hours)	Between
Vocabulary level	Independent	• As many as values of the variable	Between
Writing quality	Independent	• As many as values of the variable	Between
Lexical errors	Dependent	• Misspellings • Borrowings • Coinages • Calques • Misselection • Semantic confusion	Within

attending the last year of primary education (sixth grade), the second session of data collection took place. This time our informants had received a total of approximately 629 hours of classroom instruction. The first data collection moment or testing time will be henceforth referred to as Time 1, and the second data collection moment or testing time will henceforth be referred to as Time 2. Informants were aged between 9 and 10 years at the first data collection moment; more precisely, the mean age of learners at Time 1 was 9.39 years, and they were aged between 11 and 12 years at the second moment of data collection, with the mean age of participants at Time 2 being 11.39 years.

In the design of this study, the amount of instruction and level of proficiency co-occur with age. To determine the English level of the participants at the two testing moments and to check whether proficiency developed and increased as experience with the language increased, informants were asked to complete two level tests consisting of a cloze procedure and a reading comprehension test. An analysis of the cloze procedure and reading comprehension test yielded results expected in general language proficiency in English: level of proficiency increases with the amount of instruction, as illustrated in Table 5.3, which shows the characteristics of the participants, such as their age, amount of

Table 5.3 General characteristics of participants at both testing times

	Mean age	Hours of instruction	Mean score cloze¹ (%)	Mean score reading (%)
T1	9.39	419	33.9	24.39
T2	11.39	629	46.8	34.28

¹Percentage of right responses

instruction at both testing times and their proficiency level[2] as measured by the cloze and the reading comprehension tests.

All participants were native Spanish speakers. Some learners were not included for some of the analysis because they had not attended class the day the data-collection session took place, or their handwriting was so unintelligible that their compositions remained illegible to the researcher, or their compositions were not written in English. Further information about this will be given in due course in the corresponding section. Rather than volunteers, entire classes were selected for testing. Thus, we used 11 classes in four schools which were tested twice with an interval of two years. Students' names and grade levels were removed and replaced by identification numbers. With regards to the gender variable, it should be noted that male participants totalled 162 (57.24%) and female participants totalled 121 (42.75%).

Materials

The instruments used for the study consisted of a written composition, two vocabulary size tests – the 1000 Word Test (1k) and Nation's Vocabulary Levels Test of the 2000 words, 2k frequency band (VLT 2k) – and two tests of general proficiency – a cloze test and a reading comprehension test. In order to obtain demographic and academic information about the participants, they were given a questionnaire to complete as part of the research study. These instruments of data collection will be explained in more detail in the corresponding sections below.

Written composition

A written composition was used for the study as the elicitation procedure to obtain real language from learners. Participants were allotted a total of 30 minutes to complete the composition task. No minimum length or word constraints were placed on students, and they were encouraged to write as much as they could.

The composition task consisted of writing a letter to a prospective English host family where the learner introduced himself or herself and talked about his or her family, home town, school, hobbies, main interests and anything else about his or her life that he or she deemed interesting to the host family. The composition topic used here was selected because of the following reasons:

(1) It imposed little or no constraints as to the type of language and content to be used by the informants. Instead, the free nature of the writing task allowed students to deploy as much linguistic knowledge in English as possible. Differences between learners in proficiency were ruled out, since the topic did not especially direct the learner to the use of either specific grammatical structures or particular lexical items.
(2) It was guaranteed that informants would have something to write about, and differences in the resulting essays with regards to content and length because of different subject knowledge were eliminated. It was assumed that the specific and personal information required from learners was available to them and thus the task could be performed more easily, a very important fact, considering the young age of the participants. It seemed reasonable to select a familiar topic related to the learner's experience, if the writing task 'is intended to elicit a fluent sample of writing under test conditions without advanced preparation' (Read, 2000: 198).
(3) It was employed to elicit data in a much larger national project within which this study is framed. This allows for comparison with other learners, thus permitting further research.

Participants were given oral and written instructions in L1 Spanish (see Appendix 2 for the exact wording of the instructions).

Compositions, also referred to in the literature as free writing tasks (Read, 2000: 198), were used in this study for several reasons. Firstly, compositions provide very valuable data for error analysis, since they deal with learners' performance at the production level. Secondly, compositions provide relatively spontaneous language material produced by the learner. It is commonly agreed among practitioners and second language researchers that EA should be performed on spontaneously produced language data. Compositions are considered to be the best sources for this goal (Da Rocha, 1980: 85). Besides, if the time and topic of composition are controlled, the resulting products are comparable (Wolfe-Quintero et al., 1998). Argüelles Álvarez (2004: 84), echoing Jacobs et al. (1981) and Ferris and Hedgcock (1998), believes that direct testing of writing ability, that is writing assessment through composition, is the most effective, valid and reliable method of assessing writing in the classroom.

Compositions have been repeatedly used to assess linguistic knowledge and lexical competence of ESL learners, including exploration of lexical errors (Ambroso, 2000; Celaya & Torras, 2001; Engber, 1995; Fernández, 1997; Hemchua & Schmitt, 2006; Hyltenstam, 1988; Jacobs et al., 1981; Jiménez Catalán, 1992; Lasagabaster & Doiz, 2003; Laufer & Nation, 1995; Naves et al., 2005; Palapanidi, 2009; Vázquez, 1987; Warren, 1982). Written essays have been shown to be a valid instrument for measuring linguistic and lexical proficiency. Although they do not offer an exact measure of linguistic knowledge, it is assumed that as a general indication of written production, compositions reflect the real linguistic and lexical knowledge of the learners.

Tests of receptive vocabulary level

In order to measure the receptive vocabulary size of the learners at different moments and to check whether vocabulary size increases with grade level, we administered a vocabulary size test at two levels: the 1000 Word Test and the first band of the VLTs, that is the 2000 word band. The following sections take a closer look at these tests.

VLT 2k

Developed by Paul Nation in the early 1980s, the VLTs were initially designed to help teachers create a vocabulary teaching programme that suited learners' lexical needs. However, they came to be used as estimates of receptive vocabulary size (Nation, 1990, 1993a; Read, 2000). The VLT is divided into five bands, each of which represents a level of word frequency: 2000 most frequent words (2k), 3000 words (3k), 5000 words (5k), university level (academic English words beyond the level of frequency 5000) and 10,000 words (10k) (Nation, 1990, 2001; Read, 2000). The tests are based on the frequency lists collected by West (1953), General Service List and Thorndike and Lorge's (1944) list, which were checked against the list compiled by Kucera and Francis (1967), known as the Brown Corpus.

The design of the test assumes that a learner who scores well at the 5k-word level will obtain good scores at the 2k- and 3k-word levels as well. There exist several versions of the tests designed by Nation, Laufer or Schmitt, (e.g. Laufer & Nation, 1999; Nation, 1990, 2001; Read, 2000; Schmitt et al., 2001). In particular, the version of the VLT 2k used here was taken from Schmitt et al. (2001). This is a slightly modified version of the original. A total of 60 target words were used for testing. Ten groups of six words and three definitions made up the test.

Learners had to write the number of the target word beside the appropriate definition. Each correct answer was given 1 point, so that the maximum score of the test was 30 points. Learners had 10 minutes to complete the task. Appendix 3 offers the complete VLT 2k test used here.

1000 Word Test

Although initially not included in the VLT as an independent testing level, the first 1000 words were later tested as an independent level from the 2k-word level. Nation (1993b) realised the importance and necessity to test the 1000 most frequent words since they provide high degrees of text coverage.

The format of the 1000 Word Test used in this study diverges from the original test proposed by Nation (1993b), which had a true-or-false design. Learners were originally asked to mark sentences including the target word with true or false. However, and considering that participants had the same L1, learners here had to match the target words to a Spanish translation.[3] Learners with low competence would have difficulties in understanding the definitions, because these also include words of lower frequency, and, therefore, translations were chosen to make the test here more practicable.

A total of 60 target words and 30 translations were tested and arranged in groups of six and three, respectively.

Learners had to write the number of the target word beside the appropriate translation. Each correct answer was given 1 point, so that the maximum score of the test was 30 points. A total of 10 minutes was allotted to complete the task. Appendix 4 offers the complete 1000 Word Test used here.

The research studies that have reported on the scalability of the tests (see Read, 2000, but especially Jiménez Catalán & Terrazas Gallego, 2008) serve as evidence to account for the reliability and validity of these tests (Beglar & Hunt, 1999). Many studies have used variations of the VLT to test the receptive vocabulary size of learners for descriptive, comparative or correlational purposes. Some of these studies are Clark and Ishida (2005), Pérez Basanta (2005), Cameron (2002), Qian (1999, 2002), Cobb and Horst (1999), Nurweni and Read (1999), Fan (2000), Horst et al. (1998), Laufer (1998), Laufer and Paribakht (1998) and Waring (1997).

General language proficiency level tests

To ensure an objective measure of the proficiency level of the participants in the study, they were asked to complete two proficiency level tests: a cloze procedure and a reading comprehension test. Learners were allotted 10 minutes to complete each of the two proficiency tests.

Cloze procedure

The cloze procedure was of the multiple-choice type, also called 'multiple-choice cloze' (Read, 2000: 102), where each deleted word is incorporated into a multiple-choice item. Test takers have to choose between three options. The number of multiple-choice items totalled 8 within a total number of 110 words. This indicates that on average one word is deleted every 14 words. The cloze stems from Cambridge KET coursebook, *Key English Test 1*.

The cloze procedure is thought to be an integrative measure of overall language proficiency, and a highly effective way of testing learners' general L2 knowledge (Cenoz, 2003; Muñoz, 2000; Read, 2000).

In 1979, Alderson questioned the general consensus of previous studies, arguing that the cloze procedure is a valid and reliable measure of readability, reading comprehension and global skills in EFL proficiency. He discovered that the cloze procedure correlates highly with tests of grammar and vocabulary, what he calls core proficiency, rather than with tests of reading comprehension. Echoing these findings, the cloze procedure was used here to measure general language competence. A reading comprehension test was further employed to assess learners' level in English.

Furthermore, this competence testing instrument is especially adequate for low-level learners for two main reasons. Firstly, it does not require writing ability on part of the test-takers, and secondly, the multiple-choice format reduces the range of possibilities for each blank, which makes it easier to respond (Read, 2000: 111). The multiple-choice cloze can also be marked more objectively, because the range of responses that the learners could give is limited and controlled. In addition, this type of cloze procedure is considered to be more 'learner-friendly' for providing learners with possible answers and by making it easier for them to complete (Read, 2000).

A model of the cloze test that participants had to complete appears in Appendix 5. Here instructions were also in Spanish L1.

Reading comprehension test

A reading comprehension test was employed to evaluate the learners' proficiency level in EFL. It consisted of a total of seven multiple-choice questions, where learners had to choose the correct answer from three options. The main advantage of using a reading passage to evaluate language knowledge is the presence of context (Read, 2000). Language appears and is assessed in context within a communicative situation. The reading passage used here had a total of 190 words. The reading comprehension test can be found in *KET Handbook* 2004, Read/Write Sample Test 2.

The level of reading comprehension is often considered as an indicator of general proficiency in the language. In fact, learners of different proficiency levels also display varied reading skills and perform in a different way in their reading comprehension (Codina Espurz & Usó Juan, 2000; Mecartty, 1998). It is reasonable to believe that results of a reading comprehension test will serve as indicators of the learning stage and proficiency level at which learners find themselves.

A model of the reading comprehension test that learners had to implement appears in Appendix 6. The instructions for the reading comprehension test were given in Spanish L1. A total of 10 minutes was given for participants to read the text and answer the comprehension questions. In both proficiency level tests, the cloze and reading, participants were provided with a real example from the text showing how to implement the activity.

Both proficiency tests were marked by the researcher. Because of the nature of the multiple-choice format of tests, scoring proceeded easily and quickly. Each correct answer was given 1 point, with maximum scores of 8 points for the cloze test and 7 points for the reading comprehension test. The resulting scores for the cloze and reading tests are presented as two separate measures which reflect the general language proficiency level of the participants.

Questionnaire

In order to complete the information about the participants obtained from the several data-collection instruments presented above, in the last testing session we administered a questionnaire. The questionnaire was written in L1 Spanish and the participants had 30 minutes to answer all questions (see Appendix 7).

The questionnaire contained 26 questions which were grouped into a total of five main areas. The first section was devised to obtain demographic information of the participants, such as their sex, nationality, mother tongue and date of birth. The second main section dealt with learners' FL experience. Questions in the third section tackled learners' EFL knowledge: past grades in English at school and subjective perceptions of their proficiency level in EFL. A fourth section accounted for the learning habits of the participants. And finally, a fifth section examined the beliefs and attitudes of learners towards (1) the English language, (2) the native speakers of that language and (3) the process of acquisition of EFL.

Procedures

Firstly, all data were collected in three sessions in Time 1 and two years later in Time 2. The same procedures were applied for both data-collection moments and data sets. Participants completed the general level tests, the vocabulary tests and the questionnaire, and wrote the compositions in their own classrooms in the presence of the teacher and the researcher. Learners could not make use of any dictionaries, notes, grammar books or textbooks, nor were they allowed to ask the teacher, researcher or their classmates for help.

In a preliminary correction session, the cloze procedure, the reading comprehension test, the 1000 Word Test and the VLT 2k were corrected and scored for right answers.[4] The questionnaires at Time 1 and Time 2 were coded and the results typed in into the statistical program SPSS. During this session, both the Time 1 and Time 2 data were submitted to scoring.

Compositions were collected and converted into computer readable files. All compositions were assessed in two different phases, each of them with particular objectives and procedures, but both complementary and necessary for the design of this study.

Phase 1: Composition rating with the *ESL Composition Profile*

Compositions were assessed using the ESL Composition Profile, an instrument that evaluates the quality of composition from the perspective of communicative effectiveness. Following Jacobs *et al.* (1981), compositions were read twice. In the first reading, the assessor tried to judge holistically whether the composition transmitted the message. In the second, analytic evaluation according to the descriptors took place.

The Profile consists of five rating scales, which distinguish four levels of mastery: excellent to very good, good to average, fair to poor and very poor. However, each of these scales is scored in a different way. Thus, the content scale scores up to 30, organisation and vocabulary up to 20 points each, language use scores 25 and mechanics scores 5. The maximum score is 100, and the minimum is 34.

In order to guarantee internal validity of the measure, each composition was read twice blindly by two trained raters. When there was a disagreement of more than 10 points, a third rating was implemented, in which case the score of the controversial composition was decided upon the majority opinion. Agreement was achieved when readers' scores were 10 points or fewer apart, as defined by the ESL Profile standards (see Jacobs *et al.*, 1981, and also Read, 2000: 216–217). In addition, the Pearson product–moment correlation coefficient[5] was calculated for interrater reliability[6] between the first, second and third readers.[7] Results for compositions at Time 1 revealed a correlation coefficient of $r = 0.84$, and for compositions at Time 2, $r = 0.82$.

Rater agreement procedures resulted in 36.53% of the Time 1 compositions and 55.72% of the Time 2 compositions going to a third reader. The discrepancies were resolved with the input of the third rater. An average was then calculated on the basis of two or three different scores, and this mean was used to determine the quality of composition for each composition. This single score was then correlated to lexical errors and lexical error types.

Phase 2: Error analysis

In the second phase of the analysis, compositions were scrutinised for lexical errors. Lexical errors were identified, counted, described, interpreted and subsequently classified according to their origin. The taxonomy of lexical errors designed by Celaya and Torras (2001) was also used here; two further categories were added on the basis of James's (1998: 144–154) classification of lexical errors. According to these authors, any open class word, that is nouns, adjectives, verbs and adverbs, is liable to be the subject of a lexical error (see also Engber, 1995). Consequently, a word is considered to be erroneous, and, therefore, unacceptable 'if it contains a malformation, if it is not an English word or if it violates native-like use in the context where it appears' (Celaya & Torras, 2001: 6).

Of all the steps of the methodology of EA, the identification and classification of the lexical errors is the most difficult. Erroneous productions were determined on the basis of the English norm. Dictionaries and grammar books were used to establish the standards of English for our purposes. Specifically, we used the *Collins Cobuild*

Dictionary, the *Collins Spanish–English Dictionary,* the *Oxford English Grammar* and the *Cambridge Grammar of the English Language*. Classifying lexical errors is an arduous task, because the same problem or deviation can be due to several causes, or respond to different mechanisms of production in different contexts. Furthermore, although EA is a field where classification of lexical errors cannot be made with absolute confidence, we have tried to be as systematic and objective as possible.

Six main categories of lexical errors are distinguished in the taxonomy:

(1) *Misspellings,* also frequently known in the literature as 'spelling errors' (see, e.g. Arnaud, 1992; Bouvy, 2000; Fernández, 1997; Lindell, 1973) or orthographic errors (Olsen, 1999): These are violations of the orthographic conventions of English which are generated as a result of the difficulties that learners have in coping with the 'English encoding system' (Celaya & Torras, 2001: 7), for example *biutiful* for 'beautiful', *smool* for 'small' or *guatermelon* for 'watermelon'. Some researchers prefer to ignore spelling errors, but many of the learners in this study have problems with English orthography, and as Olsen (1999) noted, these play an important role in the poor results achieved by learners, with many spelling errors in their written essays. Therefore, it is interesting to examine the processes behind misspellings.

(2) *Borrowings,* also called 'complete language shift' or 'code switching' (see, e.g. James, 1998; Naves *et al.,* 2005; Olsen, 1999), appear when the learner inserts any L1 words into the L2 syntax 'without any attempt to tailor them to the target language' (Celaya & Torras, 2001: 7), and this includes phonological or morphological adaptations. Following are some examples:

(a) My grandmother is *coja* (Eng. lame).
(b) My father is big and *lento* (Eng. slow).

We disregarded any clauses written completely in the L1.

(3) *Coinage* or 'relexification' (see, e.g. Ringbom, 1983) consists of the adaptation of an L1 word to the L2 orthography or morphology, 'so that it sounds or looks English' (Celaya & Torras, 2001: 7).

(a) My rabbit is small, very *divert* (Sp. *divertido,* Eng. funny).
(b) In mai house is famili: fatter, matter, *tater* and mai (Sp. *tato,* Eng. familiar for 'brother').

(4) *Calque* or 'literal translation' happens when a learner literally translates the word from the L1. This has to do with the transfer of semantic features from an L1 word to an L2 equivalent but with different contextual distribution (see, e.g. Zimmermann, 1986a,

1986b, 1987). In other words, learners are aware of the existence of a word and its form, but they lack knowledge of the semantic and/or collocational restrictions of that word (Ringbom, 2001: 64).

(a) My *table study* is blue and big (literal translation from mesa de estudio, Eng. desk).

(b) My favourite *plate* is pasta and rice (literal translation from plato, Eng. dish).

Ringbom (2001) distinguishes between what he calls 'semantic extension of single lexical units' (p. 64) and 'calques of multi-word units (compounds, phrasal verbs, idioms)' (p. 64). In this section, we will not apply this distinction and will refer to semantic extensions of one or several words as calque or literal translation.

(5) *Misselection*, also called 'synforms' (Laufer, 1990b, 1991a, 1992) or malapropism (see, e.g. Channell, 1988), is a confusion of formally similar items, that is pairs or triples of words that sound (phonetic similarity) or look (orthographic similarity) similar are confused and interchanged (James, 1998: 145; Laufer, 1990b, 1991a, 1992). A misselection implies the wrong selection of an already existing word in the target language, that is error word and target word are both target language words (malapropism or synform).[8]

(a) My *class* is big (class for 'classroom').

(b) I am tall and my *hear* is very long (hear for 'hair').

(6) *Semantic confusion* refers to the confusion of semantically related words; in other words, two words are confused because they are semantically similar; that is they have similar meanings but are functionally different. Here again two existing target language words are mixed up (James, 1998: 151–154).

(a) In the city there are *very* shops (very for "many").

(b) My bedroom is *great* (great for "huge" or "big").

Celaya and Torras (2001) restricted their analysis of lexical errors to interlingual errors, that is errors originated by L1 influence; but in this study, all lexical errors, interlingual and intralingual, that is errors caused by the very characteristics of the target language, have been considered.

The formal or semantic distinction is also central to the taxonomy of lexical errors in this study. This dichotomy reflects the way in which the lexicon of the L2 learners is organised, that is formal and semantic criteria of vocabulary storage, and how vocabulary is accessed in the L2 production (James, 1998: 145; see also Fernández, 1997, and Legenhausen, 1975, for examples of this approach to lexical error

Table 5.4 Distribution of lexical error categories according to source and type (cf. James, 1998: 144–154)

		Type	
		Formal	*Semantic*
Source	Mother tongue	• Borrowing • Coinage	• Calque[1]
	Target language	• Misspellings[2] • Misselection	• Semantic confusion

[1]We do not agree here with James (1998: 150) in the ascription of calques to the formal type of lexical errors in the sense that if the L2 word is a literal translation from another existing L1 word, it implies that a transfer of semantic features from the L1 word to the L2 word is taking place, as Zimmermann (1986a, 1986b, 1987) notes. Consequently, we believe that this type of lexical error can be better considered to be of the semantic rather than the formal type. Other researchers who consider calque errors as semantic errors are Ringbom (1987, 2001) and Gabryś-Barker (2006).

[2]Celaya and Torras (2001) distinguish interlingual, that is L1-oriented, from intralingual, that is target-language-oriented, errors in all the categories that they mention. In this sense, they claim for misspellings which are derived from mother tongue influence: 'This type of error [misspelling] can be explained by the fact that learners have acquired the oral English word but not its written form, and so, in order to write the word, learners use their available knowledge, that is the L1 [...] phonographic coding rules' (p. 9).

classification). Table 5.4 offers a summary of the different types of lexical errors according to these two basic distinctions.

Lexical errors in this study were classified into types or categories. However, in order to determine the reliability of the classification, a sample of 100 randomly selected compositions was scrutinised for lexical errors, and the lexical errors identified in this random sample of 100 compositions were classified by another trained teacher of EFL. The interrater reliability between both categorisations achieved a coefficient of 0.87.[9]

Analysis

Lexical errors were identified and tallied into a relative measure, so that lexical error density per composition was calculated by dividing the total number of words in the composition by the total number of lexical errors counted in that composition (i.e. accuracy ratio). The procedure used here to calculate the accuracy ratio of compositions is quite common, as suggested by Kroll (1990: 146), 'using the total number of words in a composition and tabulating the number of errors is one of the standard measures used in forming the basis for a kind of accuracy ratio'. A further measure was obtained that made it possible to determine the percentage of lexical error by dividing the number of lexical errors by the total number of words per composition. This procedure yields a decimal which translates into a percentage. The latter procedure allows for *t*-test and other measures of means comparison to be conducted to measure the differences among groups (cf. Kroll, 1990: 147). Lexical errors were classified according to their type and source.

The rest of the measures were also coded into computer-readable documents. The questionnaire was analysed to obtain relevant information for this study. The language-level tests – cloze procedure and reading comprehension – were scored for correct answers; the vocabulary size tests were also corrected and numerical data were obtained. Finally, the compositions were assessed using the *ESL Composition Profile* that judges the essay quality in English as a second language.

Firstly, we studied the two cohorts (learners at T1 and T2) separately, focusing on the description of the lexical errors at both moments, and also giving account of the general proficiency level and vocabulary level of participants at each measuring time. We then compared the results of the group at both testing times to check for any differences due to increasing amount of instruction, which co-occurred with increasing age.

Descriptive and inferential statistics were used for the analysis. Descriptive statistics included raw counts, that is simple frequency counts of particular units – words per composition,[10] lexical errors and lexical error types – and ratio measures – lexical errors per composition, lexical error types per total number of lexical errors, percentage of correct answers in the language level tests and percentage of right answers in the vocabulary tests. Firstly, we performed descriptive analysis of the data to examine whether there was any change in the lexical error production in relation to school grade; then we checked whether the differences found reached statistical significance. Inferential statistics included paired and matched (two-tailed) means comparison tests and correlation tests. Lexical error production at T1 and T2, language level at T1 and T2, and vocabulary size at T1 and T2 were submitted to statistical analysis. When the distribution of the sample variable was not normal, non-parametric correlation measures had to be used (Spearman's rho and Spearman–Brown rank–order correlations). Correlations were calculated for lexical error and essay quality, lexical error type and essay quality, lexical error and vocabulary size, and lexical error types and vocabulary size.[11] We used the SPSS 14.0 version to implement the statistical analysis.

Designing a Study to Explore Lexical Errors in Writing 127

In this chapter we explained the design of the study conducted to examine the production of lexical errors at two different stages of proficiency level. The characteristics of the learners who participated in the study and the instruments used to determine the general proficiency level, as well as the receptive vocabulary size of the learners, are accounted for. The taxonomy of lexical errors adopted is explained, and the procedures followed and analyses implemented on the data have also been the subject of examination in this chapter. The remaining chapters address the description and interpretation of the results found.

Notes

1. Although some of the subjects revealed attending private English lessons, we decided not to eliminate them from the sample, because in this research we were examining the development of the lexical error production of the *same* subjects at two different times, Time 1 and Time 2, after two years of formal instruction in English (210 hours of difference between the first and second testing moments); that is, we were doing not only a cross-sectional study but also a longitudinal one.
2. Scores were here converted into percentages of correct answers so that the measures of comparison could be conducted among the results of the cloze test and the reading comprehension test at both testing times.
3. Nation provided a colleague of the research group Grupo de Lingüística Aplicada de la Universidad de la Rioja (GLAUR) with this version of the 1000 Word Test.
4. The cloze and reading comprehension tests were scored by the researcher. We are fully indebted to other colleagues and members of the research team GLAUR for doing the scoring of the vocabulary tests (1000 Word Test and VLT 2k) and for helping in typing and scoring the compositions with the *Profile*.
5. Data were normally distributed; therefore, we used the Pearson product–moment correlation coefficient measure.
6. For very thorough discussions about the validity of different measures of interrater reliability, especially for ratings using the *ESL Profile*, we refer the reader to Polio (1997), Campbell (1990), Cherry and Meyer (1993) and Kroll (1990).
7. When the third rater was required, the correlation was calculated between the two nearest scorings, that is score rater 1-score rater 3 or score rater 2-score rater 3. When scores were not tallied, correlation coefficients were $r = 0.523$ for Time 1 compositions (rater 1 – rater 2) and $r = 0.641$ for Time 2 (rater 1 – rater 2).
8. When the misselection has its origin in the mother tongue of the subject, then we talk about the 'false friend' phenomenon. Nevertheless, we did not consider this possibility in our classification, and preferred to classify any possible instances of 'false friend' errors as calques (see Example (4)(b)).
9. Interrater reliability was calculated using the Pearson product–moment correlation coefficient test.

10. Proper names (people's names, films and book titles) were not included in the word counts, since they do not always respect grammar and lexis rules, and lexical errors in these types of words were not considered for the analysis, for example *My teacher's name is* Eba.
11. We are very grateful to the statistician Montserrat San Martín for her help with the statistical analysis regarding the decision as to what statistical test to perform on our data. Remaining errors are our own.

Chapter 6
Lexical Error Production: Changes Over Time

The purpose of this chapter is to give account of the results concerning the main types of lexical errors made by young Spanish EFL learners at two different testing moments. The chapter is organised in minor sections which report findings pertaining to the research questions and hypotheses posited above. In general terms, we observe that as proficiency increases, the production of lexical errors decreases in relative and absolute terms, especially for formal errors. Semantic errors also decrease, but their decrease is less notable than that of formal errors. Finally, the chapter concludes with a discussion and interpretation of the findings in the light of previous research-related studies.

Proficiency-Related Lexical Error Types

The first hypothesis stated that the production of lexical errors would be kept stable from the fourth to the sixth year despite the increase in age, exposure time and the proficiency of learners. At the second time of data collection, learners were two years older, had received 210 more hours of instruction in EFL and had increased their proficiency level in 12.9 percentage points of correct answers as measured by the multiple-choice cloze test and in 9.89 percentage points of correct answers following the measures of the reading comprehension test. The difference in the proficiency level is significantly higher for learners in their sixth grade, with $Z = -6.977$ for the cloze test and $Z = -6.382$ for the reading test at a significance level of $p < 0.0010$.[1]

An analysis of the identified lexical errors for T1 and T2 revealed that in absolute terms, learners produced fewer lexical errors in sixth grade than in fourth grade. Given that absolute frequency of lexical errors may be a deceptive measure because of different composition lengths, an accuracy ratio had to be calculated in order to reliably compare learners at T1 and T2. Concerning the length of composition, we observed that learners write longer compositions in sixth grade than in fourth grade.

It must be noted that proper nouns and whole sentences written in Spanish were not included in the word counts for the analysis.

Accuracy ratio or error density is a measure derived from the relationship between absolute number of lexical errors and number of words of composition. In this sense, it is reasonable to expect the accuracy ratio of sixth grade compositions to be higher than that of fourth grade compositions. In fact, this is what happened. Accuracy ratio or error density stays in complementary distribution with the percentage of lexical error. These are opposed measures, and in this sense, the results of the former correlate with the results of the latter. Both say the same thing, but explained in different terms.

A further measure counting the number of compositions excluded serves to support the statement that learners perform better in sixth grade than in fourth grade. For the first testing time, a total of 24 compositions from 273 could not be considered for error analysis, because they were mostly written in Spanish or were completely incomprehensible. In other words, 8.8% of the available compositions had to be discarded and were not included in the analysis. Nonetheless, for sixth grade, no composition had to be excluded from the analysis. At any rate for the second testing time, the total number of compositions counts up to 263, since no less than 20 participants were not present when samples of the written production in English of participants were taken. In total, 235 compositions were available for comparison, since we have 235 compositions at T1 and the compositions of the same 235 learners at T2.

Table 6.1 and Table 6.2 show the results for descriptive statistics for all measures at T1 and T2, respectively.

Non-parametric tests of means comparison, in particular Wilcoxon signed ranks tests for two matched samples, were performed with data from the 235 learners present at both data collection times to find out

Table 6.1 Descriptive statistics for lexical errors per composition, length of composition, accuracy ratio and percentage of lexical errors per composition at T1

	Maximum	*Minimum*	*Mean*	*SD*
Lexical error production	53	0	11.14	7.82
Length of composition (in words)	277	3	91.35	52.91
Accuracy ratio	91	1.5	12.22	11.86
% of lexical errors	66.7	0	14.38	9.75

Table 6.2 Descriptive statistics for lexical errors per composition, length of composition, accuracy ratio and percentage of lexical errors per composition at T2

	Maximum	Minimum	Mean	SD
Lexical error production	37	0	8.79	5.83
Length of composition (in words)	423	2	134.57	70.36
Accuracy ratio	183	1	21.71	22.84
% of lexical errors	100	0	7.66	7.35

Table 6.3 Wilcoxon signed ranks test for relative measures of lexical error production for fourth and sixth grades

	Lexical error production	Composition length (in words)	Accuracy ratio	% of lexical errors
Z value	−4.17*	−10.25*	−8.66*	−10.20*

*Significant at $p < .000$

whether differences were significant. The Wilcoxon test for means comparison revealed that for all measures tested results were significant at a significance value of $p < 0.001$, with learners in sixth grade producing significantly fewer lexical errors and significantly longer compositions. These results are presented in Table 6.3, which offers Z values and significance levels.

Figure 6.1 summarises findings for the first hypothesis graphically.

In view of the findings presented above, the first hypothesis posed for the study has to be rejected, since lexical error production decreases over 2 years' time as age and proficiency in the target language increase. Writing fluency[2] also increases from T1 to T2.

Types of lexical errors at T1 and T2

This section will examine the results by looking at the production of types of lexical errors at different testing times. As Table 6.4 shows, the most frequent category of lexical errors for learners in fourth grade is misspellings, followed by borrowings, semantic confusions, coinages, calques and misselections in decreasing order. Figures in Table 6.4 reveal that for sixth grade the order of frequency of the different lexical error

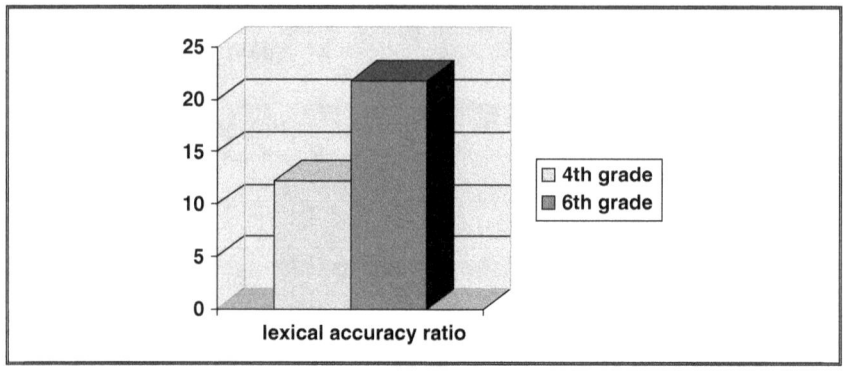

Figure 6.1 Mean lexical accuracy ratio or number of words between consecutive lexical errors

Table 6.4 Lexical error types

	Fourth grade	Sixth grade
Misspelling	7.21 (5.68)	4.56 (3.63)
Borrowing	1.78 (2.83)	0.91 (1.86)
Semantic confusion	0.61 (0.92)	0.8 (1.21)
Coinage	0.60 (1.3)	0.78 (1.53)
Calque	0.56 (0.96)	1.23 (1.56)
Misselection	0.39 (0.7)	0.52 (0.85)

Note: All measures are expressed in means (SD)

categories varies, although this variation is slight. Misspellings are again the most common type of lexical error, although their presence is considerably lower than two years before. The second most frequent category of lexical error is calques, displacing borrowings in this case to the third position. Semantic confusion, coinage and misselection are error types that do not appear in all compositions.

As can be seen in Table 6.5, the order of frequency of lexical errors changes as experience with the language increases. However, this variation is very small. The most conspicuous change refers to the decrease in the production of spelling errors and borrowings, and the increase in the production of the rest of the categories. Especially remarkable is the rise in the production of calques, which go up from

Lexical Error Production: Changes Over Time   133

Table 6.5 Order of frequency of lexical error categories

Order of frequency	Fourth grade	% over total	Sixth grade	% over total
1	Misspelling	64.72	Misspelling	51.83
2	Borrowing	15.93	Calque	13.96
3	Semantic confusion	5.5	Borrowing	10.33
4	Coinage	5.4	Semantic confusion	9.07
5	Calque	5	Coinage	8.9
6	Misselection	3.46	Misselection	5.88

the fifth to the second position of most frequent lexical error types. From the 2775 total errors in fourth grade, misspellings make up 1796 instances and 1199 occurrences at T2. The other category that decreases from T1 to T2 is borrowings going from 442 instances to 239 examples. The remaining categories increase their presence in sixth grade as follows: calques increase from 139 instances to 323 occurrences, from 152 semantic confusions in fourth grade to 210 in sixth grade, from 150 coinages at T1 to 206 coinages at T2, and finally from 96 misselections at T1 to 136 instances at T2. These differences in the order of frequency can also be observed in the examination of the proportion of the several lexical error categories.

Figure 6.2 shows the comparison of lexical error categories in their order of frequency for fourth and sixth grades.

Subsequent sections will deal with the production of each particular type of lexical error in greater detail.

Misspellings

There was a steady decrease from the lower to the higher grade in the production of spelling errors. It was, though, the most frequent category of lexical errors produced at both testing times. In order to ascertain the reduction of misspellings, the standard measure of the mean misspellings used per composition, that is by participant, was complemented with two further measures: (a) the percentage of misspellings per total number of words and (b) the percentage of learners who commit spelling errors. Here we followed Naves *et al.* (2005). The percentage of misspellings per total number of words fell drastically as grade increased from fourth to sixth. A further highly revealing measure is the proportion

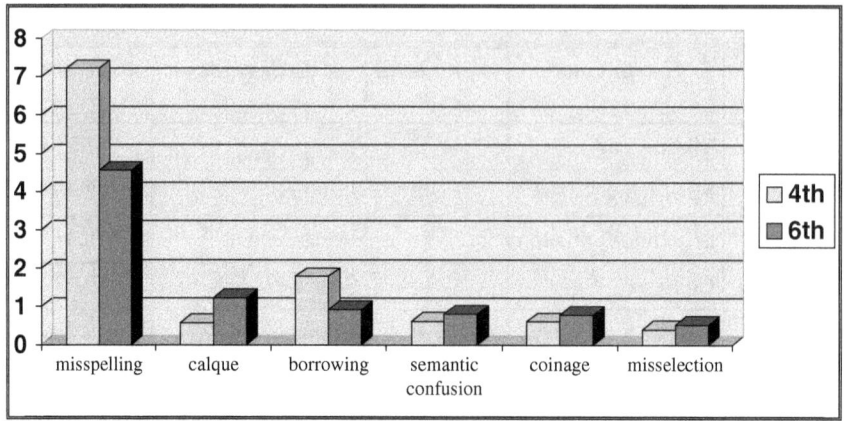

Figure 6.2 Comparison of lexical error types in order of frequency

of learners who produce misspellings. In this case, the decrease is very small. Table 6.6 presents these results.

A non-parametric test of means comparison was performed for the mean production of misspellings. The results of the Wilcoxon signed ranks test reveal that learners make significantly fewer misspellings in sixth grade than two years before ($Z = -7.07$, $p \leq 0.001$).

Borrowings

The category of borrowings followed the same pattern as misspellings, but the decrease within this category was smaller than in the former case. The production of borrowings was measured in the same three ways as misspellings: (a) the mean production of borrowings by participant, (b) the percentage of borrowings per total number of words and (c) the percentage of learners who make borrowing errors. We can observe a general and steady decrease of the production of borrowing errors for all measures considered, as can be seen in Table 6.7.

Although the decrease in the production of borrowings was not so acute in this case as in the former, the results of non-parametric tests reveal significant differences (Wilcoxon, $Z = -3.86$, $p < 0.001$), meaning that learners in sixth grade show significantly fewer borrowings than in fourth grade.

Calques

From the remaining categories of lexical errors, the one that suffers the most notable increase in its frequency of appearance is that of calques. A careful analysis and description of the results of the three different

Table 6.6 Misspellings

Grade	Raw number of misspellings	Mean misspellings	% misspellings/ total words	% subjects who produce misspellings	Mean misspellings only subjects who produce misspellings
Fourth	1796	7.21	9.22	96	7.51
Sixth	1199	4.56	4.27	92.4	4.93

Table 6.7 Borrowings

Grade	Raw number of borrowings	Mean borrowings	% borrowings/ total words	% subjects who produce borrowings	Mean borrowings only subjects who produce borrowings
Fourth	442	1.78	2.51	52.21	3.4
Sixth	239	0.91	0.77	41.44	2.2

Table 6.8 Calques

Grade	Raw number of calques	Mean calques	% calques/ total words	% subjects who produce calques	Mean calques only subjects who produce calques
Fourth	139	0.56	0.62	38.15	1.46
Sixth	323	1.23	0.90	59.7	2.05

measures implemented on calque production follows. Examination of Table 6.8 reveals that for all measures there is an increase in the production of calques as experience with the language also increases.

The production of calques increases significantly from fourth to sixth grade, as revealed by the Wilcoxon signed ranks test implemented ($Z = -6.28$, $p < 0.001$). This implies that although, in general terms, learners in sixth grade produce fewer lexical errors than two years before, they commit more errors of the calque type than they had when they were in fourth grade.

Semantic confusions

Although the increase in the production of semantic confusion is not very high, an analysis of results from all the measures considered here, with the only exception of percentage of semantic confusion per total number of words, revealed that lexical errors due to semantic confusion increase very slightly as learners pass grade and improve their proficiency in the L2. The corresponding figures for the evolution of semantic confusion in learners' written compositions are presented in Table 6.9.

A statistical test of non-parametric means comparison for two matched samples shows that although learners produce more semantic confusions in fourth grade, this difference is not significant in statistical terms (Wilcoxon $Z = -1.77$, $p = 0.077$).

Coinages

The production of coinages increases as grade and experience with the language increase; this increase is very low, though. The measure that establishes the percentage of coinages per total number of words is this time also an exception to the general rise in coinages production. Table 6.10 shows the results.

Table 6.9 Semantic confusions

Grade	Raw number of semantic confusions	Mean semantic confusion	% semantic confusions/ total words	% subjects who produce semantic confusions	Mean semantic confusions only subjects who produce semantic confusions
Fourth	152	0.61	0.75	41	1.5
Sixth	210	0.8	0.66	43.72	1.82

Table 6.10 Coinages

Grade	Raw number of coinages	Mean coinages	% coinages/ total words	% subjects who produce coinages	Mean coinages only subjects who produce coinages
Fourth	150	0.6	0.79	31.72	1.89
Sixth	206	0.78	0.62	40.68	1.92

Table 6.11 Misselections

Grade	Raw number of misselections	Mean misselections	% misselections/ total words	% subjects who produce misselections	Mean misselections only subjects who produce misselections
Fourth	96	0.39	0.47	28.91	1.3
Sixth	136	0.52	0.42	35	1.5

The results from the Wilcoxon singed ranks tests reveal that the decrease of coinages as experience with the language increases is not significant ($Z = -1.96$, $p = 0.051$). From this, we can conclude that the production of coinages remains practically the same as experience with the language and proficiency increase.

Misselections

The lexical category of misselections is the rarest in the production of learners at both testing times. Nevertheless, in spite of being the less common type of lexical error in our sample, the number of misselections increases from T1 to T2. The proportion of misselections per total number of words is an exception to this. Results are shown in Table 6.11.

A statistical analysis reveals that differences in the production of misselections over the two years are not significant (Wilcoxon $Z = -1.91$, $p = 0.056$).

Formal and Semantic Lexical Errors

This section will address the issue of the evolution of the dichotomy formal versus semantic lexical errors. The focus will be on the quantitative relationship between formal lexical errors and semantic lexical errors, on the one hand, and on the development of this relationship longitudinally from fourth to sixth grade, on the other. As in the previous reports on general and particular lexical error production, this description of the relationship between formal and semantic lexical errors over time will begin with the account of the descriptive statistics followed by the comparison between both testing times, and finally inferential statistics will be dealt with.

The category of formal lexical errors was made up by grouping the types: misspellings, borrowings, coinages and misselections. Calques and semantic confusions made up the category of semantic lexical errors. The data concerning the production of formal and semantic lexical errors are presented in Table 6.12, and Figure 6.3 illustrates the comparison of both testing times.

Comparing the production of formal and semantic lexical errors at T1 and T2, it can be noted that learners produce less formal errors in sixth grade than they did two years before. On the contrary, the production of semantic lexical errors increases with grade and proficiency level, being higher in sixth grade at T2 than in fourth grade at T1. Formal errors are still the most frequent category in sixth grade. In order to find out whether the decrease in the production of formal lexical errors was significant, a Wilcoxon signed ranks test was performed. Results revealed that formal errors are significantly more in fourth grade than in sixth grade ($Z = -6.08$, $p < 0.001$). A further Wilcoxon signed ranks test was performed to explore the significance of the increase of the frequency of semantic errors from T1 in fourth grade to T2 in sixth grade. Results are conclusive in that they show a statistically significant increase

Table 6.12 Formal and semantic lexical errors

	Fourth grade	Sixth grade
Mean formal errors per subject (SD)	9.97 (7.33)	6.76 (5.26)
Mean% formal errors (SD)	13.01 (9.79)	6.08 (7.29)
Mean semantic errors per subject (SD)	1.16 (1.45)	2.02 (2.03)
Mean% semantic errors (SD)	1.37 (1.74)	1.57 (1.5)

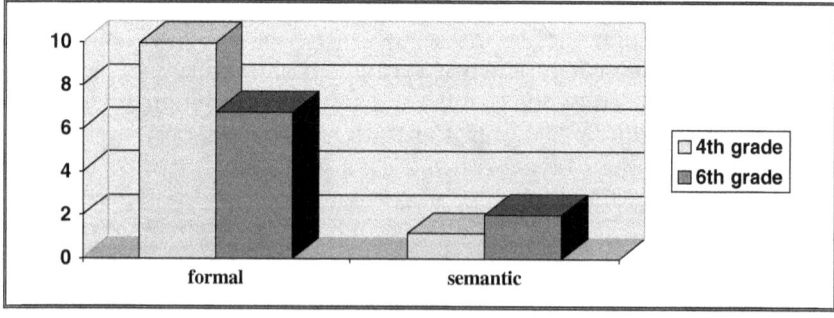

Figure 6.3 Mean formal and semantic lexical errors for 4th and 6th grade

at $p < 0.001$ ($Z = -6.198$). Likewise, a Wilcoxon signed ranks test revealed that learners produce significantly more formal lexical errors than semantic errors both in fourth ($Z = -13.21$, $p < 0.001$) and in sixth ($Z = -11.95$, $p < 0.001$) grade.

L1-Oriented and L2-Oriented Lexical Errors

The relationship over the two-year period between lexical errors originated in the mother tongue and those deriving from the influence of the target language will be discussed in the following section. When the L1 is the origin of the lexical error, such as in the cases of borrowings, coinages and calques, we talk of L1-oriented lexical errors. On the contrary, if the lexical error is originated by the influence of the L2, that is the language being learned, such as in misspellings, misselections[3] or semantic confusion, we say they are L2-oriented lexical errors.

As Table 6.13 shows, L2-oriented lexical errors are more frequent at both testing times than are L1-oriented lexical errors. Lexical errors deriving from L1 influence decrease only slightly from fourth to sixth grade. However, intralingual lexical errors show a notable decrease as learners move up grade. Figure 6.4 shows these results.

Several Wilcoxon signed ranks tests were performed to examine the statistical significance of the differences in the production in fourth and sixth grade of L1- and L2-oriented lexical errors. The decrease in the production of lexical errors derived from L1 influence was significant statistically ($Z = -3.41, p < 0.01$). For L2-oriented lexical errors there were significant differences between T1 and T2 production as well ($Z = 11.08$, $p < .01$). Similarly, we found significant differences between the production of intralingual and interlingual lexical errors for both grades (fourth grade: $Z = -10.42$, $p < 0.001$; sixth grade: $Z = -10.08$, $p < 0.001$). In other words, fourth and sixth grade learners produce significantly more

Table 6.13 L1- and L2-oriented lexical errors

	Fourth grade	Sixth grade
Mean L1 errors per subject (SD)	2.93 (3.64)	2.92 (3.34)
Mean% L1 errors (SD)	3.93 (5.05)	2.29 (2.41)
Mean L2 errors per subject (SD)	8.2 (6.05)	5.87 (4.02)
Mean% L2 errors (SD)	10.44 (7.85)	5.36 (6.93)

Part 2: Lexical Error Production in Young Spanish Learners

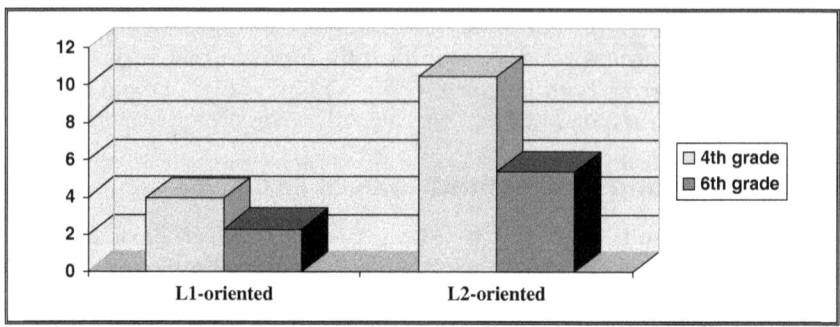

Figure 6.4 L1- and L2- oriented lexical errors for 4th and 6th grades

L2-oriented lexical errors than L1-oriented errors. The recurrent and abundant presence of misspellings may account for this.

To summarise, learners present different lexical error production behaviour as grade and experience with the language increase, as revealed by the different frequencies of the particular lexical error categories. The changes are, however, very small, and misspellings remain the most frequent type of lexical error produced after 419 and 629 hours of instruction in the L2, although their occurrence is reduced at T2. Likewise, learners at T2 also produce fewer borrowings than two years before at T1. The remaining categories of lexical errors increase slightly from T1 to T2, with misselections always as the less frequent type, and calques showing a notable increase. Semantic errors also increase at T2 and formal errors decrease. L2-oriented lexical errors are more common at both testing times, but L1- and L2-oriented lexical errors both decrease from T1 to T2. This finding suggests that there is a slight difference in the behaviour of learners in their production of particular types of lexical errors as they get more experienced with the language and their proficiency improves. Consequently, hypothesis 2 must be accepted although with the reservations expressed above.

Discussion

The findings presented in the preceding chapter reveal that as learners get older and increase their experience with the target language, they also show higher levels of proficiency. Regarding lexical errors, their written performance is also better. In other words, at T2, learners produce fewer lexical errors than they had produced two years before at T1, even though the length of their written essays increased considerably.[4] The findings of this study are also in line with the previous research in written composition and errors in the lexical component. These studies (Bradovi-Harlig & Bofman, 1989; Fernández, 1997; Grant & Ginther, 2000; Hawkey & Barker, 2004; Lennon, 1991b; Naves *et al.*, 2005) have put forward a reduction in the production of lexical errors and an increase in length in different writing tasks as experience with the language increases. Dagneaux *et al.* (1998) also found a considerable decrease in the production of errors in written compositions over two years' time and as proficiency increased. They call it an 'undeniable improvement'. Nevertheless, they also note that different types of error categories progress at different rates. Our results also suggest, in line with Dagneaux *et al.* (1998), that learners at different levels of L2 mastery will display differing amounts of lexical errors and differing essay lengths. Consequently, the proportion of lexical errors per composition appears to be an evident determiner of the proficiency level (cf. also Fernández, 1997).

Text length has also been observed in the literature (Grant & Ginther, 2000; Hawkey & Barker, 2004; Jarvis *et al.*, 2003) to be a representative measure of learners' proficiency and essay quality, so that the longer the composition, the higher the competence level of the learner. In this sense, we can conclude from the results of this study that essay length can be used to establish proficiency levels in a similar way as lexical errors.[5] This, however, contradicts to some extent Torras and Celaya's (2001: 117) claim that accuracy, that is lack of errors, develops at the expense of fluency and complexity. In our data, the decrease of lexical errors concurs with the increase in text length (cf. Lasagabaster & Doiz, 2003: 55; Wolfe-Quintero *et al.*, 1998: 4). Further research in this respect is warranted.

From our results and concurring with the findings of previous related studies, there are some indications to conclude that:

(1) learners with weaker linguistic competence in the target language (fourth graders) are more likely to make more lexical errors than do more advanced learners (sixth graders). Lexical accuracy ratio thus becomes an indicator of the proficiency level in EFL, but
(2) learners in sixth grade and with a more advanced level of language knowledge continue to make lexical errors of all types. The fact that sixth grade learners of EFL are still of limited linguistic and lexical competence may account for this.

Several explanations may account for the decrease of lexical errors with increasing proficiency. Foremost, it seems reasonable to assume that as learners get more proficient with the language and show higher receptive lexical knowledge of the first most frequent 2000 words, they will also be more lexically accurate. However, this is not always true, and studies that show a lack of decrease of error production despite increase in proficiency abound (Fernández, 1995; Cenoz, 2002; Naves & Miralpeix, 2002; Torras & Celaya, 2001). The different nature of the focus of the research may account for the differences in results.

One of the most frequently cited reasons for the lack of decrease in error production as proficiency gets higher is the nature of the tasks to be performed. Researchers claim that as learners progress in their language knowledge, the types of activities they are required to do get more difficult, and therefore, they continue making errors. Furthermore, learners at more advanced stages of language acquisition make use of more complex linguistic resources in their written production, and as a consequence the number of errors they make does not decrease. In this sense, Hyland (2003: 5) suggests that 'fewer errors in an essay may simply reveal a reluctance to take risks, rather than indicate progress'. In other words, lack of errors in an essay may indicate lack of use of complex structures rather than progress.

The second explanation for lexical error decrease in our data may be the fact that the writing task that learners had to perform is the same in both testing times. Considering that learners become more proficient and know more vocabulary at T2 than at T1, we can reasonably argue that the writing task is perceived as easier at T2. In addition, learners at T2 perform the written task for the third time since they were required to write an essay with the same composition topic in fourth, fifth and sixth grades. In this sense, we believe that the so-called test effect may also have influenced learners' better performance at T2 regarding both lexical error production, which reduces, and general essay quality, which increases.

Special attention needs to be given to L1 literacy in the improvement of accuracy in FL writing. Because of transfer phenomena, as L1 literacy grows, writing ability in the L2 will also grow. Harley *et al.* (1990: 24) wrote: 'academic skills [literacy] were significantly related across the two languages in use [L1 and L2]'. In this sense, as schooling progresses, which occurs along with the aging and proficiency development in the L2, and L1 literacy grows, the learners' ability to write in the L2 also improves and thus leads to the reduction in the production of lexical errors at T2. There are indications, inviting further investigation, that L2 proficiency and L1 literacy influence lexical accuracy in writing. However, the nature and the extent of the relationship among the three constructs are not clear yet.

Although studies dealing with writing development have concentrated on the production of advanced and older learners (Krapels, 1990: 49), Torras and Celaya (2001: 118) investigate young beginner EFL learners, with a very similar sample to ours. They believe that the application of general composing strategies and writing practice can help learners, especially low-proficiency students in developing FL proficiency. Similarly, Lasagabaster and Doiz (2003: 154) believe that learners at higher grades write longer texts and produce fewer errors, because they take advantage of school learning experience, in general, and writing experience, in particular. This empirical evidence suggests that the composing strategies and writing experiences in L1 and L2 that our participants achieved over two years of school experience, from fourth to sixth grade, explain the improvement in lexical production in terms of lexical errors.

Several further studies have demonstrated the efficacy of L1 literacy transfer in writing production (Eisterhold, 1990; Freidlander, 1990; Krapels, 1990; Kubota, 1998; Manchón et al., 2000, 2007; Silva et al., 2003). However, for this transfer to happen, a certain threshold proficiency level in the L2 is necessary (Cabaleiro González, 2003; Kubota, 1998; Weigle, 2002: 35). Whether transfer from L1 literacy skills had any crucial role in the improvement of lexical accuracy in written composition of the learners in our sample is a matter that has not been proved in this research. It would be interesting for future studies to examine the influence of L1 literacy skills in the development of lexical accuracy over time. For the time being, and until this issue is clarified, we can only speculate about its potential influence.

It seems reasonable to expect learners to keep on committing lexical errors along their way of acquiring the target language. Errors are inevitable and necessary for the development of language (cf. Fernández, 1995). Nonetheless, it is also true, as our results have shown, that as learners get more proficient, they make fewer and fewer lexical errors. This indicates a progress in the development of L2 vocabulary and shows that learners master more L2 words, or more aspects of the already known words. In this sense, lexical accuracy may be used as an indicator to distinguish among proficiency levels.

The type of lexical errors that learners produce at different stages of acquisition varies according to frequency of error. As a result, there will be some lexical errors typical of lower stages of language learning, whereas some other types will characterise learners' performance at higher levels of proficiency (cf. Lasagabaster & Doiz, 2003, for similar results regarding different types of errors as age increases). Specifically, misspellings and borrowings are most frequent at T1 and decrease their frequency at T2. Semantic confusions, coinages, calques and misselections, although generally less common than misspellings and borrowings at both testing times, tend to become more frequent as proficiency increases. In broad terms, as learners know more about the target language, they start making use of it to compensate for the lack of lexical knowledge and thus change the type of compensatory communication strategies employed to get their message across. They more frequently reduce L1 word insertions and increase literal translations. We will now examine the evolution of each lexical error category from fourth to sixth grade in detail.

Misspellings

Misspellings are the most frequent category of lexical errors at both testing times. This category of lexical errors is controversial, because it is often considered separately from lexical errors, and either it forms an independent category – orthographic or spelling errors – or it is included within the category of mechanic errors together with capitalisation, punctuation or paragraphing errors (cf. Cameron & Blesser, 2004; De Cock & Granger, 2005; Dušková, 1969; Hawkey & Barker, 2004; Jacobs *et al.*, 1981; Lasagabaster & Doiz, 2003; Valero Garcés *et al.*, 2000).

Misspellings are very frequent at the early stages of language acquisition (cf. Bouvy, 2000; Celaya & Torras, 2001; Lindell, 1973; Mutta, 1999; Olsen, 1999), but they become less and less common as proficiency increases, as this study shows (see also Bouvy, 2000; Sánchez Jiménez, 2006; Santiago & Repáraz, 1993). Likewise, FL learners in low school grades will also present many spelling errors, which decrease as learners move up through the grades (Lasagabaster & Doiz, 2003). This result mirrors Schmitt's (1998) findings that show that spelling is acquired before other dimensions of word knowledge, such as derivational forms and meanings. In this sense, as misspellings decrease, errors in other aspects of lexical knowledge will appear. Nevertheless, Alonso Alonso and Palacios Martínez (1994) found that for very advanced learners of Spanish, FL orthographic errors, including punctuation and stress marking, were also the most frequent. This concurs with the results of this study regarding the highest frequency of misspellings at T1 and T2. It would be interesting to know whether for Alonso Alonso and Palacios Martínez' learners orthographic errors are even commoner at lower-proficiency levels.

As proficiency increases, learners acquire new phonographic rules, developing further their lexical competence (cf. Sánchez Jiménez, 2006). Furthermore, more advanced learners have enjoyed more encounters with the target words both in writing and in speech and consequently can reproduce those words better with the correct spelling. Learners in sixth grade are required to write a composition with the same topic as two years before. It is reasonable to expect that at T2 learners, who are more proficient than at T1, use words they are more familiar with and therefore know how to spell them.

The origin of misspellings in our data is not obvious. Spelling errors derive from the disagreement between orthography and pronunciation in English. However, several other sources are mentioned in the literature that include influence of L1 pronunciation and spelling (Celaya & Torras, 2001; James, 1998: 134; Lasagabaster & Doiz, 2003; Olsen, 1999: 196), application of L2 phonological or orthographic rules (James, 1998: 134; Olsen, 1999: 196) and lack of match between the sequential letter probabilities, orthographic patterns or grapheme/phoneme correspondence of the target and native languages (Ellis & Beaton, 1993: 567–569). Apart from linguistic causes, spelling errors in our data seem to have their origin in a poor lexical competence and especially in lack of writing experience in the target language (Celaya & Torras, 2001; James, 1998: Chap. 6; Jiménez Catalán, 1992; Lasagabaster & Doiz, 2003; Sánchez Jiménez, 2006). Considering the mainly oral approach of FL teaching in primary education in Spain, it is not surprising that misspellings are so frequent in our data.

The misspellings we analysed generally involve doublets, that is lexical items that share meaning and have a similar form in the L1 and the L2, such as *familia* (Sp.)/'family' or *fútbol* (Sp.)/'football'. But other spelling errors in 'difficult' words in English are also observed, for example in 'beautiful' or 'birthday'. These errors could be considered 'slips of the pen' if they had not been so frequent and commonplace in the written production of the participants in our study (Bouvy, 2000: 147). Here we also agree with Zimmermann (1987: 57) when he says that 'the majority of lexical errors in an L2, particularly in the fairly well-monitored written mode, will not be slips, but rather "systematic" errors owing to lack of competence'. Probably, the low-proficiency level of the learners as manifested in their inexperience with writing in English and their lack of internalisation of the graphophonological system of English explains the overwhelming presence of spelling lexical errors in the study presented here.

The lack of agreement between the phonetic and orthographic systems of English poses a great problem for Spanish natives, especially in writing. For instance, learners have problems with certain vowel or consonant sounds, consonant clusters or silent sounds (see Moya Guijarro, 2003). When facing a writing task in English, the learners in this study usually opt between two strategies to reduce words to writing: (a) imitation of pronunciation in spelling or (b) writing words in a 'difficult' way, that is with infrequent consonant or vowel associations. It is a frequent case in the present data that learners write the English word as it is pronounced. Morris' (2001: 276) words are very enlightening in this respect:

> When L2 learners are unfamiliar with the written form of a sound sequence and therefore are unable to conjure up an appropriate letter sequence, they often produce something that is essentially a phonetic representation of the sound sequence as they perceive it.

On some occasions, these creations show good phonetic perceptions on part of the learners, for example

- *ould* for 'old' (S208, fourth),[6]
- *biutiful* for 'beautiful' (S212, fourth; S252, fourth),
- *haus* for 'house' (S252, fourth),
- *could* for 'cold' (S18, sixth),
- *ancols* for 'uncles' (S19, sixth) and
- *feivorite* for 'favourite' (S89, sixth).

This strategy is more frequent in fourth grade than in sixth grade, where examples of phonetic spelling are much rarer. In some other cases, learners opt to write the word in English as difficult as they can. This is because they think that writing is difficult in English because of the discordance between pronunciation and spelling (Olsen, 1999: 198). Furthermore, spelling in English is characterised by an abundance of consonant clusters, single vowel sounds represented by more than one letter, diphthongs, silent letters, long vowel sounds and double consonants (cf. Morris, 2001: 278) that make English spelling very difficult for Spanish learners.[7] In such cases, learners tend to omit, add or change some letter (cf. James, 1998: 150), for example

- *scool* for 'school' (S233, fourth; S256, fourth; S205, fourth),
- *havee* for 'have' (S252, fourth),
- *bahtroom* for 'bathroom' (S228, fourth; S243, fourth),
- *practic* for 'practice' (S60, sixth),

- *theacher* for 'teacher' (S100, sixth) and
- *freinds* for 'friends' (S178, sixth).

The two main causes of spelling errors mentioned above have their origin in the target language, more specifically in the disagreement between phonetic and orthographic conventions in English and the peculiar spelling of English because of, for example, consonant clusters or silent letters. Nevertheless, some other spelling errors clearly show the influence of the native pronunciation of some sounds. Observe, for example

- *broder* Spanish rendering of 'brother'. Clearly for Spaniards the *th* sound, either voiceless,/θ /, or voiced/ð /, resembles the Spanish /d/sound, and as such it is usually produced (S235, fourth; S55, sixth; S164, sixth; S170, sixth).[8]

As a consequence of that 'wrong', peculiar pronunciation of some English sounds, their written renderings of the words result in spelling errors. This phenomenon, where writing/spelling reflects non-native pronunciation, usually a wrong pronunciation, can be seen in the renderings of several sounds. These are sounds that Spanish natives have problems with. Some other times, no single problematic sound can be identified, but the renderings of some words clearly show that Spanish learners have problems with pronouncing them:

- *sabyet* for 'subject' (S144, fourth),
- *may hap beily* for 'my happy birthday' (S195, fourth),
- *brosskast* for 'breakfast' (S68, sixth) and
- *sallens* for 'science' (S246, sixth).

In a nutshell, a closer examination of the spelling errors revealed that these have their source in the 'difficult' pronunciation and spelling of some English words. There seem to be various factors that interact to account for the misspellings of certain English words. These are

(1) the failure of the learners to realise the corresponding patterns between sounds and letters in English (see Terrebone, 1973: 136),
(2) the influence of the phonetic, phonological and orthographic systems of the mother tongue (Terrebone, 1973: 137) and
(3) the lack of experience of the learners in writing and reading words in English (Jiménez Catalán, 1992: 251; Lasagabaster & Doiz, 2003: 156).

In this study, we have opted for including misspellings as a category within L2-oriented lexical errors because it is the particulars of the phonographic system that make up the main source of spelling errors (cf. James, 1998: 138). Other authors consider that, in fact, it is the discrepancy between the graphophonological systems of TL (English) and NL (Spanish in this case) which is the actual origin of these lexical errors. Consequently, the mother tongue of the learners or rather the interlingual asymmetries L1–L2 are responsible for most lexical errors encountered (Celaya & Torras, 2001; Dagut & Laufer, 1982, amongst others). Terrebone (1973) also traces back spelling errors to the influence of Spanish phonetics and uses contrastive phonetics to explain misspellings. She does not refer explicitly to the source of spelling errors, but limits her study to a description of the main types of misspellings produced by Spanish learners of English. Ellis and Beaton (1993) also believe that the difficulties learners have with the L2 come from a lack of overlap between the target and native words.

It can be concluded that misspellings imply a certain lexical knowledge of the words in question. Learners will typically know what the word means and how to use it, but they will lack knowledge of how to render the word correctly in writing. After some experience with the language, spelling errors tend to decrease.

Borrowings

Borrowings are the second most frequent category in fourth grade, but as proficiency increases they become less frequent so that at T2, borrowings occupy the third position in the frequency of appearance. This result is in line with findings from previous studies that showed a clear decrease in the use of borrowings as learners get more proficient in the L2 (Bouvy, 2000; Rokita, 2006; Williams & Hammarberg, 1998). Similarly, as learners grow older and go up grade, the presence of borrowings in their compositions becomes rarer (Celaya & Torras, 2001; Lasagabaster & Doiz, 2003; Naves et al., 2005).[9] In this sense, we believe that borrowing in our data is temporary and evolves since it depends on learners' levels of linguistic and lexical knowledge and on communicative demands.

One possible explanation for the massive production of borrowings may be lack of lexical knowledge. In this sense, when learners cannot find an adequate word in their English lexicon and when they do not know a word in English, they resort to their L1 to fill the (knowledge) gap (cf. Bouvy, 2000, who calls borrowings 'gap fillers'). When having to face the 'lexical challenge' imposed by the composition task, informants often opt for the introduction of the L1 equivalent of the unknown word in English, for example

- *My grandmother is fumando* (Eng. smoking) (S216, fourth),
- *I have got a one tortuga, is big* (Eng. turtle) (S238, fourth),
- *My mom and my father are separados y divorciados* (Eng. separated and divorced) (S17, sixth) and
- *My mejor friends is the woman Angela and Andrea* ... (Eng. best) (S193, sixth).

This may be an unconscious impulse or rather a voluntary act (Bouvy, 2000; Williams & Hammarberg, 1998). Although research investigates different instances of unconscious or non-intentional borrowing (De Angelis & Selinker, 2001; Ringbom 1987; Williams & Hammarberg, 1998), the present data suggest that this is not the case here. When borrowing unconsciously, learners are not aware that the borrowed words are not target words; they are not even aware that they do not know those lexical items in the L2 (cf. De Angelis & Selinker, 2001; Ringbom, 1987). On many occasions, our learners, however, seem to be aware of using Spanish words, because they tend to write these borrowed words within either inverted commas, or parentheses, signalling thus that there is something remarkable with those words. We can conclude in our data that borrowing usually proceeds consciously.

Borrowing is used as a compensatory communication strategy[10] (Celaya, 1992; Celaya & Torras, 2001; De Angelis & Selinker, 2001; Lasagabaster & Doiz, 2003; Olsen, 1999; Ringbom, 1987; Williams & Hammarberg, 1998). In this sense, we agree here with Bouvy (2000: 152) that 'presence of borrowings may be attributed to the discrepancy between learners' linguistic competence and their communicative needs'. The use of this communicative compensatory strategy depends upon two main factors: (a) communicative pressure and (b) the level of difficulty of the task to be performed (Bouvy, 2000: 153). Applying these two usage criteria for borrowing to our data, we observe that while condition (a) remains stable over the two years passed between T1 and T2, we assume that the task becomes easier since it is the third time (fourth, fifth and sixth grades) that learners write the composition task with the same topic. Furthermore, their lexical and general linguistic knowledge have increased over this time, so that it seems logical to believe that the task, being the same as two years before, is perceived by learners as easier.

The use of borrowings contains information about the communicative situation (Cenoz, 2001; Dewaele, 2001; Williams & Hammarberg, 1998) as it seems that insertion of L1 words in the L2 discourse without adaptation is limited to those communicative situations where speaker and hearer share L1 or both of them know the L1 of the learners. This is the communicative situation of participants in this study. Participants, teachers and researchers share the same mother tongue, that is Spanish. Therefore, learners feel safe to include Spanish words in their English texts since their audience would understand them (Dewaele, 2001). In addition to this, the fact that learners knew they were not in an exam situation and that their essays would not be assessed by the teacher did not prevent the appearance of L1 words in their writing (cf. Dewaele, 2001). This evidence seems to support Dewaele (2001: 84) in that if the learner feels that L1 insertions will not be penalised, he or she will use the L1 whenever the need arises. We may speculate that had learners considered the data collection session as an exam situation and the letter as a writing test to be included in their final grade, intrusions of the L1 may have been avoided. The main aim of learners was to communicate rather than to take an English writing test.

Calques

A calque consists in the literal translation of a word or expression from the L1 into the L2. The semantic properties of the error word are extended and transferred to the target word (cf. Ringbom, 2001; Warren, 1982). According to this, for a calque to happen, the learner has to dispose of some considerable lexical knowledge of the L2 in order to being able to literally translate and render the Spanish L1 idea with English L2 words. This idea finds further support in Warren's (1982) study, which found calques, or 'equivalence errors', to be the most numerous in the essays of university students. In our data, calques are 9% more frequent in sixth grade than in fourth grade. They go from the fifth to the second position in the frequency of appearance in learners' productions.

The following examples from our data illustrate this:

- *Mys fathers is Nerea and Manolo* (Sp. padres, Eng. parents) (S168, fourth),
- *I like ballhand* (Sp. balonmano, Eng. handball) (S226, fourth),
- *I want to pass a very good time with you* (Sp. pasar, Eng. have, spend) (S14, sixth) and
- *Madrid is very big have very people and very cars very houses a park of atraccions* ... (Sp. parque de atracciones, Eng. fun fair) (S207, sixth).

Bearing in mind the relationship between word difficulty and types of lexical errors commented on above, it may be suggested that the proficiency level of the participants at T1 is too low to allow them to resort to calques (also coinages) because these imply transfer of semantic features, semantic extension and overgeneralisation. In short, they require a deeper knowledge of the L2 phonographemic, morphological and semantic systems, and a more developed L2 lexicon. This is the reason why in the production of learners, calques appear in a greater proportion at T2 than at T1 (cf. Bouvy, 2000; Celaya & Torras, 2001). In her account of the main lexical errors produced in scientific articles in English by Spanish intermediate English users, Carrió Pastor (2004) observed that calques were very frequent.

Our research suggests that the more semantically oriented nature of calques with respect to the more formally oriented borrowings accounts for the higher frequency of the former in sixth grade. It seems reasonable to argue that the changing degrees of lexico-semantic competence a learner may possess will have consequences on literal translation, and relexification, among other phenomena (Ambroso, 2000; Ringbom, 1983, 1987, 2001). In this sense, formal lexical errors deriving from L1 influence, that is borrowings and coinages, will be more frequent at the early stages of acquisition in fourth grade, being slowly replaced by semantic lexical errors originated in the L2 at more advanced stages in sixth grade. The works of Ellis (1997) and Singleton (1999: 152) support this argument. They claim that learning the semantic aspects of words is a more demanding task than learning the form of words. The former will require some kind of explicit and conscious learning, but learning the form of lexical items can proceed from implicit and unconscious learning (cf. also VanPatten *et al.*, 2004).

A more detailed account of the evolution of semantic and formal errors over time will be given below; suffice to say here that the evolution in the frequencies of the production of borrowings and calques over 2 years' time corresponds with the gradual progress from organisation by form to organisation by meaning of the mental lexicon as proficiency in the L2 increases (Gabryś-Barker, 2006; Ringbom, 2001: 65).

Calques derive from the conjunction of communicative need and lack of lexical knowledge (Bouvy, 2000). In this sense, we believe them to be the result of a compensatory strategy. It is probable that this compensatory communication strategy is applied unconsciously, because learners seem to believe that the words they are calquing are in fact English words, contrary to what had happened before with borrowings.

Semantic confusions

As learning proceeds and L2 proficiency increases, the production of semantic confusion also increases, although very slightly. A semantic confusion is the result of the mixing up of two words which are similar in meaning but have different usage distribution. Usually these words belong to the same semantic field. Some examples of semantic confusion in our data are

- *I have got very fridns* ('very' for 'many') (S57, fourth),
- *My favourite sing is HIM* ('sing' for 'music group') (S189, fourth),
- *My fan is Pau Gassol* ('fan' for 'idol') (S51, sixth) and
- *My favourite eat is potatoes* ('eat' for 'food') (S167, sixth).

Semantic confusions in our data can be explained by alluding to the complexity and subtleties of semantic relations (Fernández, 1997: 72). Moreover, in many cases the semantic confusion does not derive from a failure in choosing the correct word between two, but rather from the use of the only word the learner knows. This word must bear some semantic resemblance to the intended word. For instance, in the following sentences

- *My uncle name is Ana* (S226, fourth) and
- *My years is thirty the April* (S280, sixth),

the error words – *uncle* and *years* – are semantically related to the intended words – *aunt* and *birthday*. In these cases we cannot tell for sure whether the learners are confusing two semantically related words they possess in their lexicons – in this case *aunt* and *uncle* or *year* and *birthday* – or whether they are using the only word they know and assuming for this the meanings of other related words. In most cases, we believe learners are not conscious of using an incorrect word.

Semantic confusions can be thought to be semantic overextensions of the words learners know. These overextensions of meaning are also very typical of the early stages of L1 lexical acquisition (Singleton, 1999). Considering the developing L2 linguistic and lexical competence of participants, it seems reasonable to believe that at T2, learners know more words and know words better than at T1. Consequently, it follows that from having knowledge of more words, learners also have greater chances of confusing those words in their essays. The semantic networks of learners develop and enlarge as their proficiency and lexical knowledge increase, so that when they have to choose a word from the network, several semantically related words are activated and, on some occasions, learners select the wrong one. At T2, learners have more associated words to choose from than at T1, and as revealed by the lexical errors of the semantic confusion type, they choose the wrong word more frequently than at T1. These results provide evidence in support of the theories that point to a change from a formally organised lexicon to a semantically structured one, as proficiency increases.

Moreover, semantic confusions also point to an incomplete and unstable knowledge of the meaning or meanings of the target words. One can argue that learners have some knowledge of the core meaning of the intended word and of the target word; however, they have no full knowledge of the semantic properties of the words. We deduce this, because learners show knowledge of the semantic field the error and intended word belong to. Nevertheless, they do not master the complete range of meanings of these words, and as a result semantic confusions arise. Drawing from the example above, learners know that the word *uncle* belongs to the semantic field of 'family relatives', but they are unaware of the semantic restrictions of that word; namely, it can only be applied to the male brother of the father or mother. Thus, we say learners have partial knowledge of the word *uncle*.

This finding of semantic confusions increasing with proficiency reflects the findings of Ringbom (1987, 2001) and Channell (1988), which showed that semantic confusions are more typical of more advanced learners. Carrió Pastor (2004) found that semantic confusions were very frequent in the production of academic articles by intermediate English learners.

Coinages

Coinage errors although not very frequent in our data are very illustrative of the lexical acquisition process. This process shows itself to be a creative process deriving from the assimilation of TL spelling, pronunciation and even morphological rules. There is a slight increase in the production of coinage errors from fourth to sixth grade. As in preceding cases, this increase in the frequency of coinages is related to the higher proficiency and lexical knowledge of learners. As a consequence, it follows that in order for some lexical errors to be produced, learners must have reached a certain L2 proficiency level.

Coinages result from the adaptation of an L1 word to the L2 graphophonemic rules so that it sounds or looks English. The use of coinages implies, therefore, that the learner possesses some knowledge of the orthographic or phonetic conventions of the L2 and generalises them.

In this sense, it can be derived from the data that coinages will appear in the productions of somehow more proficient learners (cf. Celaya & Torras, 2001). The present findings regarding the higher frequency of calques and coinages at T2 than at T1 coincide with previous results that found a positive relationship between grade/age and the ability to create new words in the L2 or words that resemble those of the L2 (Celaya & Ruiz de Zarobe, 2008; Celaya & Torras, 2001). The greater language awareness of older and more proficient learners and their ability to analyse and dissect language into parts explains the more frequent appearance of calques and coinages in those learners' essays.

Our results point to learners abandoning simple recourse to the L1, that is borrowing, and beginning making a creative use of TL rules, particularly in formal contexts and as they get more proficient in the L2 (cf. Dewaele, 1998; Ringbom, 2001: 63, 2006: 40). Lexical inventions that derived from L1 influence might be both intentional and unintentional. This result confirms the findings of preceding research by Ringbom (2001, 2006) and Dewaele (1998). Errors of creativity, for example coinages, or calques are evidence that the learner is growing in the use of language.

We believe that resort to coinages which tailor the L1 word to the English conventions is the result of a compensatory strategy to compensate for lack of lexical knowledge. Singleton and Little (1991: 73) mention three main reasons why learners 'create' new words in the L2. The lexical creations could (a) 'result from an incomplete mastery of orthographic conventions', (b) derive from 'cross-linguistic influence at work' or, finally, (c) they may be 'a consequence of deficient coding in memory of items encountered in the language input' (see also Dewaele, 1998). It is likely that a number of sources combine to produce lexical creations in our learners. It is also likely that the lack of knowledge of L2 target words compels learners to create new words making use of the knowledge they have: (a) L1 and (b) some English phonographemic rules.

Coining new words seems to be a conscious strategy with learners trying to make use of the only knowledge they have to communicate. The psycholinguistic origin of coinages may lie in the closeness between Spanish L1 and English L2 lexis. When a learner does not know a word in the L2, he or she tries out adapting a Spanish word to English morphology (orthographic and phonological rules) (cf. Dewaele, 1998: 480ff). This is a very intelligent strategy as it works quite often, for example:

- *contribución* (Sp.) → contribution (Eng.),
- *nacionalidad* (Sp.) → nationality (Eng.),
- *proceso* (Sp.) → process (Eng.) and
- *combinación* (Sp.) → combination (Eng.).

However, some other times this strategy fails and gives rise to a lexical error of the coinage type:

- *My favourite equip it's Alavés* (Sp. *equipo*, Eng. team) (S133, fourth),
- *My grandnny name is Antonia and lots of familiars* (Sp. *familiares*, Eng. relatives) (S217, fourth),
- *I got colch of Bart Simpson* (Sp. *colcha*, Eng. eiderdown) (S140, sixth) and
- *What's asignatures is Peter & Helen's favourites?* (Sp. *asignatura*, Eng., subject) (S236, sixth).

Misselections

Misselections are the least frequent category of lexical errors identified in our data. The production of misselections increases slightly from T1 to T2 in about 2.5%, and more learners produce misselections at T2 than at T1. These examples taken from our data illustrate the phenomenon of misselection:

- *My eat chiken, a meat, and fruit salad ais youth* (youth for yogurt) (S26, fourth),
- *I'm a long hear, brown eyes, and I am a tall* (hear for hair) (S76, fourth),
- *My arrive is General Urrutia n° 76, 5° A* (arrive for address) (S92, sixth) and
- *I meat a lot of childrens* (meat for meet) (S239, sixth).

As can be observed in the examples above, the prerequisite for a misselection error to happen is formal similarity between the target and the error word. Two words that look or sound similar may be confused in learners' writings. Our data confirm Laufer's (1991a) findings which distinguish different types of similarities that may lead to confusion of two words:

(1) same number of syllables (see also Channell, 1988: 88), for example *I leave on la Calle de la Cigüeña* for *live* (S161, sixth),
(2) same stress pattern (see also Channell, 1988: 88), for example *I like go four your house* for *for* (S169, sixth),
(3) shared phonemes, for example *buy buy* for *bye bye* (S26, fourth),

(4) same initial consonants or consonant clusters, for example *I lake swimming* for *like* (S177, fourth) and
(5) same syntactic class, for example *I go to school by car and something on foot* for *sometimes* (S107, sixth).

However, she also observes that L2 learners do not always store these properties correctly in the lexicon. The most crucial feature of misselections in our data is that both the target and the error words exist in the L2 (James, 1998: 146).

That misselections are scarce in our data is not at all surprising, bearing in mind that previous studies with misselections or synforms (similar target words) (Channell, 1988; Duškova, 1969; Laufer, 1990a, 1990b, 1991a; Zughoul, 1991) were done on more advanced learners than the participants in this study. From our data, and confirming previous research studies, it follows that in order for misselections to happen learners have to have achieved a certain level of lexical knowledge. As Laufer (1991a: 323) notes, the vocabulary of learners who use synforms frequently was good enough to communicate. The more words a learner has in stock in the mental lexicon, the higher the possibility for that learner to confuse two formally similar words. Our results point in this direction, with learners in sixth grade producing more instances of misselections than in fourth grade.

James (1998: 146) states that misselections derive in fact from 'double ignorance': on the one hand, from ignorance of the target word, and on the other, from ignorance of the error word. The misselections produced by the participants in our study derive from the lack of lexical knowledge of the meaning of the error and the target word. This mirrors James' (1998) findings. Moreover, we believe that (a) this ignorance is but a partial ignorance, since learners have some approximate knowledge of either word form, word meaning or both, and (b) this ignorance can be indeed claimed for all types of confusions in our data.

From careful consideration of the present data, it seems that there is a threshold level beyond which misspellings and borrowings tend to decline, but other types of lexical errors such as calques, coinages, semantic confusions and misselections start increasingly appearing in learners' production. It is likely that the latter group of lexical errors involve higher levels of lexical knowledge or general language knowledge.

Formal and semantic lexical errors

At T1 as well as at T2, formal lexical errors are more frequent than semantic lexical errors. The data reveal that formal lexical errors decrease from fourth to sixth grade, but semantic lexical errors become slightly more frequent as L2 proficiency increases. The distinction between formal and semantic lexical errors looked at in this study shows us how L2 lexical items are stored and accessed during SLA (Channell, 1988; James, 1998; Legenhausen, 1975; Meara, 1984; Mutta, 1999; Warren, 1982; Zimmermann, 1987). Moreover, this distinction also allows us to learn more about the nature of the lexical competence of our participants (Nation, 1990).

There are two main sources of formal lexical errors in our data (Zimmermann, 1987). Firstly, lack of lexical knowledge may lead learners to make up or build a new lexical item. Most usually, they rely on formal similarities with either the L1 equivalent or other L2 words. Secondly, learners fail to remember the form of the target word correctly and produce something that resembles it formally. Likewise, content-oriented lexical errors derive either from the inability of the learners to retrieve a word correctly or from their lack of knowledge of the target word.

Following Laufer (1991a) (see also Meara, 1983, 1984; Zimmerman, 1986b), we believe that just as L1 errors are used to determine some properties of the L1 lexicon (Channell, 1988), lexical errors in L2 may be indicative and shed some light on the structure of the L2 lexicon. Concurring with previous studies (Bouvy, 2000; Celaya & Torras, 2001; Laufer, 1991a), our present findings show confusion because of semantic relatedness and formal similarity. These two types of lexical errors serve as evidence to support the theory of an organisation of the L2 mental lexicon that is driven by formal as well as semantic associations. Channell (1988), Meara (1983) or Henning (1973) point to this dual structure of the L2 learner's mental lexicon. Some evidence of this can be seen in the following examples of formal and semantic lexical errors:

- *I leave opposite the town hall* for *live* (S198, sixth) – formal lexical error and
- *My blond is brown* for *hair* (S61, sixth) – semantic lexical error.

In these examples, words are stored according to their form: *live* and *leave* may be stored together and therefore they are confused in production. Similarly, *blond* and *hair* also seem to be stored next to each other because they share semantic field and are frequently used together. This fact supports previous studies that showed that semantic associations in the mental lexicon are first syntagmatic in less-proficient learners such as the participants in our study (Meara, 1983; Verhallen & Schoonen, 1998; Wolter, 2002).

From these data, it follows that words are arranged in formal and semantic networks. This arrangement is not arbitrary, but follows a systematicity based on proficiency. Our data show that formal lexical errors are more typical of lower proficient learners, fourth graders, while semantic lexical errors increase with proficiency and are more common in the language production of more advanced students, sixth graders. The findings of this study corroborate previous results found with association tests and lexical error analysis that beginner language learners will store words in the lexicon through formal (phonetic and orthographic) associations. But as learning progresses, new lexical items seem to enter semantic networks rather than formal networks (Ellis & Beaton, 1993; see also Meara, 1983; Wolter, 2002; Zimmermann, 1987). The results obtained in this study are similar, with formal lexical errors decreasing from fourth to sixth grade and semantic lexical errors showing an increase from T1 to T2. A high number of formal lexical errors point to less-proficient learners, whereas an increasing presence of semantic lexical errors characterise the production of more advanced learners.

Our findings and interpretation of the results mirror those of preceding research, where highly advanced learners produced more content than form-oriented lexical errors (Bouvy, 2000; Fernández, 1997; McNeill, 1990; Ringbom, 1987, 2001; Zimmermann, 1987: 61). Errors with word forms are significantly more important for learners at lower levels of proficiency in writing since the formal aspect creates a major source of confusion in vocabulary learning, especially among beginning to intermediate learners of EFL (Gu, 2003: 14; Gu & Leung, 2002; Hawkey & Barker, 2004: 148). Ringbom (2001) states that differences in frequency in lexical error production were 'linked with a gradual progress from organization by form to organization by meaning as the learners' [...] proficiency [in the foreign language] develops' (p. 65), which is also reflected in our findings. As a consequence of the decrease of formal lexical errors as proficiency increased, we might conclude that the formal aspects of words are easier to learn than semantic aspects, which are more resistant to acquisition (Fernández, 1997: 70).

Interpretation of our findings in the light of previous research (especially Fernández, 1997; Meara, 1996; Ringbom, 2001; Zimmermann, 1987) suggests that for semantic lexical errors to appear, learners have to achieve a certain threshold lexical level. Upon passing that threshold, it seems that semantic lexical errors will start to increase their presence in learners' production. Formal lexical errors will be present since the earliest stages of acquisition but become less as learning progresses.

The results of this study regarding evolution of formal- and content-oriented lexical errors from T1 to T2 as learners gain in proficiency are suggestive of the existence of transitional stages in the acquisition of the L2 lexicon (cf. Meara, 1983). Lexical acquisition shows a certain developmental pattern evident in the type of lexical errors that learners make at each particular phase or stage of the acquisition process. From formal knowledge of words, learners acquire semantic aspects of lexical items as they get more proficient. Ideally, this development would end with knowledge of all aspects of a word, that is spelling, pronunciation, core meaning, peripheral meanings, collocations, syntactic, frequency and so on. This last stage would resemble native-like lexical knowledge. This result lends evidence and supports preceding studies which suggest that vocabulary acquisition is a process that develops in stages (Ellis, 1997; Ellis & Beaton, 1993; Jiang, 2000; Palmberg, 1987; Schmitt & Meara, 1997; Viberg, 1996). An analysis of our research findings support Singleton (1999: 139) in that semantic integration is the 'most challenging component of the acquisition of any word' and 'until integration is properly under way the learner is bound to rely heavily on formal cues when dealing with the item in question'.

In sum, our results offer some preliminary evidence on how L2 learners structure and restructure their L2 lexicon as a result of being exposed to an increasing amount of the L2. Furthermore, our findings shed light on the issue of lexical access. The next section will give an account of this matter.

L1-oriented and L2-oriented lexical errors

One of the most prominent distinctions in error analysis is that of L1 or L2 derived errors. The relevance of this distinction is justified empirically since myriad studies have shown the important part that the L1 plays in acquiring an L2. In this study we have focused on the lexical errors produced by L1 influence as compared to those produced by L2 influence. Thus, among the former, we distinguish borrowings, calques and coinages, and among the latter, misspellings, semantic confusions and misselections.

This study reveals that lexical errors derived from L1 influence are recurrent all through the second phase of primary education in fourth and sixth grades. And although the tendency is to decrease, L1-oriented lexical errors are considerable at both testing times. Lexical errors derived from L2 are more frequent both at T1 and T2 than are L1 lexical errors. The findings of this research concur with those of previous studies: that as proficiency in the L2 increases, influence of the L1 decreases (Bouvy, 2000; Fernández, 1997; Herwig, 2001; LoCoco, 1975; Naves et al., 2005; Olsen, 1999; Ringbom, 1987; Williams & Hammarberg, 1998; Sánchez Jiménez, 2006; Tremblay, 2006). Taylor (1975) also noticed that the performance of beginner learners showed more instances of transfer than that of more advanced learners.

Our data also support previous studies that report younger learners to transfer most (Lasagabaster & Doiz, 2003) but contradict preceding studies by Gost and Celaya (2005), Cenoz (2001, 2003) and Celaya and Torras (2001), which found that older learners and late starters transfer more than younger students. The reason for the contradictory results between these studies and ours may be the fact that they examine the production of learners who had started learning English at different ages but had received the same hours of instruction, whereas in our study, age, proficiency and hours of instruction co-occur. In line with previous studies (Gost & Celaya, 2005), our results suggest that older and more proficient learners fall back on the L1 in different ways and show different types of transfer than younger and less-proficient students. As our learners get older and more proficient, they start adapting the L1 words to the L2 phonographemic rules; that is, they coin new words on the basis of old L1 lexical items and they start translating from the L1 into the L2, calquing L1 words or expressions using L2 words (Celaya & Torras, 2001; Naves et al., 2005). More specifically, at T1, borrowings are the most common transfer error, whereas at T2, calques are the most frequent transfer error category. Coinages also increase from T1 to T2.

The ability to create new L2 words seems to increase with proficiency and age. This is because more proficient participants resort to transfer of meaning, rather than to transfer of form (Gabryś-Barker, 2006; Ringbom, 2001). Lexical transfer is not a homogeneous phenomenon, but a multifaceted one responding to varied stimuli and purposes. In the light of our results, lack of vocabulary in the L2 might cause participants to use L1 words (Celaya & Torras, 2001; Dewaele, 1998; Naves et al., 2005; Tremblay, 2006; Viladot & Celaya, 2006). This study clearly indicates that learners use Spanish as a reference in the L2 writing process (cf. Olsen, 1999: 201). Regarding the L1-oriented lexical errors in our data, we can speculate about different sources. The young learners in our study seem to draw on their L1 to spell foreign words, since, as Celaya and Torras (2001) explain, the burden of learning both the meaning and the form of the target words is too heavy for them to learn words completely. They may just have some partial, incomplete knowledge of the target words and only an approximate rendering of the target word is possible. As revealed by our results, L1 borrowing in L2 writing may be due to several factors such as (a) inability of the learner to access or activate the intended item at the moment of performance, (b) knowledge is incomplete and does not apply to all possible situations and (c) knowledge is incomplete and can only approximate target items (Gabryś-Barker, 2006: 144).

We believe that the need to communicate collides with the lack of lexical knowledge in the L2. To overcome this problem, young learners may decide to resort to their L1 including L1 words in the L2 discourse (Bouvy, 2000; Ecke, 2001). This is considered one of the most important compensatory communication strategies (Bouvy, 2000; Celaya, 1992; Ecke, 2001; James, 1998; Olsen, 1999). Poulisse (1993) provides a very detailed account of communication strategies used by L2 learners. In particular, she refers to compensatory strategies that 'are used to solve lexical problems' (p. 61). Among the most prominent of these compensatory strategies, she mentions code switching, foreignising and literal translation. These are strategies found in our data, which gave rise, respectively, to borrowing, coinages and calque lexical errors. Poulisse (1993: 164–165) highlights that research on communication strategies has shown that communication strategy use is proficiency-related and so less-proficient learners use more communication strategies, although no conclusive results could be found for L1-based ones (cf. Zimmermann, 1987). It seems that in our case the low proficiency of learners at both testing times, together with the necessity to communicate and to carry on with the writing task, may have induced learners to transfer from the L1.

According to Bouvy (2000: 155), the higher the communicative pressure, the stronger the transfer. This may explain why in the present data, transfer from the L1 is frequent but not extremely common. The type of task to be performed may account for this transfer rate. Writing a composition is not an immediate task such as an oral interview, for example, and learners have enough time to plan their writing, to think about the content and form of the essay, to retrieve L2 words and to revise their production (cf. Gabryś-Barker, 2006: 144). During data collection sessions we observed that the 30 minutes allotted to complete the writing task were sufficient for learners to write at ease and that they had time to revise their writings, which they were encouraged to do. Therefore, the communicative pressure is reduced with the writing task and the sufficient time. Because learners were not under pressure, transfer rates in our data are moderate and L1-oriented lexical errors fewer than L2-oriented. In line with research on error production, we observe that not only do L1-oriented lexical errors tend to decrease as proficiency increases, but especially L2-oriented lexical errors get reduced in sixth grade.

Conclusion

This chapter has presented the results for lexical error production at two different levels of proficiency. Learners in sixth grade make fewer lexical errors than two years before; their compositions are longer and more accurate. Misspellings are the most common category of lexical errors in general, and formal and L2-oriented errors are more frequent in fourth grade than in sixth grade. Semantic lexical errors surpass formal ones in frequency in sixth grade but not in fourth grade. These data show an evolution in the way learners organise their lexicon from a more formal structure where the L1 serves a clear reference and scaffolding to a more semantically based network with a more developed and sophisticated use of the L1. Similarly, we can conclude that the learners' L1 serves as scaffolding from which they build their knowledge of the L2 as evidenced by the considerable amount of different types of lexical errors derived from L1 influence.

Notes

1. The critical assumption of normality in the distribution of the sample – that is the sample follows a normal distribution – was not met for the cloze and the reading tests in fourth and sixth grades. Therefore, we used non-parametric tests for two related samples, specifically the Wilcoxon signed ranks method to test for significant differences between the means of two matched samples (results of the cloze and reading tests for subjects in fourth and sixth grades). The Z represents the results of this measure.
2. Writing fluency is usually operationalised as the composition length (Wolfe-Quintero et al., 1998).
3. The false friend phenomenon (of which we found no instances in our data) is an exception to this, since false friends are derived from the mother tongue.
4. Wolfe-Quintero et al. (1998: 4) also note that an increased fluency, that is learners write more, and an increased accuracy, that is learners produce fewer errors, as proficiency progresses are two basic assumptions in studies about language development in writing. The third basic assumption refers to learners producing grammatically and lexically more complex writing as they become more proficient (Wolfe-Quintero et al., 1998: 4).
5. Some studies (Hawkey & Barker, 2004; Morris & Cobb, 2004; Torras & Celaya, 2001; Engber, 1995) have put forward that range of vocabulary in writing, that is the type/token ratio, is a distinguishing feature of proficiency levels. Analyses conducted with our participants have revealed that for our data the type/token ratio also increases with the proficiency level, and so subjects produce more different words at T2 than at T1, thus corroborating previous research (Jiménez Catalán & Ojeda Alba, 2007).

Lexical Error Production: Changes Over Time 163

6. Examples will be provided to illustrate the statements. Subjects will be identified in each case with a capital S (standing for subject) and a number before the example. Subjects in fourth grade have the numbers 1–283, with the coding fourth, and informants in sixth grade are numbered from 1 to 283, with the coding sixth. For instance, if an example is provided from learner 84 in fourth grade, the coding will look like this: S84, fourth.
7. It is worth mentioning here that Spanish spelling is very regular, with practically absolute agreement between pronunciation and spelling.
8. Compare also: *moder* (mother), *mader* (mother), *fader* (father), *de* (the).
9. For opposite results, that is an increase in the use of borrowings as grade and age increase with constant amount of exposure, see Gost and Celaya (2005) and Cenoz (2001, 2003).
10. However, as Olsen (1999: 200) notes (see also De Angelis & Selinker, 2001), communication may not always be successful upon using this strategy. As will be pointed out below, only when the reader/receiver of the message shares the L1 of the writer/learner does the communication have any possibility of succeeding.

Chapter 7
Lexical Errors in Writing Quality

In this chapter, we will examine the role of lexical errors in the global assessment of writing. Vocabulary has been traditionally seen as a positive indicator or predictor of the quality of a written text. In this sense, here we observe that lexical errors or a low lexical accuracy ratio implies a lower grade in the composition. The role of the different types of lexical errors which influence to different degrees the quality of the composition will be examined and discussed. We will also tackle the evolution of the categories of lexical errors as written composition score predictors across proficiency levels.

Lexical Errors as Predictors of the Quality of Written Composition

This section will attempt to establish the extent to which lexical errors relate to essay quality. Identifying the role of lexical errors as negative predictors of the quality of composition will be the main focus of the present section. Bearing in mind that the number of lexical errors is an absolute measure which may affect results, a relative measure – percentage of lexical errors – was used instead. The percentage of lexical errors in a composition is a measure resulting from the division of the absolute number of lexical errors per composition by the total number of words per composition, and multiplied by 100. The percentage of lexical errors is a complementary measure to accuracy ratio or error density. This measure allows for tests of means comparison and correlation analyses to be conducted to measure the differences among groups.

The results of descriptive analysis of participants in fourth and sixth grades are shown in Table 7.1. Here we will focus on the results of writing ability assessment and on the relationship between writing ability and lexical errors. Learners in sixth grade obtained higher scores on their compositions after evaluation with the *Profile*, specifically 66.79 points, than they had obtained two years earlier in fourth grade, in particular 56.99 points.

Differences in lexical error production as well as in composition length, accuracy ratio and percentage of lexical errors per composition

Table 7.1 Mean production of lexical errors, composition length, percentage of lexical errors, accuracy ratio and Profile composition score

	Grade fourth	Grade sixth
Mean number of lexical errors (SD)	11.14 (7.82)	8.79 (5.83)
Mean number of words (SD)	91.73 (52.94)	134.57 (70.36)
Mean percentage of lexical errors (SD)	14.38 (9.75)	7.65 (7.35)
Mean accuracy ratio (SD)	12.22 (11.86)	21.71 (22.84)
Mean composition score (SD)	56.99 (12.23)	66.79 (8.61)

are significant between the two testing times. The Wilcoxon signed ranks test for essay quality revealed that differences are also statistically significant between T1 and T2 ($Z = 10.755$, $p < 0.001$). In other words, learners write significantly better compositions in sixth grade than they did two years earlier. This concurs with previous literature on the issue. For example, Johns and Mayes (1990: 265) conclude that more proficient learners produce higher quality writings than do learners with lower L2 proficiency levels.

We will now look at the nature of the relationship between lexical errors and quality of composition, and we will examine to what extent lexical errors contribute to the detriment of essay quality. The results of the correlation analyses indicate that lexical errors contribute negatively to the assessment of quality of composition. As results presented in Table 7.2 show, at T1 the percentage of lexical errors produced by learners in each composition correlates significantly with the score obtained with the *Profile* ($r = -0.646$, $p < 0.001$). The correlation coefficient is slightly weaker for T2 data but equally significant ($r = -0.562$, $p < 0.001$).[1] In other words, lexical errors contribute negatively to the evaluation of the quality of the written composition, and so the more the lexical errors in every 100 words, the worse the overall score will be obtained by the composition.

Table 7.3 presents the values of R^2 of the correlation coefficients. The R^2 values account for the extent to what lexical errors contribute to predicting the assessment of essay quality using the *Profile*. Thus, the percentage of lexical errors per composition explains negatively 42% of the variance of the score on essay quality at T1 and 32% at T2. This implies that although there are other factors contributing to assessing quality of writing, lexical errors play an extremely important role in that

Table 7.2 Spearman rho correlation coefficients between percentage of lexical errors and scores of the Profile for fourth and sixth grades

	% *lexical errors/Profile score*
Fourth grade	−0.646*
Sixth grade	−0.562*

*Significant at $p < .001$

Table 7.3 R^2 of the correlation coefficients between percentage of lexical errors and scores of the Profile for fourth and sixth grades

	Lexical errors/Profile score
Fourth grade	0.42
Sixth grade	0.32

assessment, especially in low grades. As experience with the language and proficiency increase, this negative influence of lexical errors reduces its predictive power and other elements of the writing start being important to determine essay quality. We can think of the use of synonyms, use of sophisticated words and use of adequate words as a few of discourse aspects that may influence the assessment of essay quality.

To summarise, hypothesis 3 that posited the negative role of lexical errors in the assessment of essay quality can be accepted in view of the results presented above. The analyses of inferential statistics have proved that the percentage of lexical errors per composition contributes in a significantly negative way to the score of the quality of the composition. Correlation coefficients are quite strong, especially for fourth grade. From these data, it can be concluded that the presence of lexical errors in a written composition will result in a significant decrease of essay quality. However, it seems that as proficiency in the L2 increases, the role of lexical errors weakens in favour of other compositional aspects.

Changes over Time in the Relationship between Lexical Errors and Essay Quality

This section will address the extent of the influence of each of the different lexical error types identified in assessing written composition in English. We found that it would be very interesting to discern how much

Lexical Errors in Writing Quality 167

of the 42% in fourth grade and 32% in sixth grade of the variance of the score devoted to lexical errors was explained by the different categories of lexical errors considered in this study. Upon observation of the relatively weak influence of each particular lexical error type on the writing score, we decided that it would make no sense to carry out a regression analysis, since there are also other things predicting composition score apart from lexical errors. The results from a regression analysis would reveal extremely small prediction patches with big statistical errors.

The first subsection will deal with results for T1, and the second subsection will focus on the examination of influence of lexical error categories in essay score at T2.

Lexical error types and essay quality at T1

Several correlation analyses between lexical error types and composition score were performed. Since the sample did not meet the normality assumption, Spearman correlation tests were chosen as the statistical tests. The absolute production of lexical errors of each type per composition was the measure selected to perform the correlation analyses.[2] The results of the correlation analyses are shown in Table 7.4.

The figures in the table indicate that only two types of lexical errors contribute in some way to significantly predicting EFL composition score: borrowings and calques. We will examine these in order of importance.

The presence of borrowings, that is insertion of L1 words in the English discourse, negatively affects the quality of the essay, and so

Table 7.4 Spearman rho correlation coefficients between composition score and lexical error types at T1

	Composition score
Misspelling	− 0.024
Borrowing	− 0.326*
Calque	0.200*
Semantic confusion	0.059
Coinage	− 0.069
Misselection	− 0.022

*Significant at $p < 0.01$

compositions with many instances of borrowings will obtain worse scores. More specifically, borrowings negatively account for 10.62% of the variance of the composition score. This figure is obtained from the multiple regression correlation coefficient $R^2 = 0.1062$. On the contrary, the presence of calques, literal translations from the L1 into the L2, positively contribute to explain essay score. In other words, the more the calques in a composition, the higher the score of that composition will be. In particular, 4% of the variance of the composition score is accounted for by the presence of calques. The more the calques, the higher the composition score. This result was very surprising, since all categories of lexical errors, except calques and semantic confusions, contribute negatively to the composition score.

The remaining categories of lexical errors, that is misspellings, coinages, semantic confusions and misselections, do not offer significant correlations with essay score. In other words, they contribute minimally to the assessment of writing. In the cases of misspellings, borrowings, coinages and misselections, the effect of their presence is negative, resulting in lower essay scores. Nonetheless, semantic confusions have a positive impact on the evaluation of writing. In general terms, these correlation coefficients are somehow weak. This corroborates the idea that there are some other factors influencing the composition score.

In order to offer more complete results, we decided to group the lexical error categories again into the dichotomies formal/semantic and L1-oriented/L2-oriented lexical errors and show the influence of members of each of the dichotomies to the assessment of the composition score. Table 7.5 presents the results of the correlation analysis between formal and semantic lexical errors and essay score.

From the results of the correlation analyses, we can see that formal lexical errors contribute significantly to the composition score in a negative way and semantic errors exert a similarly important influence in essay evaluation, but their presence results in positive scoring of the

Table 7.5 Spearman rho correlation coefficients between composition score and formal and semantic lexical errors at T1

	Composition score
Formal errors	− 0.188*
Semantic errors	0.188*

*Significant at $p < 0.01$

Table 7.6 Spearman rho correlation coefficients between composition score and L1-oriented and L2-oriented lexical errors at T1

	Composition score
L1-oriented errors	− 0.241*
L2-oriented errors	− 0.022

*Significant at $p < 0.01$

learners' writing. When many formal lexical errors are present in the essay, lower grades will result. On the contrary, the more the semantic lexical errors, the higher the composition score will be. Formal lexical errors account for 3.53% ($R^2 = 0.0353$) of the variance of learners' essay score. Similarly, semantic lexical errors also explain 3.53% ($R^2 = 0.0353$) of the variance of the composition score.

The second main distinction among lexical error categories concerned origin of the error, that is L1 or L2. Table 7.6 shows the extent to which each of these categories serves to predict assessment of learners' essays.

Lexical errors originating in the L1 contribute negatively to the evaluation of students' written compositions. By contrast, L2-oriented lexical errors do not show an important influence in essay score. More specifically, the presence of L1-oriented lexical errors explains 5.80% ($R^2 = 0.0580$) of the variance of the composition score. In short, L1-oriented lexical errors serve to predict the composition score to a considerable extent, and so the more the lexical errors from the L1 origin, the lower the composition score. In the case of L2-oriented lexical errors, no significant correlations were found. But it was also observed that the more the lexical errors derived from L2 influence, the lower the composition score. To sum up, lexical errors deriving from L1 will have a more negative impact on writing assessment than do lexical errors deriving from L2.

Lexical error types and essay quality at T2

In sixth grade we generally noted lower correlations between lexical error categories and composition score, except for misselections. This category increases its impact on essay score at T2. The exact figures appear in Table 7.7. Spearman correlation coefficients were calculated between composition score and number of lexical errors of each category produced per composition.

Table 7.7 Spearman rho correlation coefficients between composition score and lexical error types at T2

	Composition score
Misspelling	− 0.008
Borrowing	− 0.104*
Calque	0.179**
Semantic confusion	− 0.005
Coinage	− 0.043
Misselection	0.106*

*Significant at $p < 0.5$
**Significant at $p < 0.01$

Correlation coefficients vary slightly at T2 from those in fourth grade. In sixth grade, three lexical error categories show significant effects on essay score: calques, misselections and borrowings, in this order. Calques are the category that has a greater positive impact on the composition score. In particular, the presence of calques accounts positively for 3.20% ($R^2 = 0.0320$) of the variance of the score in sixth grade. Likewise, misselections also contribute positively to the composition assessment. Specifically, they explain 1.12% ($R^2 = 0.0112$) of the variance of the score. On the contrary, borrowings negatively affect the writing assessment. So the presence of borrowings explains 1.08% ($R^2 = 0.0108$) of the variance of the score given to the learner's composition.

The significant correlation coefficient between misselections and essay scores introduces a novelty in sixth grade, since two years earlier this lexical error category had no significant effect on the composition score. At T2, misselections seem to affect more positively learners' composition than they did at T1. A very surprising result comes from the positive and significant correlations between calques and misselections and the composition score. Nevertheless, their positive contribution to evaluating writing is very weak.

Turning now to the analyses of the extent of the contribution of formal and semantic lexical errors to the assessment of learners' composition in sixth grade, we observe that correlation coefficients are lower than in fourth grade, meaning that although these types have a negative impact on the composition score, this effect is smaller. In sixth grade the tendency found two years before is reversed. From the figures in Table 7.8, it can be observed that formal lexical errors have a more negative effect on the assessment of compositions than do semantic lexical errors. However, this impact is not significant and almost negligible. On the contrary, semantic lexical errors show a significant positive effect on the composition score. So the presence of semantic lexical errors positively accounts for 2.28% ($R^2 = 0.0228$) of the variance of essay score.

Table 7.9 presents the results of the Spearman correlation analyses between L1- and L2-oriented lexical errors and the composition score. The amount of the variance of the score that lexical errors in these categories account for is extremely small and non-significant.

In sum, the results reported in this section show that different categories of lexical errors have different impacts on the assessment of learners' compositions. In fourth grade, borrowings and calques have a greater effect on essay score. But although the presence of borrowings in the composition has a negative impact, the presence of calques in the composition has a positive effect. At T2, borrowings, calques and misselections have a significant effect on the assessment of written work of learners. Borrowings negatively affect essay score, but the presence of calques and misselections has a positive effect on the evaluation of written assignments. For the remaining categories at both testing times, a minimal and non-significant effect on essay score can be observed.

Formal lexical errors seem to have a greater significant negative effect on the composition score than do semantic lexical errors at T1. Nonetheless, in

Table 7.8 Spearman rho correlation coefficients between composition score and formal and semantic lexical errors at T2

	Composition score
Formal errors	− 0.027
Semantic errors	0.151*

*Significant at $p < 0.01$

Table 7.9 Spearman rho correlation coefficients between composition score and L1-oriented and L2-oriented lexical errors at T2

	Composition score
L1-oriented errors	0.047
L2-oriented errors	0.010

sixth grade, semantic lexical errors show a significant positive effect on the essay score, whereas formal lexical errors show extremely weak effects. Similarly at T1, L1-oriented lexical errors show a greater negative impact on the assessment of learners' writings than do lexical errors deriving from L2. At T2, positive, non-significant effects are observed for L1- and L2-oriented lexical errors on essay score.

According to the data analysed and presented above in this section, hypothesis 4 that claimed for the different degrees of influence of the different lexical error categories in the assessment of writing is to be confirmed. The data allow us to conclude that lexical errors belonging to different categories will have a different impact on the score of the learners' written work. Furthermore, this tendency will vary as L2 proficiency increases.

Discussion

Lexical errors and essay quality

Accuracy or lack of errors is deemed as a crucial component in writing assessment despite the fact that nowadays communicative approaches have prevailed and the communicative effectiveness of a text is made prevalent over other text features when rating essay quality. Hawkey and Baker's (2004: 142) statement conveys the essence of this issue:

> ... even in a language teaching and testing world where communicative approaches hold sway, with emphasis on message rather than form, accuracy plays a key part in the impact of communication on interlocutors.

In the previous sections, we have attempted to ascertain the relationship between lexical accuracy and composition score. Results have revealed that there is a highly significant correlation between lexical accuracy and writing assessment. More specifically, we have found a strong negative correlation between percentage of lexical errors and composition score. In other words, the more the lexical errors in a composition, the lower the score obtained by that composition in an analytic scoring.

This result means that lexical errors, or rather absence thereof, are good predictors and indicators of quality of composition. So a composition that displays many lexical errors will obtain lower scores. The solid correlation coefficient could be expected considering that few lexical errors displayed in a composition point to higher productive lexical knowledge. In other words, if a learner makes few lexical errors, this learner is showing some knowledge or control of vocabulary in use.

In this study, we used the *Profile* as the measure to assess learners' writing proficiency. It is important to note in this respect that the *Profile* makes judgements about writing quality or writing proficiency based on communication effectiveness, and not on accuracy. Raters are not trained to be mediated by errors in their assessment. In this sense, lexical errors seem to distort communication, since their presence in an essay will make the score low on communicability.

So far there have been a number of studies that have demonstrated the relationship between accuracy and proficiency so that both constructs develop linearly; the higher the proficiency, the higher the accuracy (cf. Wolfe-Quintero *et al.*, 1998). Wolfe-Quintero *et al.* (1998) offer a very detailed account of the studies that investigated the relationship between accuracy and proficiency, or grade. They report that in general terms both constructs relate significantly, although some measures of accuracy reveal higher levels of significance than others. For example, they mention that a potentially very useful measure would be the number of error-free words per total number of words. In this study we have used this very measure of lexical accuracy that determines the number of error-free words between two consecutive lexical errors. This measure is complementary with the percentage of lexical errors per composition (cf. Kroll, 1990).

It is a general assumption in the literature on SLA that errors are related to proficiency (Engber, 1995; Grant & Ginther, 2000; Mutta, 1999; Olsen, 1999). For example, although Olsen (1999) does not perform statistical analyses to ascertain the relationship between the presence of errors in compositions and low grades, he repeatedly states that the abundance of errors has contributed to the low scores in his learners' essays (p. 195). Similarly, Meara *et al.* (2000: 346) claim that compositions with a restricted range of vocabulary and a high proportion of lexical errors will tend to be rated poorly irrespective of the other merits or demerits of the text. This relationship between errors and proficiency is also observed in our data. As learners go up grade and gain in general proficiency and in receptive vocabulary knowledge, they write longer essays, essays with fewer lexical errors and essays that obtain higher scores.

The findings of several research studies have illustrated the correlation between lexical errors and proficiency. Bardovi-Harlig and Bofman (1989) found that lexical errors correlated better with pass/fail judgements than did morphological errors. Grant and Ginther (2000) have put forward that lexical error production contributes negatively to predicting essay quality, and so the more the lexical errors displayed in a composition, the lower the score that piece of writing will be given. When accuracy was measured as communicative success of text, Cumming et al. (2005) found that it correlated highly with writing proficiency, and so better rated compositions were more accurate. Mutta (1999: 339–340) also observed that the presence of errors in learners' compositions had a damaging effect on evaluation. Our results also mirror this observation. Likewise, Engber's (1995) results revealed a moderate correlation ($r = -0.43$, $p < 0.01$) between percentage of lexical errors and writing quality score as measured by the Test of Written English.

Our results concur with those of Jarvis et al. (2003), who had already found that although significant correlations between text features were identified, these tend to be only low to moderate. Engber's (1995) correlation coefficient is slightly weaker than ours for fourth grade, but resembles much the coefficient found for lexical errors and essay score for learners in sixth grade. The lexical proficiency of the learners may have been decisive in the establishment of the correlation between errors and writing quality. For instance, Linnarud (1986) in Engber (1995) found a low, non-significant correlation between lexical errors and quality score of the written production of advanced learners. From this result, Linnarud concluded that lexical errors in composition probably did not have much effect on comprehension. In this sense, we agree with Engber (1995: 149) that lexical errors made by advanced learners such as Linnarud's may be understandable in context and therefore may not impede successful comprehension. However, if we observe the lexical errors made by intermediate and beginner learners, such as Engber's and ours, there are clearly some lexical errors that distort communication and cannot be understood by the reader. This may explain why for intermediate and especially beginner learners, the correlations between lexical errors and essay score are stronger.

Apart from the understandability of lexical errors as proficiency increases, other factors may be influencing scoring to a greater extent than at earlier stages of acquisition and that explain the different correlation strengths at T1 and T2. For example, as learners get more proficient their discourse may get more sophisticated, they may use more words and more synonyms, and words may be used in a better and more appropriate way.

Our findings point to lexical errors as objective writing evaluation criteria. Argüelles Álvarez (2004) has expressed her concern about finding objective and fair instruments to assess writing compositions (direct testing approach to writing). The establishment of a series of well-defined descriptors to evaluate essays can enhance the reliability and validity of the testing instrument. In this sense, lexical errors and lexical error categories are well-defined descriptors of essay quality and can serve as fair testing criteria.

Although lexical errors account for a high percentage of the variance of the composition score, there are some other writing aspects that also influence essay score. Jarvis *et al.* (2003) showed that writing assessment may be determined by the use of a combination of features rather than by the use of a single feature. The argument of having several scoring rubrics is supported by the results in Cumming *et al.* (2005). These authors' findings show that higher rated essays are longer, have more different words, have longer and more clauses, demonstrate greater accuracy, have better quality propositions and claims in the arguments and have more summaries of source evidence.

Therefore, lexical errors explain just a part of the total score, confirming previous literature that writing teaching and writing assessment proceed not from a single approach but from a combination of several approaches that complement each other. In this sense, the approach of writing as a product accounts for the fact that lexical errors influence writing quality. Nonetheless, accuracy but also other key aspects such as fluency or (grammatical and lexical) complexity are important in evaluating essays.

Fluency or length of composition is relevant in composition assessment, and so the longer an essay, the better the score it will get. The length of composition is indicative of proficiency (Cumming *et al.*, 2005; De Haan & van Esch, 2005; Grant & Ginther, 2000; Hawkey & Barker, 2004; Jarvis *et al.*, 2003; Martínez Arbelaiz, 2004). There may be two explanations for this relevance of text length. One may refer to the amount of content or information contained in the longer essays. So we echo Freidlander's (1990: 115–116) contention that although length is not a direct measure of quality, a longer essay implies an essay richer in information. For the second explanation we agree with Reid (1990: 195) who states that mere length does not ensure writing quality, but 'essay length is often indicative of development within paragraphs, structural completeness, and fluency'. In this sense, we have observed that the production of lexical errors seems to be relevant with respect to composition score when compositions start getting longer, that is, from 50 words onwards. For shorter compositions, the percentage of lexical errors seems less important in writing assessment.

But vocabulary proficiency is perhaps the most relevant indicator of the quality of composition (see, e.g. Santos, 1988) and 'range of vocabulary is thus possibly a feature distinguishing proficiency level' (Hawkey & Barker, 2004: 152). If vocabulary is a key factor in assessing writing, then an essay containing a large, rich and varied vocabulary will score better and an essay containing many lexical errors will be a poor scorer. Our present finding adds further support to the previous research that establishes vocabulary to be a key aspect in assessing writing quality. The importance of lexical knowledge in writing, be it in the form of words used in compositions or of lack of lexical errors, cannot be denied.

In summary, lexical errors have been found to be important quality predictors that may be used in writing assessment to complement evaluation of the type performed by the *Profile*. A previous research (Bacha, 2001) suggests that holistic essay scoring can benefit from the aid of other analytic measures. The different lexical error categories can take up this role, which we will now discuss.

Lexical error types and essay quality

Not all lexical errors have the same value or contribute equally to writing assessment. Some lexical errors are judged to be more negative than others. Hawkey and Barker (2004: 148) indicate that the negative impact on the reader of certain categories of errors may be greater than that of others. However, they do not specify which categories are more negative. They nevertheless suggest that errors' gravity may be proficiency-dependent. This implies that an error may be considered more serious at one proficiency level than at another. For example, at a higher proficiency level an error typical of lower stages of acquisition will be considered serious. Judgements on error gravity follow from communicability criteria, and so the errors that distort communication most are judged to be the most serious (see, e.g. Ellis, 1994; Fayer & Krasinski, 1987; James, 1977; Johansson, 1978; Khalil, 1985; Lindell, 1973; Picó, 1987; Politzer, 1978; Santos, 1988).

Our results show some slight discrepancies in the correlations between lexical error types and composition scores at both testing times. This could serve as support of Hawkey and Barker's claim just stated. However, we could not find a systematic behaviour in the correlations as proficiency increased. It may be that for some considerable differences to be appreciated learning stages might be further apart than our T1 and T2 are. At this point, we must again remember that the instrument used to assess writing in this study, the *Profile*, was independent of errors; that is, it was not based on errors for the assessment. Nevertheless, we believe that errors implicitly and tacitly influence raters' assessments. Moreover, errors are frequently used as the assessment criteria. For instance, James (1977) and Enkvist (1973) note that the writing assessment can proceed from the error evaluation, and so the final score of a composition will depend on the number of errors it contains.

While the contribution of lexical errors to essay score is quite complex, some tendencies and trends can be observed. From the categories that show a significant correlation with essay score, borrowings are the ones that most negatively affect the assessment of writing. The more the borrowings in a composition, the lower the score. This result was not surprising, since borrowings were mere insertions of L1 words in the L2 writing, and in this sense, learners using borrowings did not show any L2 word knowledge. In other words, borrowings do not count as L2 words and therefore they score negatively. In addition to this, borrowings may distort communication to a great extent, because they imply a code switching. A change in code might impose a greater cognitive demand from the reader and devalue writing.

Calques and misselections merit special attention since in our data they contribute positively to essay score. Calques imply a literal translation, that is the use of L2 words to express L1 concepts. When using calques, learners are demonstrating at least some lexical knowledge because they use English words. This seems to be valued positively in the assessment of writing with the *Profile*. Likewise, in sixth grade misselections also show a positive significant correlation with essay score. Again we believe that the fact that a misselection implies the confusion of two existing target words may account for raters valuing positively this word knowledge. It also seems from the results at T2 that showing knowledge of some English words, even when they are confused, is positive. The higher presence of misselections in sixth grade than in fourth grade may also account for the correlations being significant at T1 but not at T2. Santos Rovira (2007) concludes that lexical errors of the word choice type, either misselections or semantic confusions, do not distort communication, because although the terms/words used are erroneous in the context they are understood by the reader.

At T1, formal lexical errors contribute negatively to essay score. It may be that although formal lexical errors, such as borrowings or coinages, may distort communication to a great extent, spelling errors have minimal impact on the communicability of the message. A word that contains a spelling error is usually easily recognisable by the reader and so it does not impede comprehension. Our results support Sánchez Jiménez (2006: 176), who observed in his data that spelling errors on their own do not interrupt communication. In our data, the massive presence of misspellings does not contribute to poorer composition scores. One possible reason for this may be that misspellings are not judged to be serious errors (Enkvist, 1973). Hughes and Lascaratou (1982) also found that non-native speaker judges, such as ours, were lenient on gravity evaluation of spelling errors. However, when spelling errors give rise to lexical confusions, they are considered to be more serious (see Lindell, 1973: 94).

Surprisingly enough, at both testing times, semantic lexical errors show significant positive correlations with the composition score. The production of semantic confusions and particularly of calques results in better writing assessments. It seems that showing some word knowledge, even when this is partial or imperfect, outstands communicability. In this research we observe that formal lexical errors correlate negatively with essay score, but semantic lexical errors show a positive correlation. We cannot find a plausible explanation for this phenomenon other than that of the competing criteria just mentioned: lexical competence versus communicative success. This interpretation can be seen in the light of Khalil's (1985) results that point to errors affecting naturalness more than intelligibility. That is, errors seem to have a more negative effect on the naturalness of the message than on the intelligibility of the message. Albrechtsen et al. (1980: 389) found that errors in content words did not impede communication, because of the choice of semantically related words, that is semantic confusions. Moreover, context might aid understanding of utterances containing errors. Like Hawkey and Barker (2004), we can speculate that at this proficiency level, formal lexical errors contribute to a higher extent to the communicative effectiveness of the message than do semantic lexical errors. At higher stages of acquisition this trend may be reversed.

Finally, regarding the contributions of L1- and L2-oriented lexical errors we could observe that there were significant correlations in fourth grade only. More specifically, L1-oriented lexical errors showed a negative effect on the total score of the composition. These results are in line with the preceding interpretation of the L2 lexical knowledge criterion being decisive in writing assessment. It is worth noting at this point that at T1 the bulk of lexical errors derived from L1 influence is made up of borrowings, yet at T2 it is calques, the most prominent category of L1-oriented lexical errors. This may explain why correlations are significant at T1 but not at T2.

Borrowings and coinages can greatly distort communication, except for the cases where the addressee understands the L1 of the learners. It seems that learners resort to L1-based communication strategies when they know their addressee speaks their L1. This is also the case with our learners:

In foreign language acquisition the learner knows that the rest of the class and sometimes the teacher, too, are native speakers of his/her L1. This is probably why transferring from L1 may seem to him/her the best or the easiest solution. (Celaya, 1992: 57)

Up to this point our argument that borrowings and L1 influenced lexical errors in general exert a negative effect on the reader may seem contradictory with the above claim by Celaya (1992) taking into account that writer and reader/rater share the same L1. However, previous research (Khalil, 1985) has shown that raters judge errors as serious or unintelligible basing on what they think are unintelligible errors, not on real measures of unintelligibility or interpretability. In other words, some errors that could be easily interpreted were judged by raters to be unintelligible (Khalil, 1985). In this sense, our raters, who understood borrowings and L1 influenced lexical errors, seemed to have considered, nevertheless, that these were very negative for the writing. It is likely that had raters been native speakers of English, results regarding the relationship between lexical error types and essay quality would have been very similar. It is worth pointing out that non-native judges who are teachers of English were found to be more severe and strict than native judges – teachers or not (Fayer & Krasinski, 1987; Hughes & Lascaratou, 1982). This suggests that non-native judges as ours might feel especially annoyed with the language problems they can recognise as their own (Fayer & Krasinski, 1987). Furthermore, communicative effectiveness of the message or intelligibility may depend upon other factors such as irritability (Fayer & Krasinski, 1987). If the rater feels irritated or annoyed by the learners' message, then this message could fail to communicate and it would be judged as unintelligible.

In sum, it is hoped that the results of the analysis, cautiously interpreted, might be sufficiently concrete to have some practical application to teaching. From the examination of the relationship between lexical error types and essay quality, we have achieved a realistic ranking of the types of lexical errors that need to be remedied and taught in the classroom.

Conclusion

This chapter has presented and discussed data concerning the relationship between lexical errors and writing quality. In general, we observe that as lexical accuracy increases, composition score increases as well. Moreover, statistical analyses reveal that the presence of lexical errors in compositions account for over one third of the variation of the score. As learners' proficiency increases and their compositions get more lexically accurate, the influence of lexical errors on the final score diminishes, and the display of more elaborated discourse, more correct grammar and more sophisticated vocabulary might gain importance in determining or assessing learners writing. Likewise, we could suggest that borrowings exert a negative influence on the score, whereas calques have a positive one. Similarly, the presence of formal and L1-oriented errors results in a worse assessment of the composition.

Notes

1. Qian (1999: 286) notes that '[i]n the behavioural sciences, a correlation r of 0.50 is generally regarded as indicating a "large correlational effect size" (Cohen, 1988: 80), or at least a "moderate positive relationship" (Hamilton, 1990: 481)'. Wolfe-Quintero *et al.* (1998: 8) believe a correlation coefficient of $r = 0.65$ or above is strong enough to consider it as indicative of a high correlation.
2. The relative measure of percentage of lexical errors per total number of words per composition was not chosen as the measure for the present analyses, because it may yield deceiving results. While considering the proportion of lexical errors committed every 100 words, this measure allows for comparisons among the lexical errors of each type produced on different occasions. In the same line, it takes into account the amount of lexical errors of each type to establish correlations, and so the most frequent category would also be the one that show the greatest impact on essay score. This would distort the real picture.

Chapter 8
Lexical Errors and Receptive Vocabulary Knowledge

This chapter gives account of the relationship between lexical errors and receptive vocabulary knowledge. In an attempt to examine the nature of lexical errors, we wanted to establish a relationship between the number of words the students know receptively and the words they use incorrectly in compositions.

Lexical Errors as Negative Indicators of Vocabulary Knowledge

The last issue addressed in this research was the relationship between receptive word knowledge and the different categories of lexical errors. In this section, we will explore how misspellings, borrowings, coinages, calques, misselections and semantic confusions relate to receptive knowledge of vocabulary as measured by using the 1000 Word Test (WT) and the 2000 frequency band of the Vocabulary Levels Test (VLT).

The figures in Table 8.1 indicate that learners produce lexical errors of different types in different quantities. Furthermore, lexical error production also shows development from fourth to sixth grade, with some lexical error categories being more common at T2 than at T1, as has been already explained.

Likewise, figures from Table 8.2 also indicate a development in receptive lexical knowledge of learners in this study. As revealed by the scores obtained in the two different tests of receptive vocabulary knowledge, learners know more words receptively at T2 than they did two years before at T1. Furthermore, learners have progressed in their lexical knowledge, and data suggest that as proficiency and experience with the language increase, receptive lexical knowledge increases as well. Figure 8.1 shows the evolution of receptive word knowledge graphically.

These results are extremely interesting (see Table 8.1); although the total number of lexical errors produced decreases with grade, the production in some categories of lexical errors does in fact increase. Nevertheless, receptive knowledge of L2 vocabulary increases with grade.

Table 8.1 Absolute numbers of lexical errors distributed into categories at T1 and T2

	Grade 4	Grade 6
Misspellings	1796	1199
Borrowings	442	239
Coinages	150	206
Calques	139	323
Misselections	96	136
Semantic confusions	152	210
Total	2775	2313

Table 8.2 Mean scores of receptive word knowledge at T1 and T2

	1000 Word Test	*2000 VLT*
T1	16.76 (SD 4.00) 55.86%	5.33 (SD 3.35) 17.76%
T2	21.52 (SD 3.42) 71.73%	9.41 (SD 4.90) 31.36%

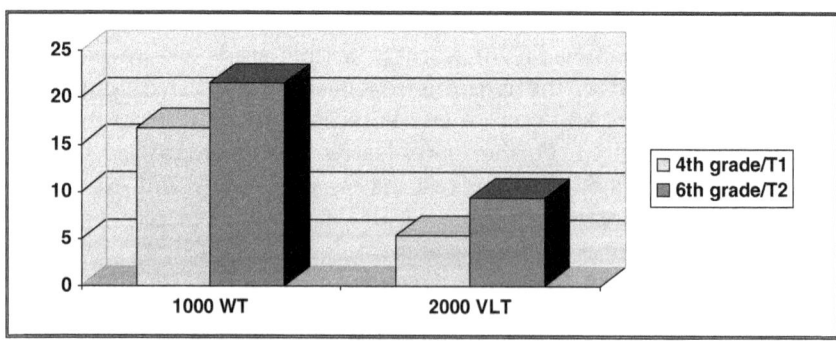

Figure 8.1 Receptive word knowledge of 1000 WT and 2000 VLT at T1 and T2

Examination of how these measures of lexical knowledge relate may throw quite newsworthy results. We will now explore this issue in detail.

Table 8.3 shows the results for the correlation analyses between the different categories of lexical errors and receptive word knowledge as measured by the 1000 WT and the 2000 VLT at T1. As can be observed from the table, only two types of lexical errors show significant correlations with receptive word knowledge. For the 1000 WT, the more the borrowings contained in learners' composition, the lower the scores of the test will be. However, for calques, the more calques produced in a composition, the higher the receptive word knowledge of learners of the first and second most frequent 1000 words will be. In other words, learners who produce more calques also know more words receptively of the first 2000 most frequent words, as measured with the 1000 WT and the 2000 VLT.

Other correlation coefficients, although non-significant, also reveal very interesting results. In all cases, except for borrowings for both tests and semantic confusions for the 1000 WT, there are positive correlations. This means that participants who produce more lexical errors also show receptive knowledge of more words. Although this result may seem contradictory at first sight, it is quite easily explained. Although learners are showing lack of knowledge in some aspect of the words in question, in fact they know some other aspects of those words. For example, if a learner misspells a word, it is evident that he or she lacks

Table 8.3 Spearman rho correlation coefficients between lexical error categories, lexical accuracy ratio and receptive vocabulary knowledge at T1

	1000 WT	*2000 VLT*
Misspellings	0.062	0.091
Borrowings	− 0.139*	− 0.117
Coinages	0.061	0.077
Calques	0.164**	0.186**
Misselections	0.108	0.041
Semantic confusion	− 0.067	0.044
Lexical accuracy ratio	0.232**	0.172**

*Significant at $p < 0.01$
*Significant at $p < 0.5$

full formal/orthographic knowledge of the word. Nevertheless, he or she also shows knowledge of some aspect of the meaning of the word or its syntactic constraints by using it appropriately. By contrast, it seems obvious that borrowings imply absolute lack of word knowledge, and consequently, those learners who borrow most will also deploy lower levels of receptive word knowledge.

When comparing the lexical accuracy ratio of the composition with the receptive word knowledge of the learners, we observe that both measures correlate significantly. The more words learners know receptively, the more lexically accurate are their essays. In other words, the fewer lexical errors per total number of words will be indicative of learners knowing more words receptively. Correlation coefficients are not very high, but significant. Correlations are higher for receptive knowledge of the first 1000 most frequent words.

This hypothesis relates the main dimensions within the field of lexical competence, namely vocabulary size or breadth and depth of vocabulary knowledge, or quality of word knowledge. The results of this research show that these two dimensions are closely related. Having receptive knowledge of a word does not necessarily imply full command of all the aspects of that word, but having partial knowledge of a word serves to increase vocabulary size.

An inspection of Tables 8.4 and 8.5 shows that correlations were very weak between scores on the 1000 WT and formal and semantic lexical

Table 8.4 Spearman rho correlation coefficients between formal and semantic lexical errors and receptive vocabulary knowledge at T1

	1000 WT	*2000 VLT*
Formal errors	0.009	0.049
Semantic errors	− 0.088	− 0.078

*Significant at $p < 0.01$

Table 8.5 Spearman rho correlation coefficients between L1- and L2-oriented lexical errors and receptive vocabulary knowledge at T1

	1000 WT	*2000 VLT*
L1-oriented errors	− 0.032	0.015
L2-oriented errors	0.058	0.094

errors at T1. These correlations were, nevertheless, positive. This indicates, thus, that the more the lexical errors produced by learners, the more the first 1000 most frequent words they knew receptively. The relationship between scores on the 2000 VLT and formal and semantic lexical errors shows similar results. However, in this case, the correlation between semantic errors and receptive knowledge of words from the 2000 most frequent words is significant.

Correlations between scores on the two tests of receptive vocabulary knowledge and L2-oriented lexical errors are positive but extremely weak. Figures for L1-oriented lexical errors show inconsistencies. In any case, the correlation, be it positive or negative, is very low.

Table 8.6 shows that for T2 every different category of lexical error correlates with a different extent with receptive vocabulary knowledge as measured by the 1000 WT and the 2000 VLT. Furthermore, the nature of this relationship is also different for each type. We will now examine the categories in more detail.

Learners who make misspellings in sixth grade show lower level of receptive vocabulary size of the first 2000 most frequent words. However, correlations are very low and not significant. It seems that in sixth grade, learners are using words with which they are so unfamiliar that they even lack knowledge of their general meaning. It may also be that those most misspelled words belong to other frequency bands, that is are of lower frequency than the first 2000 words.

Table 8.6 Spearman rho correlation coefficients between lexical error categories, lexical accuracy ratio and receptive vocabulary knowledge at T2

	1000 WT	*2000 VLT*
Misspellings	−0.110	−0.111
Borrowings	−0.198*	−0.059
Coinages	−0.052	0.071
Calques	0.248*	0.191*
Misselections	−0.006	0.051
Semantic confusion	0.006	−0.001
Lexical accuracy ratio	0.312*	0.263*

*Significant at $p < 0.01$

By the same token, and as was to be expected, the more borrowings in a composition, the lower was the receptive knowledge level of words from the 1000 WT and the 2000 VLT. This relationship is significant for the 1000 WT, but not for the 2000 VLT. It seems quite reasonable that the more the L1 equivalents a learner uses, the fewer words this learner will know receptively. Coinages and misselections show negative correlations with scores on the 1000 WT but positive correlations with the 2000 VLT. These results may seem a bit confusing. We can argue that whereas vocabulary tests are receptive in nature, lexical errors derive from productive language use. In this sense, we can assume that learners recognise words but have problems with their productive use.

For semantic confusions, we find amount of misselections correlating negatively with the scores on the 2000 VLT and positively with the results of the 1000 WT. However, the correlation coefficients are so small for coinages, misselections and semantic confusions that results may rather point to lack of relationship between these categories and receptive vocabulary knowledge. Finally, calques show significant positive correlation coefficients with scores on the tests of receptive vocabulary knowledge, especially with the 1000 WT. This means that the more the calque errors or literal translations appear in a composition, the more the receptive word knowledge is shown by the learners.

In general terms, when lexical accuracy is correlated with receptive word knowledge of the first 1000 and 2000 most frequent lexical items, results show significant correlation coefficients. As happened two years before, participants who make fewer lexical errors in their compositions show higher receptive knowledge of the 1000 and 2000 most frequent words in the L2. Correlation coefficients are higher for the first level of the frequent words than for the second level and higher than for fourth grade for both levels tested. This can be thought to be quite logical since as learners know more words they produce more lexically accurate essays.

Data from sixth graders point to inconclusive and contradictory results regarding the nature of the relationship between scores on tests of receptive vocabulary knowledge and formal, semantic, L1-oriented and L2-oriented lexical errors. Formal lexical errors correlate significantly and negatively with scores on the 1000 WT but non-significantly with scores on the 2000 VLT. The more formal lexical errors a learner produces, the lower will his or her receptive vocabulary knowledge be. Semantic lexical errors show positive and significant correlations with scores on both tests, so that the more the semantic lexical errors produced by learners, the higher the receptive word knowledge of the first 2000 most frequent words.

Very low correlation coefficients were found for L1- and L2-oriented lexical errors. Lexical errors originating in the L1 show positive correlations with scores on the 1000 WT and 2000 VLT. On the contrary, lexical errors that derive from the L2 show negative correlations with receptive word knowledge of the first 2000 most frequent words. Results are presented in Tables 8.7 and 8.8.

To sum up, we may conclude that the different types of lexical errors show different degrees of relationship with receptive word knowledge of words belonging to the first 2000 most frequent lexical items of English. This is true for learners in fourth and sixth grades and for the nature of this relationship. Our last hypothesis which claimed that all different types of lexical errors correlate with similar extents to word knowledge must be rejected. Lack of knowledge of different word aspects influences in differing degrees receptive word knowledge measured by the 1000 WT and 2000 VLT. These results point to a relationship between depth of knowledge and receptive vocabulary size, although the nature of the relationship is variable. Depending on the category of lexical error being analysed, that is depending on the aspect of word knowledge the learner lacks, we find a positive relationship – the more the lexical errors of that type, the higher the word knowledge; or a negative one – the more the lexical errors of that type, the lower the level of receptive word knowledge.

Table 8.7 Spearman rho correlation coefficients between formal and semantic lexical errors and receptive vocabulary knowledge at T2

	1000 WT	2000 VLT
Formal errors	-0.164^{**}	-0.094
Semantic errors	0.191^{**}	0.167^{**}

*Significant at $p < 0.01$

Table 8.8 Spearman rho correlation coefficients between L1- and L2-oriented lexical errors and receptive vocabulary knowledge at T2

	1000 WT	2000 VLT
L1-oriented errors	0.025	0.106
L2-oriented errors	-0.113	-0.093

In general terms, results revealed that learners who displayed higher levels of receptive word knowledge in the 1000 and 2000 frequency bands also produced more lexically accurate essays with fewer lexical errors per total number of words written. Correlation coefficients were higher for the first one thousand words than for the second thousand.

Semantic lexical errors show significant positive correlations with receptive knowledge of words belonging to the 1000 and 2000 frequency levels. For formal lexical errors, results are more conflicting and depend on grade. In fourth grade, low positive correlations are found, and in sixth grade, significant negative correlations are found with scores on the 1000 WT. No significant correlations are found either for fourth or sixth grade between receptive word knowledge of the first 2000 most frequent words in English and L1- and L2-oriented lexical errors. Apart from low correlations, inconsistencies in the nature of the relationship can be attested depending on the grade.

Discussion

This section examines the results of the relationship between the dimensions of receptive vocabulary size and vocabulary depth as measured by the production of vocabulary errors. In other words, we correlate the results of receptive word knowledge of the first 1000 and 2000 most frequent words in English with the lexical errors found in the compositions of the learners. Results revealed powerful correlations between the ratio of the total number of words and production of lexical errors and the scores obtained by learners on the receptive vocabulary tests. Our findings show three main trends.

Firstly, while learners may show receptive knowledge of many words belonging to the first 1000 and 2000 most frequent words, they may not know them all correctly. In other words, they may lack knowledge of how to spell them correctly, of meaning nuances or of how to use them correctly in context, just to mention some word knowledge components. Furthermore, this also points to lack of knowledge of some other aspects of these words.

For the first 1000 words, the correlation coefficient was higher than for the 2000 most frequent words. A possible explanation for this may be that most of the words used in the written compositions belong, in fact, to the most common 1000 words. If comparable means for the scores in the 1000 WT and in the vocabulary section of the *Profile* were found, they would confirm this explanation. It would be interesting to analyse the lexical profile of the learners' compositions in order to find out the proportion of words belonging to each of the frequency levels (cf. Laufer, 2005; Laufer & Nation, 1995). Further research in this respect is warranted.

From the correlation coefficient found between the percentage of correct words free from lexical errors per composition and score in the 2000 frequency band of the VLT, it can be assumed that in their written compositions learners use some words from the second most frequent 1000 words in English and that these are more likely to be affected by a lexical error than the first 1000. These results seem to be true for both testing times.

Despite the solidness of the correlation coefficients, results suggest that learners use words from other frequency bands in their compositions, which may also be prone to lexical errors. This is so, because correlation coefficients are highly significant but could be higher. This is not surprising, especially if we bear in mind that Spanish is participants' L1 and most words of Latin origin are included in the lists of fairly less frequent words (3000 frequency band, Academic Word List, 5000 frequency band and so on) (Nation, 1990). It is reasonable to assume that Spanish learners would know a considerable number of words from Latin origin that belong to lower-frequency bands (cf. Pérez Basanta, 2005). Future studies should concentrate on examining the relationship between lexical error production in terms of accuracy ratio and receptive knowledge of words at higher levels of frequency, that is less frequent words. Elaboration of the lexical profile of the participants' compositions could also be very revealing in clarifying this issue.

Secondly, results show that the more the receptive knowledge learners possess, the more lexically accurate the essays they produce. This is in line with a previous research that has linked word knowledge and quality writing (see, e.g. Engber, 1995; Grant & Ginther, 2000; Goodfellow et al., 2002; Hawkey & Barker, 2004; Jarvis et al., 2003; Laufer & Nation, 1995; Lee, 2003; Morris & Cobb, 2004; Santos, 1988). It seems that the more words learners know receptively, the more correct words they can produce in composition. Correlations are significant but moderate. As lexical accuracy is only one of the several different dimensions of word knowledge, stronger correlations could not be expected.

This result can be interpreted in the light of the general implicit assumption of the literature on L2 vocabulary acquisition that 'active vocabulary knowledge can reasonably be extrapolated from measures of receptive knowledge. This assumption is not an implausible one' (Meara & Fitzpatrick, 2000: 20). Laufer and Nation (1995) conclude from their study with the Lexical Frequency Profile that learners' vocabulary size is reflected in their vocabulary use in composition. Takala (1984) also looks at the link between the passive and active vocabularies in his research study.

Lexical accuracy ratio also appears to have some potential as a diagnostic tool. Our results suggest that the lexical accuracy of learners' essays broadly corresponds with the size of their receptive vocabulary knowledge (cf. Meara & Fitzpatrick, 2000, for results with the Lex30). Interrelating different types of lexical competence, that is lexical accuracy ratio and receptive word knowledge, may be a first exploratory step towards a deeper understanding of vocabulary acquisition (Schmitt & Meara, 1997: 19).

However, while previous research (Laufer, 1998; Laufer & Paribakht, 1998; Meara & Fitzpatrick, 2000) has observed that as passive vocabulary increases, it will give rise to an increase in active vocabulary and an increase in the gap between passive and active vocabulary. Our research results show contradictory findings. In our study we observe that for T2, correlations between receptive word knowledge and lexical accuracy are higher than for T1. We dare speculate that a reduction in the gap between the words learners know receptively and how they can produce them correctly in composition is more likely.

Two main explanations may account for this result. Firstly, it may be that the low level of learners accounts for this difference. They may have not reached a sufficient lexical competence for this increasing gap to be reproduced in their data. Participants of previous studies are older and more proficient than our informants. These results suggest that our learners are below the threshold level of passive vocabulary size beyond which the gap passive–active expands. The second main reason alludes to the fact that learners may not know more words productively, but that some of the words which they already know are produced more accurately. That is, they may not have acquired new words, but improved the knowledge of these already known words. These results lend support to previous research by Fan (2000), who demonstrated that the relationship is not as straightforward as it appears to be, since no evidence to indicate a consistent ratio between passive vocabulary knowledge and vocabulary produced in composition could be found. Moreover, Schmitt and Meara (1997) suggest that beginning students may have a wider range between the two types of word knowledge (receptive and productive). As learners proficiency progresses this gap is likely to narrow. Our results lend support to this statement.

The third trend that can be derived from the results refers to the relationship between breadth and depth of vocabulary knowledge.

Breadth of vocabulary knowledge refers to the receptive vocabulary word knowledge of the first 2000 most frequent words in English. The depth of vocabulary was measured with lexical errors. We tried to find which dimensions of lexical competence or word knowledge correlate best with receptive vocabulary knowledge. We found two main results worth mentioning.

Borrowings correlated negatively with receptive word knowledge, pointing to the fact that the more words learners know, the fewer the borrowings in their compositions. This result seems quite common-sense because as we have said before borrowings derive from the tension between the need to communicate and the lack of lexical knowledge. To compensate for this lack of knowledge of L2 words, learners tend to include L1 words in their discourse. As learners know L2 words, they can use them and stop resorting to L1 lexical items.

By contrast, calques showed a positive correlation with receptive word knowledge. This result implies that the more words a learner knows receptively, the higher the number of calques that the learner will produce. This is again quite reasonable since calques involve the use of L2 words with the same distributional meaning as their equivalents in the L1. So the more the words learners know receptively, the higher the possibility of learners to translate literally words or expressions from their L1 to their L2. This is closely related with another finding of this study, which finds semantic lexical errors correlate positively with receptive word knowledge of the most frequent 2000 words. Correlations are not significant for the rest of the lexical error categories.

Receptive word knowledge measured with the 1000 WT and the 2000 frequency band of the VLT taps the knowledge learners have regarding the link between form and meaning of words. However, these tests do not measure other types of word knowledge, such as syntactic restrictions, collocations or knowledge of register. This explains why although learners show receptive knowledge of some words, they still commit lexical errors regarding, for example, the spelling of those words and the semantic distribution of the words.

It should be noted here that the purpose of this study was not to establish the active or passive vocabulary size of learners or to determine the depth dimension of word knowledge. We wanted to examine how lexical errors and lexical accuracy ratio relate to receptive vocabulary knowledge. We believed it would be interesting to explore the nature of these relationships to observe the role of lexical errors in vocabulary size. These findings suggest that there may be some basic patterns in the development of L2 vocabulary acquisition and that examination of lexical error production could help to tease this pattern out. Nevertheless, this line of argument is not straightforward and the assumptions behind it need to be explored in more detail.

Conclusion

This chapter has offered a report of the study of the relationship between lexical errors and receptive vocabulary knowledge. We can conclude that there is a powerful correlation between the receptive knowledge of the learners and the lexical accuracy of their compositions, and so the bigger the receptive word knowledge, the more lexically accurate the compositions are. By contrast, we found out the nature of the relationship between lexical competence and lexical errors is variable in the sense that different types of lexical errors relate in varying degrees to receptive word knowledge. Word frequency, word origin and intralexical factors are used to explain this variability to the extent of the correlations.

Chapter 9
Some Concluding Remarks

In this final chapter which acts as a global conclusion of the book, we will look at the pedagogical implications of our research findings. We will also give account of some of the limitations of the study acknowledging its main shortcomings, and finally we will end the chapter and the book with a section on suggestions for further research.

A personal interest in finding out how vocabulary acquisition develops over time in young beginner learners and the type of lexical errors they make during that process was the starting point of the present research. We wanted to inquire into the vocabulary acquisition process in English FL as it manifests in the lexical errors produced by low-proficiency learners and to explore the role of lexical errors in writing quality and vocabulary level. We highlight the nature of the relationship between lexical error production and writing quality and between lexical error production and receptive vocabulary knowledge. This study has aimed to put lexical errors in the centre of the frame. This section summarises what we have learned and found out in this work and pulls together the central issues and findings of the study.

The main objective of this study was to identify the categories of lexical errors made by primary school learners and examine how these changed over two years time. In addition to the main objective, we were interested in exploring the extent of the influence of the different lexical error types in writing assessment, as well as in establishing the degree of relationship between lexical accuracy ratio and receptive word knowledge, on the one hand, and between lexical error categories and receptive vocabulary knowledge, on the other hand.

Along the review of prior studies on lexical issues, we have noticed the need to further examine the process of L2 lexical acquisition and use by young beginner learners within an educational context. Most studies that address vocabulary learning in children focus rather on bilingual development in infants in a second language context than on the acquisition of a foreign language. Besides, lexical errors are seldom chosen as the instrument of language data elicitation and analysis of lexical knowledge. Despite the research findings that point to the valuable contribution of lexical errors to the process of vocabulary acquisition, to quality assessment and to research on L2 learning and use (Ambroso, 2000; Engber, 1995; Fernández, 1997), actual instructional and research approaches to EFL have not reflected this. Probably the lack of consensus regarding the definition and above all the classification of lexical errors is responsible for this neglect in the use of lexical errors as a tool to improve and enrich lexical learning and teaching.

This is a preliminary study that tries to shed some light on the field of lexical error analysis, vocabulary acquisition processes by Spanish young beginner learners of English and factors that affect writing quality. This research aims to be comprehensive but not exhaustive. Just as it tries to identify the foundations of lexical error production by Spanish primary school learners, so it is itself a foundation on which to build greater understanding of the field of lexical errors. This study focused on the very beginning stages of vocabulary learning, and we agree with Meara (1984) and Ellis and Beaton (1993: 609) that 'one cannot assume that learning occurs in similar ways at different stages of proficiency'. However, this research by interrelating different types of word knowledge and lack thereof contributes to some extent to the development of an explanatory model of vocabulary acquisition (cf. Schmitt & Meara, 1997).

An analysis of the data revealed that lexical error production decreases as L2 proficiency increases and as learners go up grade, that is from fourth grade to sixth grade. This decrease can be observed in absolute terms, that is total number of lexical errors per composition, and in relative terms, that is number of lexical errors per 100 words (percentage of lexical errors) or number of correct words between two consecutive lexical errors (lexical accuracy ratio). The decrease is significant. The decrease in relative terms is higher than the decrease in absolute terms because parallel to the decrease in the raw number of lexical errors, length of composition, that is number of words per composition, increases. We have tentatively argued for three main causes for the production of lexical errors, namely (a) lack of lexical knowledge, (b) native language transfer or interference and (c) lack of practice. We may conclude that many lexical errors would disappear if practice of free expression, that is essay writing, increased (cf. Santos Rovira, 2007).

We believe that the implicit assumption in the literature that fluency and accuracy in writing increase with proficiency (Wolfe-Quintero *et al.*, 1998: 4) is true, at least for our data. In the light of this result, we can conclude that the lexical accuracy ratio and the percentage of lexical errors per composition, that is fluency and accuracy measures combined, are evident determiners of proficiency levels, at least at the early stages of acquisition.

Two main factors combined may account for the decrease in lexical errors in writing production: (a) increased L2 proficiency and (b) increased L1 writing ability, that is L1 literacy skills. In this sense, it seems safe to conclude that as learners get more proficient in the L2, they produce fewer lexical errors. This points to learners mastering more L2 words or more aspects of L2 words, and so lexical errors may distinguish among L2 proficiency levels. But not all lexical error categories are shown to display the same pattern of evolution over the 2 years between T1 and T2. The most noteworthy changes in lexical error production refer to the considerable decrease of misspellings, and especially of borrowings, and the notable increase in the presence of calques from T1 to T2. Also and very importantly, too, more learners make semantic confusion mistakes, calques and misselections at T2 than at T1, but the difference is very small. In absolute terms, the order of frequency of lexical errors is very similar for both testing times, with misspellings being the most frequent category and misselections the least frequent lexical error type at T1 and T2.

From the data it can be concluded that different types of lexical errors indicate the proficiency of learners, and so by identifying the frequency of certain categories of lexical errors, we can predict the acquisition stage the learner is at. Accordingly, higher numbers of calques, semantic confusions, coinages and misselections will imply higher levels of general language proficiency and will be typical of learners in higher school grades. In this sense, an increase in the production of calques, semantic confusions, coinages and misselections is a sign of lexical development.

We observed that formal lexical errors are more frequent than semantic lexical errors at both testing times. Nevertheless, whereas formal lexical errors decrease from fourth to sixth grade, errors caused by meaning orientation increase over two years. From the results of this study we can conclude that lexical development undergoes a series of stages. It seems that learners will first learn the formal aspects of words, for example their spelling, with the knowledge of the basic meaning coming later and the development of associative knowledge coming last. In the light of our results, we may argue that learners have problems discerning between words that look similar or have similar meanings, especially when they have already mastered the form and core meaning of the target and error words. As the learner incorporates new words in his or her lexicon, he or she tends to store them together with formally similar words first and semantically similar words later. In production, learners will tend to confuse those similar words stored together which pinpoints the incomplete, unstable and partial knowledge learners have of those words.

Considering intra- and interlingual lexical errors, the tendency for L1-oriented lexical errors is to decrease from T1 to T2. Learners' L1 has proved to be an important factor in L2 lexical use and writing performance. Nevertheless, as proficiency increases and learners use more L2 words productively, the use of their L1 diminishes. The L1 is always recurrent and very important in SLA, although it is more frequent at lower proficiency levels than at higher levels. Despite the pervasive presence of L1 influence, we have observed that learners at different stages of acquisition display different transfer behaviour. In other words, whereas fourth graders borrow L1 words and insert them without any adaptation in the L2 discourse, sixth graders most frequently calque from their L1 or coin new words based on L1 lexical items which learners tailor so that they sound or look English. We believe that the collision between the need to communicate and the lack of L2 lexical knowledge lead to L1 use.

This study has also confirmed that lexical errors play a significant role in the assessment of writing and determination of essay quality. This result is not surprising, since it supports previous findings that highlight the role of lexical accuracy as a crucial component in writing assessment. In addition, it seemed reasonable to assume that an abundance of lexical errors will exert a negative influence on composition if we bear in mind that vocabulary knowledge plays a positive role in writing quality. If a rich and varied vocabulary is typical of high-quality writing, a piece of writing with many lexical errors will be of poor quality.

Especially relevant to writing quality are lexical errors at lower levels of proficiency, that is at T1. It seems that at more advanced levels lexical errors do not result in much communication breakdown, since lexical errors may be more easily understood from context. Furthermore, other aspects may be influencing the quality of the compositions written by more proficient learners such as the lexical variety, a more sophisticated discourse and use of more synonyms. In short, the lexical accuracy ratio of a composition is a measure indicative of progress, and so the higher the ratio, the better the writing. Moreover, this finding also contributes to strengthen the arguments which suggest that vocabulary is a key aspect in assessing writing.

An analysis of the data also confirmed our initial assumption that the different types of lexical errors will contribute in different ways to the quality of the composition, because not all lexical error categories are equally serious and negative. In particular, borrowings were judged to be the most negative lexical errors. When a learner produces a borrowing, it is a sign of lack of lexical knowledge, because the learner is not showing any knowledge of L2 words. The presence of borrowings involves a code switching which may impose more cognitive demands, and as a consequence, this type of lexical error is considered more negative. Calques and misselections were found to contribute positively to essay score. The fact that they show L2 lexical knowledge may account for this result. We may dare speculate that showing some L2 lexical knowledge is a stronger evaluation criterion than communicative success itself. This seems particularly true when assessing young beginner learners' essays produced in an FL learning context. The remaining categories of lexical errors show no significant contribution to writing quality. Especially remarkable is the case of misspellings. Despite their overwhelming presence in our data, spelling errors have no influence whatsoever in the scoring of compositions.

Our final aim was to relate productive vocabulary knowledge as measured by the lexical accuracy ratio of compositions to receptive vocabulary knowledge, and in addition, we wanted to determine the nature of the relationship between depth of word knowledge as measured by the different lexical error types and receptive vocabulary size. From the significant correlation coefficients, we can conclude that learners either show partial knowledge or complete lack of knowledge of words in the 1000 frequency band and especially in the 2000 frequency band. Because correlations between the lexical accuracy ratio and receptive word knowledge were just moderate, we believe that learners (a) do not know some of the words belonging to these frequency bands and (b) may be using words from other frequency bands in their essays, for example words from Latin origin which belong to lower-frequency bands.

From the results in this study we also observe that the higher the receptive word knowledge of the learners, the higher the lexical accuracy ratio of their compositions. This result relates receptive and productive vocabulary knowledge, confirming previous findings that the higher the receptive knowledge, the higher in turn the vocabulary in use. Furthermore, we also noted that the gap between both types of lexical knowledge is less as proficiency increases.

Finally, results confirmed that different types of lexical errors, as evidence of lack of knowledge of different aspects of words, relate differently to receptive vocabulary size. In other words, whereas borrowings show negative correlations with receptive vocabulary size, calques show positive correlation. These results imply that the higher the receptive vocabulary size of learners, the more calques will they produce in writing and the fewer borrowings, at least at the beginning stages of acquisition.

On the whole this study contributes to our understanding of the process of lexical acquisition and development in young beginner learners. The findings of this study suggest that although no definitive statements can be made concerning vocabulary instruction, they have some important pedagogical implications.

Pedagogical Implications

Error analysis stands out as a useful methodology to guide FL teaching. From the results of the error analysis, language instruction programmes can be devised that focus on the most relevant aspects depending on the errors identified. Thus, learners can be aided to work on the errors they make in order to find a remedy to those errors based on the causes that have originated them (Sánchez Jiménez, 2006: 109).

This study has revealed that as proficiency increases, lexical error production in writing decreases and length of composition increases. Fernández (1997) believes that the increasing number of sociocultural and linguistic experiences of learners with the target language contributes to reducing the number of lexical errors and improving written fluency. In this sense, we echo a suggestion by Fernández (1997: 75–76) that learners should be provided with rich and varied sociocultural and linguistic experiences with the L2, where learners are required to interact and negotiate meaning in order to improve and enrich their vocabulary knowledge and use.

From the data we have concluded that the presence of lexical errors in writing, especially of misspellings, may derive from the lack of L2 writing experience and given the young age of our learners also of L1 writing. The prevalence of the communicative approach in classroom teaching has prioritised face-to-face or oral communication skills over written ones. It can be argued that little attention has been paid to the teaching of English spelling in the primary schools considered here. Previous studies have also shown concern about the neglect of spelling instruction in primary education (Meijers, 1992), in L2 teaching (Brown, 1970) and in the Spanish school system (Santiago & Repáraz, 1993), for instance.

From the massive presence of misspellings at low levels of acquisition and considering the important role of writing in SLA (Harklau, 2002), we advocate for the extensive practice of writing in the L2 classroom. By practicing writing, learners are expected to improve their general language skills, and in particular, their writing of lexical items. We believe, nevertheless, that primary school learners of English in the Spanish school context would benefit from a structured or directional approach to spelling and pronunciation, as explicit instruction would raise orthographic and phonetic awareness. Opportunities should also be provided to practice writing and saying new unfamiliar words in the English classroom. We agree with Sánchez Jiménez (2006: 177–178) that teaching high-frequency words that are common prey to misspellings[1] may be highly recommendable to remedy spelling errors.

Knowledge of derivational and compositional morphology plays an important role in the development of spelling skills. The ability to spell correctly is very much linked and somehow derives from the mastery of word morphology (see Carlisle, 1989). It goes without saying that being aware of the form of suffixes and prefixes that combine with substantive, verbal, adjectival or adverbial roots may be of much help when facing the difficult task of having to spell in English. For instance, the cognitive spelling load of words such as *beautiful, needless or impossible* is reduced if learners are shown what parts these words are composed of and how these parts or morphemes are spelled. Pérez Basanta (1999) considers morphological analysis as one of the most relevant vocabulary learning strategies and suggests that teachers should show and foster the use of this strategy to help learners acquire L2 vocabulary.

Instructing young learners in the basic morphological rules of English can assist them not only in spelling (Sánchez Jiménez, 2006: 177–178) but also in expanding their vocabulary and enriching their vocabulary knowledge, for instance by creating lexical fields of the type *mean, meaning, meaningful, meaningless, meaningfulness*. Learners should be made aware that words are made up of morphemes they can combine to form other words (see Beheydt, 1987). This approach can change a seemingly endless memorisation process into a 'confident search for pattern and regularity leading to orthographic awareness and consequent increased word knowledge' (Goldsmith, 1995: 124). This could be a way of helping learners reduce confusion of similar word forms or misselections.

In the light of the idea that the idiosyncratic pronunciation of a language group is responsible for abundant spelling errors, it is logical to expect that teachers would inform their pupils about the pronunciation of English and about the relationship between orthography and pronunciation in the L2. The discrepancy between the way words are pronounced in English and how they are spelled is a frequently cited source of confusion and of spelling, also pronunciation, difficulties. Deschamps

(1992) proposed showing learners how this relationship works and providing them with some simple graphematic rules, avoiding complicated theoretical explanation at the early stages (cf. Sánchez Jiménez, 2006: 177–178).

Considering the data of the present research regarding formal and semantic errors and echoing previous studies, it may be concluded that the mental lexicon is organised in semantic and formal networks. It seems important that new vocabulary is introduced formally and semantically in oral and written forms. Learners should be taught and encouraged to make their own lexical associations when learning new words aided and fostered by activities in which vocabulary is presented in semantic fields (Channell, 1988: 94). In theory, we agree with Channell (1988: 93) that establishing both formal (phonological) and semantic associations would be the most helpful method to recall vocabulary and reduce misselections, calques and semantic confusions. However, this claim still requires empirical testing.

Semantic lexical errors are relevant because they become more prominent as learning progresses as our results have shown. Therefore, L2 semantic associations, which are complex for the learner, will demand higher attention in classroom. Presentation of semantic fields and typical associative networks will enhance acquisition (Fernández, 1997; Gu, 2003). In this sense, in the light of the results that learners seem to acquire first the formal aspects of words and afterwards the semantic or meaning aspects, we call for classroom activities that focus on meaning, particularly at higher proficiency levels (McNeill, 1996). We believe that learners may benefit from being made aware of related words, that is from the same word family, and 'indeed benefit from activities which require them to say these words' (McNeill, 1990: 118).

By contrast, Nation (1990) and Waring (1997) discourage learning words in semantic sets, since this carries the danger of lexical items interfering and competing with each other in word learning and retrieval. However, we believe that if words belonging to the same semantic field are introduced together and learners informed about their semantic components, syntactic restrictions and use, the presence of calques and of semantic confusions could be reduced considerably. Moreover, taking into account that our data revealed that these lexical errors appear as learning progresses, this type of activity of semantic associations and componential analysis should be carried out especially at more advanced stages of acquisition. Pérez Basanta (1999) also advocates for these types of vocabulary learning activities which she refers to as semicontextualised.

Warren (1982) proposes error-specific activities to end problems of equivalence errors or calques. Echoing Warren (1982), we suggest that when a semantic equivalence error appears, for example *My favourite plate is pasta and rice* (S27, 4th), we can make learners figure out the meaning of the target word by analysing its semantic feature components. In order to do this, we can provide students with sentences in their mother tongue, each including a different semantic feature of the error word. In the present example the two explanation sentences could be

(1) *El plato típico de La Rioja son patatas con chorizo.* (Eng. typical dish) and
(2) *Mi abuela me ha regalado unos platos con dibujos de flores.* (Eng. plate, dish).
In this way, learners should see and learn the differences of the words.

Considering that errors derived from confusions based either on form (misselections) or on meaning (semantic confusions) result from double ignorance (a) of the target word and (b) of the error word (cf. James, 1998; Warren, 1982), we believe learners should be informed of the relationship meaning–form of both words: the target and the error word.

Vocabulary teaching has concentrated on extensive reading and contextual guessing as a result of a tradition of communicative L2 teaching (Laufer, 2006; Pérez Basanta, 1999). However, the results of this study indicate the need for explicit vocabulary instruction that would result in an intensification of the learning of words. Vocabulary exercises that focus on isolated lexical items, as well as on context-embedded vocabulary, are called for to increase retention and recall of vocabulary (see Laufer, 2006). In this line, Cobb (2003: 413) is in favour of the teaching of vocabulary in context to prevent learners from making lexical errors and furthermore insists on the explicit instruction of prefabricated phrases.[2]

Lee (2003) proved that explicit vocabulary teaching increases not only receptive vocabulary knowledge but also productive vocabulary use in free composition. Hence, he calls for systematic explicit vocabulary instruction and teaching of word learning strategies comprising strategies to enhance word learning, word memory and word recall to improve writing (see also Pavičić Takač, 2008). Likewise, writing practice can be a tool to improve vocabulary knowledge and general L2 competence (see also Muncie, 2002). The selection of writing topics related to the vocabulary being taught in explicit instruction and to pre-writing reading activities maximises, according to Lee (2003: 551), vocabulary learning opportunities.

The value of explicit instruction has been proved in the literature over the years (Agustín Llach, 2009b; Laufer, 2005, 2006; Nation, 1993b; Torras & Celaya, 2001). Torras and Celaya (2001) concluded that the teaching methodology used with learners who started with EFL at a later stage favoured their linguistic development. Explicit teaching of the linguistic system and form-focused activities with metalinguistic basis promote language awareness and this contributes to improving language knowledge and use. Examination of children's L2 spelling errors has shown that contact with the L2, even when it is intensive, does not lead inevitably to learner uptake of the correct spelling of words (Morris, 2001). The findings of previous studies and of our own strengthen the case for focus-on-form instruction in the L2 classroom, particularly to overcome spelling errors. In Morris' (2001: 285) words:

> From a basic communicative perspective, the learners certainly get their messages across in a rudimentary way in spite of the missing and misspelled words. However, if there is a desire to move the learners onto a higher level of formal competence, pedagogic support is clearly required.

We believe that teaching and promoting the use of vocabulary learning strategies other than simple memorisation or rote learning will enhance lexical acquisition. Helping learners to develop their strategic competence either by teaching them new learning strategies or by reinforcing the use of exiting ones is one of the best ways to contribute to successful L2 vocabulary acquisition (Beheydt, 1987; Pavičić Takač, 2008). Harley *et al.* (1990: 23) already pointed to the need of more classroom activities designed to increase the lexical resources of learners. Some of these strategies may be guessing from context, using mnemonic techniques, such as the keyword technique, using dictionaries, building original sentences with the new words, note taking, repetition, or forming mental images of the word, associating, classifying, and interconnecting words (Beheydt, 1987; Brown & Rodgers, 2002; Ellis & Beaton, 1993; Gu, 2003; Pérez Basanta, 1999).

De Cock and Granger (2005) advocate the use of error analysis in the design of mono- and bilingual dictionaries. After identifying the lexical items that cause problems and the lexical aspects that cause most difficulty to a particular group of learners, for example Spanish learners of English, lexicographers could include specific information regarding those problematic areas in dictionaries so that learners can benefit from previous research on lexical error analysis.

Teaching young learners to write in the L1 and introducing them to general composing strategies is thought to contribute to improving lexical accuracy and may also benefit L2 proficiency. Including extended writing practice and explicit teaching of composing strategies in L1 and L2 education in primary school, as well as encouraging transfer process from L1 literacy to L2, can be a good way of developing L2 writing ability (Torras & Celaya, 2001). This is in line with the results found regarding L1 influence in L2 writing processes. Instructors ought to incorporate comparisons of the L1 and L2 phonographemic systems. Instances of agreement between pronunciation and spelling in Spanish are greater than in English. This fact can lead young beginner learners to the false belief that the correspondence between a sound and a letter in their L1 is equivalent in English. A contrastive analysis of some aspects of vocabulary, orthography and phonetics, for example, is called for (see Swan, 1997). This comparison of L1–L2 lexical systems may prove very useful in L2 vocabulary instruction. Teachers should always be aware that learners draw on their previous linguistic knowledge, usually L1, but also L3, to compensate for deficiencies in lexical knowledge (Odlin, 1989). Consequently, highlighting the similarities and differences between the L1 and L2 lexical systems regarding different aspects of the lexical items can lead to improvements in vocabulary learning, recall and use (Swan, 1997). Harley *et al.* (1990: 23) express their conviction that 'students would benefit from more focused classroom input alerting them to lexical characteristics of [...] [*the foreign language*] that are different from [...] [*the mother tongue*]'. The results from our data mirror these findings.

Lasagabaster and Doiz (2003) suggest that translation exercises could be beneficial when dealing with L1-derived lexical errors. Comparing and contrasting the L1 and the L2 can help learners organise and structure words in their L1 and L2 mental lexicons, detecting the similarities and differences. This will result in an improvement of the writing skill (Lasagabaster & Doiz, 2003: 156).

Furthermore, increasing the motivation of our learners to learn vocabulary and practice at home is also essential in helping reduce the presence of lexical errors in their writings. A positive attitude towards lexical learning is the starting point for a successful SLA. Vocabulary learning is not an easy task that requires little effort on part of the learner. The English learner has to work hard to learn, recall and use vocabulary satisfactorily. Showing learners the advantages of practicing and the effectiveness of activities and exercises will prove beneficial to the learning process. Moreover, Medina Bellido (1997) also argues for the tailoring of teaching and evaluation practices to the learning manner of the learners to further increase their motivation and improve their attitudes towards English.

Considering the results presented in this study regarding the production and the types of lexical errors, we propose a two-pronged approach: reactive and proactive. A reactive approach to vocabulary would imply the immediate and spontaneous correction of the lexical errors that appear during class time. This intervention may move in a continuum of explicitness from very implicit vocabulary practice to very explicit vocabulary learning exercises. A proactive intervention is a kind of a priori, since based on the lexical deficiencies collected from previous learners' groups, it predicts the lexical errors that learners will produce. Consequently, the syllabus and materials will be planned beforehand. Both interventions can take the form of theoretical explanations and/or practice exercises, either remedial or preventive or both.

Reactive intervention takes the form of error correction and is very popular in the literature. There exists an abundance of research in the area of error correction. Issues such as what, when and how to correct are dealt with in this field of study. Although an extensive report of error correction would be beyond the scope of this research, suffice it to mention that teachers can use error correction sheets with symbols for each different error type that will help the student identify the errors. Students should be encouraged to correct their errors on their own. Learners can also be required to collect their own errors and classify them according to their frequency, source and so on (see, for instance, among many others Chandler, 2003; Muñoz Basols, 2005).

The findings presented in this study corroborate partially the results of previous research that relate measures of lexical richness, particularly lexical error production, and overall language proficiency (see Engber, 1995). This gives an idea of the importance of vocabulary in the writing process. It is essential that teachers stress the relevant and influential role of vocabulary in writing quality. Furthermore, vocabulary has been proved to be an integral measure of academic success (see, e.g. Verhallen & Schoonen, 1993, 1998). It is reasonable to think, therefore, that expanding the vocabulary of the learners will bring forth an improvement in their general language competence and in their school performance.

Those deviations that have a more negative effect on writing should be dealt with first (Khalil, 1985: 346). Learners should be informed of the types of lexical errors that are most negative for their writings, for example borrowings, and be encouraged to be creative in the new language, since calque errors, for example, contribute positively to writing assessment. Teaching some word formation rules, collocational patterns or pragmatic distribution of lexical items may also contribute to reducing the number of lexical errors in compositions and, thus, to enhancing the quality of a student's writing. The development of communicative strategies of the paraphrase type and fostering creative language has clear positive consequences for the quality of composition, since these strategies help the learner to get the message across and to complete the communication process. This is in line with Khalil's (1985: 346) contention that 'emphasis on the development of those skills required to communicate effectively should be reflected in the writing and sequencing of teaching materials'.

Enlarging the learners' receptive vocabulary size results in higher degrees of lexical accuracy ratio and therefore in better composition scores. It is important, then, to increase the number of words learners know as well as to improve the quality of that word knowledge in order to observe improvements in writing quality. Explicit vocabulary teaching as well as extensive reading and writing practice seem good ways to make learners' lexical store richer and lexical errors fewer.

Limitations of the Study

The most obvious limitation has to do with how lexical errors are classified. Classification of (lexical) errors is somehow subjective since errors can be due to one or several sources which interrelate to give rise to the lexical error. Nevertheless, this subjectivity is present in any study using error analysis, and hence it is to some extent inevitable. Overall, the general counts of lexical errors may be quite accurate, because it is easier to determine what is a lexical error than to assign an instance of lexical error to a particular category.

Regardless of the theoretical efforts to design an exhaustive and complete taxonomy, in practice, we believe that all taxonomies of lexical errors leak in the same place; that is, some lexical errors in the corpus can be classified in two or even three valid ways, and some other errors defy categorisation and seem not to belong to any of the linguistic and psycholinguistic categories proposed. Lack of objectivity and certain degree of arbitrariness and subjectivity are common caveats in error classification and explanation.

As far as the basic aim, error analysis, is to account for the mental processes underlying the lexical errors and to assign causes to those lexical errors, it seems, for practical purposes, almost impossible to determine unequivocally the genesis of lexical errors. It cannot be claimed *precisely* and *categorically* what causes a particular learner to make a particular error. The researcher is thus compelled to use some guessing, speculation and inferring as the basis for some groupings and assignation of each lexical error to its corresponding category. Despite this subjectivity, this taxonomy of lexical errors can be said to be quite reliable since we have tried to define each individual category neatly and precisely, leaving little room to arbitrariness.

In addition, although the different types distinguished in the present classification were thought to include all possible instances of lexical errors, other classifications may also have been valid, for example those considering addition, omission or confusion of lexical items or those that base on the distinction among word classes, that is noun, verb, adjective, adverb, to classify the error.

One further weakness of the present research design has to do with the instruments of data collection. Considering Da Rocha's (1980: 85) claim that compositions cannot yield reliable data, the limitation of compositions as data collecting techniques for studies on error analysis regards the reliability of learner's language. The main point made by this statement is that compositions may not reflect the actual language knowledge of the informants, providing misleading or confusing evidence of learner's language competence. This drawback is closely related to the notion of 'avoidance'. When faced with a complex structure or a difficult lexical item, the learner may avoid using it and will look for alternative forms of expression of his or her initial thought or he or she may change that thought or even abandon it completely. There is no way to establish how far the language displayed in compositions is a good, poor, large or small representation of actual participant's knowledge.

Despite admitting this drawback, the design of this study fits perfectly its goals and characteristics. Compositions are here the best method for data collection because these young learners, who tried their best to produce real, correct and accurate English, and their low proficiency level practically ruled out any possibility of avoidance, since they do not possess alternative means to express their thoughts. More specifically, their lexical competence is too limited to allow them to search for simpler lexical items or to use paraphrase or lexical simplification. Lexical errors in the sample are genuine, spontaneous and real. Obviously, in the data obtained, the learners have not displayed all they know or do not know about English, but one can be quite sure that the lexical errors they have produced are manifestation of gaps in their lexical knowledge.

A further limitation regarding the composition as the instrument of data collection concerns the use of a single composition topic. Different composition topics have been proved to give rise to quantitative and qualitative differences in lexical error production (Agustín Llach *et al.*, 2005). Had we used more than just one composition topic, we might have come to more definite conclusions.

The proficiency level tests (cloze test and reading comprehension test), in spite of being, in general, valid and reliable instruments to determine the language level of the participants, are also levelled with some criticism. The main limitation of the multiple-choice answering format pointed out in the literature refers to the fact that learners may choose the right word simply by a process of elimination. Here participants had over 33% chance of choosing the correct word among the three alternatives. Other drawbacks of this procedure are that the learner may know a meaning of the requested word other than the one sought or that they may know the meaning of the distractors rather than of the target word (see Read, 2000: 77-78; Wesche & Paribakht, 1996: 17).

Furthermore, the results of this study are based on the lexical error analysis of the compositions of 283 Spanish learners performed when they were in fourth and sixth grades of the primary school. Hence, there is a danger in extrapolating these findings beyond the context of the foreign language classroom in Spanish-speaking contexts of primary education. These results are and should be seen as preliminary and generalisation must be done carefully and with caution.

Further Research

The job of describing through empirical research how the process of lexical acquisition in young beginner learners of English develops is far from complete. Research in the field is beginning, but much more is required in order to allow for more definitive conclusions regarding the nature of vocabulary acquisition and use in English by young beginner learners and regarding the role of lexical errors as predictors and landmarks of that process and also to make L2 teaching to less-proficient learners more effective. Although this research has pointed to the relevant role of lexical errors as predictors of writing quality and indicators of receptive word knowledge, still some further studies are needed that provide conclusive results on these issues. Areas in need of investigation are lexical errors and lexical development in young beginner learners, and the writing assessment research agenda would include the following:

- How does L1 literacy skills, for example writing ability, correlate with lexical error production? How does this relationship evolve with time and proficiency progression?
- How do fluency and accuracy evolve with time and proficiency development? How do these measures of writing development relate to lexical complexity?
- What is the nature of the relationship between lexical error production in terms of accuracy ratio and receptive knowledge of words at higher levels of frequency, that is less frequent words?
- What is the lexical frequency profile of learners' compositions? And how does that profile relate to lexical errors in composition?
- How do lexical errors relate to other measures of lexical richness in learners' compositions? How does this relationship evolve with time and increasing proficiency and lexical knowledge?
- How do lexical errors relate to general academic success for male and female performance?
- Is there any relationship between production of lexical errors and motivation and interest in the foreign language and school work, in general?
- What is the effect of different teaching programmes on lexical development and lexical error production?
- How will production of lexical errors evolve with increasing experience of the learners with the foreign language? What types of lexical errors will be most prominent at advanced stages of acquisition?
- Will lexical error production in quantitative and qualitative terms of Spanish young beginner learners resemble that of learners of comparable profile but with different mother tongue?
- Does lexical error production in writing correspond to lexical error production in speaking; for example, will there also be as many mispronunciations of lexical items as there were misspellings?
- How do perceptions of lexical proximity between target and native language affect lexical production?
- How do perceptions of lexical difficulty between target and native language affect lexical production?

Answers to these and other research questions would help develop a more precise theory to base pedagogy on as well as more effective teaching practices.

In this final paragraph we would like to return to our motivation for carrying out this study, which is excitement and wonder at how lexical acquisition in a foreign language proceeds and how children develop and use their foreign language lexical knowledge. We hope that this study will help researchers, teachers and learners to realise the importance of lexical errors and the need for future studies in the field that contribute to further clarification of the role of lexical errors in the process of lexical development and writing assessment.

Notes

1. He calls this type of words *demonios ortográficos* (orthographic demons) (Sánchez Jiménez, 2006: 177) because they tend to be frequently misspelled. In our data such 'orthographic demons' are 'beautiful', 'football', 'swimming' or 'birthday'.
2. See Pérez Basanta (1999) for an insightful review of the techniques and activities aimed at vocabulary practice and learning; also see Gu (2003).

Appendices

Appendices   211

Appendix 1: The ESL Composition Profile

ESL COMPOSITION PROFILE

STUDENT _____ DATE _____ TOPIC _____

SCORE	LEVEL	CRITERIA	COMMENTS
CONTENT	30-27	**EXCELLENT TO VERY GOOD:** knowledgeable • substantive • thorough development of thesis • relevant to assigned topic	
	26-22	**GOOD TO AVERAGE:** some knowledge of subject • adequate range • limited development of thesis • mostly relevant to topic, but lacks detail	
	21-17	**FAIR TO POOR:** limited knowledge of subject • little substance • inadequate development of topic	
	16-13	**VERY POOR:** does not show knowledge of subject • non-substantive • not pertinent • OR not enough to evaluate	
ORGANIZATION	20-18	**EXCELLENT TO VERY GOOD:** fluent expression • ideas clearly stated/supported • succinct • well-organized • logical sequencing • cohesive	
	17-14	**GOOD TO AVERAGE:** somewhat choppy • loosely organized but main ideas stand out • limited support • logical but incomplete sequencing	
	13-10	**FAIR TO POOR:** non-fluent • ideas confused or disconnected • lacks logical sequencing and development	
	9-7	**VERY POOR:** does not communicate • no organization • OR not enough to evaluate	
VOCABULARY	20-18	**EXCELLENT TO VERY GOOD:** sophisticated range • effective word/idiom choice and usage • word form mastery • appropriate register	
	17-14	**GOOD TO AVERAGE:** adequate range • occasional errors of word/idiom form, choice, usage *but meaning not obscured*	
	13-10	**FAIR TO POOR:** limited range • frequent errors of word/idiom form, choice, usage • *meaning confused or obscured*	
	9-7	**VERY POOR:** essentially translation • little knowledge of English vocabulary, idioms, word form • OR not enough to evaluate	
LANGUAGE USE	25-22	**EXCELLENT TO VERY GOOD:** effective complex constructions • few errors of agreement, tense, number, word order/function, articles, pronouns, prepositions	
	21-18	**GOOD TO AVERAGE:** effective but simple constructions • minor problems in complex constructions • several errors of agreement, tense, number, word order/function, articles, pronouns, prepositions *but meaning seldom obscured*	
	17-11	**FAIR TO POOR:** major problems in simple/complex constructions • frequent errors of negation, agreement, tense, number, word order/function, articles, pronouns, prepositions and/or fragments, run-ons, deletions • *meaning confused or obscured*	
	10-5	**VERY POOR:** virtually no mastery of sentence construction rules • dominated by errors • does not communicate • OR not enough to evaluate	
MECHANICS	5	**EXCELLENT TO VERY GOOD:** demonstrates mastery of conventions • few errors of spelling, punctuation, capitalization, paragraphing	
	4	**GOOD TO AVERAGE:** occasional errors of spelling, punctuation, capitalization, paragraphing *but meaning not obscured*	
	3	**FAIR TO POOR:** frequent errors of spelling, punctuation, capitalization, paragraphing • poor handwriting • *meaning confused or obscured*	
	2	**VERY POOR:** no mastery of conventions • dominated by errors of spelling, punctuation, capitalization, paragraphing • handwriting illegible • OR not enough to evaluate	

TOTAL SCORE _____ READER _____ COMMENTS _____

Appendix 2: The Composition Task

COMPOSITION
2005/2006

COLEGIO _____

CURSO _____ FECHA _____

APELLIDOS _____ NOMBRE_____

Imagina que vas a vivir con una familia inglesa en Oxford durante un mes. La familia se llama Mr. y Mrs. Edwards y tienen dos hijos: Peter y Helen. Escríbeles una carta <u>en inglés</u>, preséntate y háblales de tu ciudad, tu colegio, tus hobbies y cualquier otra cosa interesante que desees añadir.

Tiempo: 30 minutos

Appendix 3: The 2000 Vocabulary Levels Test

2,000 WORD LEVEL TEST
2005/2006

COLEGIO _____
CURSO_____ FECHA_____
APELLIDOS _____ NOMBRE _____

Este es un test de vocabulario. En la parte izquierda te presentamos grupos de seis palabras inglesas y a su derecha, los significados de sólo tres de ellas. **Escribe** junto a éstos, el **número** de la palabra inglesa correspondiente a dichos significados. Observa el siguiente ejemplo:

EJEMPLO	
1 business	
2 clock	____ part of a house
3 horse	____ animal with 4 legs
4 pencil	____ something used for writing
5 shoe	
6 wall	

→

RESPUESTA CORRECTA	
1 business	
2 clock	_6_ part of a house
3 horse	_3_ animal with 4 legs
4 pencil	_4_ something used for writing
5 shoe	
6 wall	

1 coffee		1 adopt	
2 disease	____ money for work	2 climb	____ go up
3 justice	____ a piece of clothing	3 examine	____ look at closely
4 skirt	____ using the law in the right way	4 pour	____ be on every side
5 stage		5 satisfy	
6 wage		6 surround	

1 choice		1 bake	
2 crop	____ heat	2 connect	____ join together
3 flesh	____ meat	3 inquire	____ walk without purpose
4 salary	____ money paid regularly for doing a job	4 limit	____ keep within a certain size
5 secret		5 recognize	
6 temperature		6 wander	

1 cap		1 burst	
2 education	____ teaching and learning	2 concern	____ break open
3 journey	____ numbers to measure with	3 deliver	____ make better
4 parent	____ going to a far place	4 fold	____ take something to someone
5 scale		5 improve	
6 trick		6 urge	

1 attack		1 original	
2 charm	____ gold and silver	2 private	____ first
3 lack	____ pleasing quality	3 royal	____ not public
4 pen	____ not having something	4 slow	____ all added together
5 shadow		5 sorry	
6 treasure		6 total	

1 cream		1 ancient	
2 factory	____ part of milk	2 curious	____ not easy
3 nail	____ a lot of money	3 difficult	____ very old
4 pupil	____ person who is studying	4 entire	____ related to God
5 sacrifice		5 holy	
6 wealth		6 social	

Appendix 4: The 1000 Word Test

1,000 WORD LEVEL TEST
2005/2006

COLEGIO_____
CURSO_____FECHA_____
APELLIDOS _____ NOMBRE_____

Este es un test de vocabulario. En la parte izquierda te presentamos grupos de seis palabras inglesas y a su derecha, la traducción en castellano de sólo tres de ellas.
Escribe junto a cada palabra en castellano, el **número** de la palabra inglesa que tenga el mismo significado. Observa el siguiente ejemplo:

EJEMPLO	
1 dog	
2 house	___ negro
3 girl	___ nariz
4 fork	___ casa
5 black	
6 nose	

→

RESPUESTA CORRECTA	
1 dog	
2 house	_5_ negro
3 girl	_6_ nariz
4 fork	_2_ casa
5 black	
6 nose	

1 could
2 during   ___ podía/pude
3 this   ___ durante
4 piece   ___ para
5 of
6 in order to

1 kill
2 reply   ___ avanzar
3 advance   ___ responder
4 appoint   ___ matar
5 divide
6 receive

1 indeed
2 what   ___ mi
3 along   ___ en efecto
4 my   ___ algo
5 some
6 away

1 moment
2 separate   ___ separado
3 worse   ___ momento
4 free   ___ amarillo
5 heavy
6 yellow

1 church
2 scene   ___ coche
3 hour   ___ problema
4 trouble   ___ hecho
5 fact
6 car

1 spring
2 danger   ___ hermana
3 stone   ___ peligro
4 product   ___ piedra
5 sister
6 subject

1 meet
2 leave   ___ poner
3 put   ___ dar
4 give   ___ utilizar
5 use
6 begin

1 example
2 breadth   ___ anchura
3 fear   ___ miedo
4 desert   ___ ayuntamiento
5 bit
6 town hall

1 wind
2 room   ___ hombre
3 line   ___ línea
4 enemy   ___ noche
5 night
6 man

1 surround
2 shoot   ___ quedar bien
3 paint   ___ advertir
4 fit   ___ disparar
5 command
6 warn

Appendix 5: The Cloze Test

Cloze Test

COLEGIO_____CURSO_____FECHA

APELLIDOS_____NOMBRE_____

1) Lee la información sobre los dinosaurios.
2) Elige la palabra que crees más adecuada (A, B ó C) para cada hueco.
3) Marca la respuesta correcta con un círculo en la parte de las respuestas.

Dinosaurs

No one has ...**0**... seen a dinosaur. The last dinosaur died about 60 million years ago, a long time ...**28**... there were any people on the earth. ...**29**... knows for sure why they all died. The nearest living relatives of dinosaurs are birds.

Dinosaurs didn't all look the same. There were more ...**30**... 5000 kinds. Some were very small, ...**31**... others were giants. The largest were bigger than any other animals that ever lived ...**32**... land. The Brontosaurus, for example, was twenty metres long, and it ...**33**... plants. The Tyrannosaurus Rex was not as ...**34**... , but it was stronger. It had sharp teeth for eating meat. Also it could run fast ...**35**... it had long back legs.

EJEMPLO			RESPUESTA
0 A ever	B never	C yet	Ⓐ

RESPUESTAS

28	A that	B when	C before
29	A everybody	B people	C nobody
30	A than	B that	C as
31	A as	B but	C or
32	A in	B on	C at
33	A ate	B eat	C eats
34	A bigger	B biggest	C big
35	A that	B because	C where

Appendix 6: The Reading Comprehension Test

COLEGIO_____ CURSO_____ FECHA_____ Tiempo
10 minutes

APELLIDOS_____NOMBRE_____

1) Lee el artículo sobre Ingrid McFarlane y contesta a las preguntas marcando con un círculo la respuesta correcta.

Ingrid McFarlane
Zoo Keeper

When I left school at eighteen, I got a job at a zoo as a student keeper. Now, five years later, things have changed – I have passed my exams and I am a full animal keeper.

The money is not good. I only get £9,000 a year. You have to be outside in rain and snow, which is hard work, and you get very dirty. But this doesn't matter to me because animals are the most important thing in my life!

There are a hundred monkeys and fifty deer in my part of the zoo and I give them their food and clean their houses. I also need to watch them carefully to be sure that they are all well. In fact, rhinos are my favourite animals and so last year I went to Africa with a colleague for a month to study them.

The zoo is open every day and I work five different days each week. I live in a small flat twenty minutes away and I get up at ten to seven and start work at eight. The first thing I do when I get home at quarter past five is have a shower!

EJEMPLO
0   Ingrid left school
    A   five years ago.
    B   nine years ago.
    C   eighteen years ago.   RESPUESTA
                                               (A)

RESPUESTAS

21	Ingrid would like to	A	take some exams.
		B	earn more money.
		C	change her job.

22	How does Ingrid feel about working in bad weather?	A	She hates getting dirty.
		B	She doesn't mind it.
		C	She likes the snow.

23	If Ingrid doesn't check the monkeys,	A	they may become ill.
		B	they may get hungry.
		C	they may run away.

24	The animals Ingrid likes best are the	A	monkeys.
		B	deer.
		C	rhinos.

25	Ingrid travelled to Africa	A	to have a month's holiday.
		B	to visit a colleague there.
		C	to learn more about some animals.

26	The zoo is open	A	only five days a week.
		B	seven days a week.
		C	on different days every week.

27	Ingrid arrives at her flat in the evening at	A	five fifteen.
		B	twenty past five.
		C	ten to seven.

Appendix 7: The Questionnaire

CUESTIONARIO

COLEGIO _____

CURSO _____ FECHA DE NACIMIENTO _____

APELLIDOS _____ NOMBRE _____

Marca con una cruz la respuesta que corresponda:

1. Sexo
   - ❏ Hombre
   - ❏ Mujer

2. Nacionalidad
   - ❏ Española
   - ❏ Otras. Especifica _____

3. Lengua materna
   - ❏ Español
   - ❏ Otras. Por favor, especifica _____

4. ¿Recibes clases particulares de inglés fuera del colegio?

   ❏ Sí   ❏ No   ❏ He ido, pero ya no voy

5. En caso de recibas o hayas recibido clases de inglés fuera del colegio, especifica:

   ➢ **durante cuantos años:**
   - ❏ menos de un año   ❏ un año   ❏ dos años   ❏ tres años
   - ❏ cuatro años   ❏ cinco años   ❏ más de cinco años

   ➢ **durante cuantas horas a la semana:**
   - ❏ 1 hora   ❏ 2 horas   ❏ 3 horas   ❏ 4 horas   ❏ 5 horas   ❏ más de 5 horas

   ➢ **cuál ha sido el motivo**
   - ❏ Había suspendido y quería aprobar
   - ❏ En el colegio saco buenas notas pero quería mejorar
   - ❏ Me gustan mucho los idiomas y me divierte aprenderlos
   - ❏ Complacer a mi familia

6. ¿Has estado en algún país de habla inglesa?
   - ❏ No
   - ❏ Sí
     - ➢ ¿Cuándo? _____
     - ➢ ¿Durante cuánto tiempo? _____
     - ➢ ¿Has ido a clases de inglés allí? ❏ Sí   ❏ No

7. ¿Has ido a colonias o campamentos de inglés alguna vez?
   - ❏ No
   - ❏ Sí
     - ➢ ¿Cuándo? _____
     - ➢ ¿Durante cuánto tiempo? _____

8. ¿Cuál fue tu nota en inglés el año pasado en tercero de primaria?

   - ❏ Progresa adecuadamente (P.A.)   ❏ Necesita mejorar (N.M.)
   - ❏ Otro. Especifica cual _____

CUESTIONARIO
2005/2006

9. INDICA CON UNA CRUZ COMO TE RESULTA:

- *Leer en inglés (entender un texto escrito)*

  ☐ Muy difícil   ☐ Difícil   ☐ Normal   ☐ Fácil   ☐ Muy fácil

  ➢ En el caso de que hayas respondido difícil o muy difícil, selecciona con una cruz el motivo:

  ☐ Por la aparición de vocabulario que no entiendo
  ☐ Por la aparición de estructuras gramaticales que no entiendo
  ☐ Por la escritura de algunas palabras inglesas
  ☐ Otra dificultad: especifica cuál _____

- *Entender el inglés hablado (personas nativas hablando inglés, tu profesor, cinta, televisión, etc)*

  ☐ Muy difícil   ☐ Difícil   ☐ Normal   ☐ Fácil   ☐ Muy fácil

  ➢ En el caso de que hayas respondido difícil o muy difícil, selecciona con una cruz el motivo:

  ☐ Por la presencia de vocabulario que no entiendo
  ☐ Por la aparición de estructuras gramaticales que no entiendo
  ☐ Porque los sonidos ingleses son difíciles de entender
  ☐ Otra dificultad. Especifica cuál _____

- *Escribir correctamente en inglés*

  ☐ Muy difícil   ☐ Difícil   ☐ Normal   ☐ Fácil   ☐ Muy fácil

  ➢ En el caso de que hayas respondido difícil o muy difícil, selecciona con una cruz el motivo:

  ☐ Por falta de vocabulario
  ☐ Por la aparición de estructuras gramaticales que no entiendo
  ☐ Porque no sé escribir ciertas palabras
  ☐ Otra dificultad. Especifica cuál _____

- *Hablar correctamente en inglés*

  ☐ Muy difícil   ☐ Difícil   ☐ Normal   ☐ Fácil   ☐ Muy fácil

  ➢ En el caso de que hayas respondido difícil o muy difícil, selecciona con una cruz el motivo:

  ☐ Por falta de vocabulario
  ☐ Por falta de estructuras gramaticales
  ☐ Porque no sé pronunciar ciertas palabras
  ☐ Otra dificultad. Especifica cuál _____

CUESTIONARIO
2005/2006

10. ¿Cómo describirías tu nivel de inglés?

❏ Muy bueno ❏ Bueno ❏ Regular ❏ Malo

11. ¿Cuánto tiempo le dedicas al inglés en casa (sin contar las clases de inglés que puedas recibir)?

❏ Menos de media hora ❏ Entre media hora y una hora
❏ Entre una hora y dos ❏ Más de dos horas. Especifica el número _____

12. Ese tiempo que le dedicas al estudio del inglés en casa, ¿en qué lo empleas?

❏ Leer libros o revistas en inglés ❏ Ver la tele en inglés
❏ Oir música en inglés ❏ Estudiar vocabulario
❏ Hacer los deberes ❏ Otros. Especifica _____

13. ¿Sueles leer en inglés en casa?

❏ Sí, a diario ❏ A menudo ❏ Casi nunca ❏ Nunca

14. Por favor, pon una 'X' en la casilla que corresponda de entre las siete que te presentamos (incluida la sombreada). La casilla sombreada te guía para que sepas el término medio de las opciones que te presentamos.

El aprender inglés es ....

Necesario							Innecesario
Feo							Bonito
Difícil							Fácil
Atractivo							No atractivo
Agradable							Desagradable
Poco importante							Importante
Inútil							Útil
Interesante							Aburrido

PON UNA 'X' EN LA CASILLA QUE CORRESPONDA

15. Me gusta aprender inglés

Totalmente de acuerdo	De acuerdo	Ni a favor ni en contra	En desacuerdo	Totalmente en desacuerdo

16. El aprender inglés es importante

Totalmente de acuerdo	De acuerdo	Ni a favor ni en contra	En desacuerdo	Totalmente en desacuerdo

CUESTIONARIO
2005/2006

17. El aprender inglés es aburrido

Totalmente de acuerdo	De acuerdo	Ni a favor ni en contra	En desacuerdo	Totalmente en desacuerdo

18. Quiero aprender mucho inglés

Totalmente de acuerdo	De acuerdo	Ni a favor ni en contra	En desacuerdo	Totalmente en desacuerdo

19. Me gustan las clases de inglés

Totalmente de acuerdo	De acuerdo	Ni a favor ni en contra	En desacuerdo	Totalmente en desacuerdo

20. Me interesa aprender inglés

Totalmente de acuerdo	De acuerdo	Ni a favor ni en contra	En desacuerdo	Totalmente en desacuerdo

21. Aprender inglés es una pérdida de tiempo

Totalmente de acuerdo	De acuerdo	Ni a favor ni en contra	En desacuerdo	Totalmente en desacuerdo

22. Me esfuerzo por aprender inglés

Totalmente de acuerdo	De acuerdo	Ni a favor ni en contra	En desacuerdo	Totalmente en desacuerdo

23. El inglés me vendrá muy bien para encontrar trabajo cuando sea mayor

Totalmente de acuerdo	De acuerdo	Ni a favor ni en contra	En desacuerdo	Totalmente en desacuerdo

24. Me gustaría hablar y escribir muy bien en inglés

Totalmente de acuerdo	De acuerdo	Ni a favor ni en contra	En desacuerdo	Totalmente en desacuerdo

25. En las clases de inglés intento aprender todo lo que puedo

Totalmente de acuerdo	De acuerdo	Ni a favor ni en contra	En desacuerdo	Totalmente en desacuerdo

26. Quiero dominar muy bien el inglés para poder comunicarme con otros niños que hablan esa lengua

Totalmente de acuerdo	De acuerdo	Ni a favor ni en contra	En desacuerdo	Totalmente en desacuerdo

References

Adolphs, S. and Schmitt, N. (2004) Vocabulary coverage according to spoken discourse context. In P. Bogaards and B. Laufer (eds) *Vocabulary in a Second Language* (pp. 39–52). Amsterdam: John Benjamins.
Agustín Llach, M.P. (2007) Lexical errors as writing quality predictors. *Studia Linguistica* 61 (1), 1–19.
Agustín Llach, M.P. (2009a) Lexical L1 transfer in Spanish EFL writing. Paper presented at the XXVII International AESLA Conference, Ciudad Real, 26–28 March 2009.
Agustín Llach, M.P. (2009b) The effect of reading only, reading and comprehension, and sentence writing in lexical learning in a foreign language. *RESLA* 22, 9–34.
Agustín Llach, M.P., Fernández Fontecha, A. and Moreno Espinosa, S. (2005) Responding to different composition topics: A quantitative analysis of lexical error production *Glosas Didácticas* 13, 133–141.
Agustín Llach, M.P. and Jiménez Catalán, R.M. (2007) Measuring lexical knowledge through lexical accuracy ratio. *Language Forum: A Journal of Language and Literature* 33 (2, Special Issue: New Trends in Vocabulary Acquisition), 65–84.
Agustín Llach, M.P. and Terrazas Gallego, M. (2008) Gender differences in receptive vocabulary size in EFL primary school learners: A longitudinal study. Paper presented at the XXXII International AEDEAN Conference, Palma de Mallorca, 13–15 November 2008.
Agustín Llach, M.P. and Terrazas Gallego, M. (2009) Examining the relationship between receptive vocabulary size and reading and writing of primary school learners. *Atlantis* 31 (1), 11–29.
Al-Othman, N.M.A. (2004) The relationship between gender and learning styles in Internet-based teaching – A study from Kuwait. *The Reading Matrix* 4 (1), 38–54.
Albrechtsen, D., Henriksen, B. and Faerch, C. (1980) Native speaker reactions to learners' spoken interlanguage. *Language Learning* 30, 365–396.
Alderson, J.C. (1979) The cloze procedure and proficiency in English as a foreign language. *TESOL Quarterly* 13 (2), 219–227.
Alonso Alonso, M.R. and Palacios Martínez, I.M. (1994) Expresión escrita y transferencia: Análisis de errores en la lengua escrita de estudiantes de español como segunda lengua. *REALE* 2, 23–38.
Altenberg, B. and Granger, S. (2002) Recent trends in cross-linguistic lexical studies. In B. Altenberg and S. Granger (eds) *Lexis in Contrast* (pp. 3–48). Amsterdam: John Benjamins.
Álvarez Castrillo, C. and Diez-Itzá, E. (2000) Competencia léxica y rendimiento académico en alumnos de segundo de Bachillerato. *Aula Abierta* 76, 185–195.

Ambroso, S. (2000) Descripción de los errores léxicos de los hispanohablantes: análisis de la producción escrita de IT, el certificado de competencia general en italiano como L2. In E. de Miguel, M. Fernández Lagunilla and F. Cartoni (eds) *Sobre el lenguaje: miradas plurales y singulares* (pp. 53–72). Madrid: Arrecife.
Anderson, J.C. and Freebody, P. (1981) Vocabulary knowledge. In J.T. Guthrie (ed.) *Comprehension and Teaching* (pp. 77–117). Newark, DE: International Reading Association.
Andreou, G., Vlachos, F. and Andreou, E. (2005) Affecting factors in second language learning. *Journal of Psycholinguistic Research* 34 (5), 429–438.
Anglin, J.M. (1985) The child's expressible knowledge of word concepts: What preschoolers can say about the meanings of some noun and verbs. In K.E. Nelson (ed.) *Children's Language* (Vol. 5, pp. 77–120). Hillsdale, NJ: Erlbaum.
Ard, J. and Gass, S. (1987) Lexical constraints on syntactic acquisition. *Studies in Second Language Acquisition* 9, 233–252.
Argüelles Álvarez, I. (2004) Evaluación y calificación de resúmenes de textos expositivos en el aula de ILE/IFE: la guía 'BABAR'. *Ibérica* 8, 81–99.
Arnaud, P. (1992) Objective lexical and grammatical characteristics of L2 written compositions and the validity of separate-component tests. In P. Arnaud and H. Béjoint (eds) *Vocabulary and Applied Linguistics* (pp. 133–145). London: MacMillan Academic and Professional Ltd.
Arnaud, P. and Béjoint, H. (eds) (1992) *Vocabulary and Applied Linguistics*. London: Macmillan.
Atai, M.R. and Akbarian, I. (2003) The effect of exposure on EFL learners' acquisition of idioms with reference to proficiency levels. *Indian Journal of Applied Linguistics* 29 (1), 21–34.
Bacha, N. (2001) Writing evaluation: What can analytic versus holistic essay scoring tell us? *System* 29, 371–383.
Barcroft, J. (2004) Effects of sentence writing in second language lexical acquisition. *Second Language Research* 20 (4), 303–334.
Bardovi-Harlig, K. and Bofman, T. (1989) Attainment of syntactic and morphological accuracy by advanced language learners. *Studies in Second Language Acquisition* 11, 17–34.
Beheydt, L. (1987) The semantization of vocabulary in foreign language learning. *System* 15 (1), 55–67.
Beglar, D. and Hunt, A. (1999) Revising and validating the 2000 word level and university word level vocabulary tests. *Language Testing* 16 (2), 131–162.
Berg, E.C. (1999) The effects of trained peer response on ESL students' revision types and writing quality. *Journal of Second Language Writing* 8 (3), 215–241.
Berko Gleason, J. (ed.) (1997) *The Development of Language* (4th edn). Boston: Allyn and Bacon.
Berkoff, N.A. (1981) Error analysis revisited. In G. Nickel and D. Nehls (eds) *Error Analysis, Contrastive Linguistics and Second Language Learning*. Papers from the 6th International Congress of Applied Linguistics (pp. 5–17). Lund 1981. Heidelberg: Groos.
Blum, S. and Levenston, E.A. (1978) Universals of lexical simplification. *Language Learning* 28, 399–415.
Blum-Kulka, S. and Levenston, E. (1983) Universals of lexical simplification. In C. Faerch and G. Kasper (eds) *Strategies in Interlanguage Communication* (pp. 119–139). London: Longman.

Bogaards, P. and Laufer, B. (eds) (2004) *Vocabulary in a Second Language*. Amsterdam: John Benjamins.
Bouvy, C. (2000) Towards the construction of a theory of cross-linguistic transfer. In J. Cenoz and U. Jessner (eds) *English in Europe: The Acquisition of a Third Language* (pp. 143–156). Clevedon: Multilingual Matters.
Brown, H.D. (1970) Categories of spelling difficulty in speakers of English as a first and second language. *Journal of Verbal Learning and Verbal Behaviour* 9, 232–236.
Brown, J.D. and Rodgers, T. (2002) *Doing Second Language Research*. Oxford: Oxford University Press.
Bruce, I. (2005) Syllabus design for general EAP writing courses: A cognitive approach. *Journal of English for Academic Purposes* 4, 239–256.
Bruton, A. (2007) Vocabulary learning from dictionary reference in collaborative EFL translational writing. *System* 35, 353–367.
Brutten, S., Mouw, J. and Perkins, K. (1986) The effects of language group, proficiency level, and instruction on ESL subjects' control of the {D} and {Z} morphemes. *TESOL Quarterly* 20 (3):553–559.
Burling, R. (1978) Language development of a Garo and English-speaking child. In E. Hatch (ed.) *Second Language Acquisition: A Book of Readings* (pp. 54–76). Rowley, MA: Newbury House.
Burstall, C., Jamieson, M., Cohen, S. and Hargreaves, M. (1974). *Primary French in the Balance*. Slough: NFER.
Cabaleiro González, M.B. (2003) La escritura en L1 y L2: estudio empírico. *RESLA* 16, 33–52.
Cameron, L. (1994) Organizing the world: Children's concepts and categories, and implications for the teaching of English. *ELT Journal* 48 (1), 28–39.
Cameron, L. (2001) *Teaching Languages to Young Learners*. Cambridge: Cambridge University Press.
Cameron, L. (2002) Measuring vocabulary size in English as an additional language. *Language Teaching Research* 6 (2), 145–173.
Cameron, L. (2003) Challenges for ELT from the expansion in teaching children. *ELT Journal* 57 (2), 105–112.
Cameron, L. and Blesser, S. (2004) Writing in English as an additional language at key stage 2. Research Report RR586. ON WWW at http://www.dfes.gov.uk/research/data/uploadfiles/RR586.pdf.
Camp, R. (1993) Changing the model for the direct assessment of writing. In M.W. Williamson and B. Hout (eds) *Validating Holistic Scoring for Writing Assessment: Theoretical and Empirical Foundations* (pp. 45–78). Cresskill, NJ: Hampton Press.
Campbell, C. (1990) Writing with others' words: Using background reading text in academic compositions. In B. Kroll (ed.) *Second Language Writing: Research Insights for the Classroom* (pp. 211–230). Cambridge: Cambridge University Press.
Carlisle, J. (1989) Knowledge of derivational morphology and spelling ability in fourth, sixth, and eighth graders. *Applied Psycholinguistics* 9, 247–266.
Carrió Pastor, M.L. (2004) Las implicaciones de los errores léxicos en los artículos en inglés científico-técnico. *RAEL* 3, 21–40.
Carroll, J.B. (1969) Psychological and educational research into second language teaching to young children. In H.H. Stern (ed.) *Languages and the Young School Child*. London: Oxford University Press.

Carson, J. (2001) Second language writing and second language acquisition. In T. Silva and P.K. Matsuda (eds) *On Second Language Writing* (pp. 191–200). Hillsdale, NJ: Erlbaum.
Cassany, D. (1989) *Describir el escribir*. Barcelona. Paidós Comunicación.
Celaya, M.L. (1992) *Transfer in English as a Foreign Language: A Study on Tenses*. Barcelona: Promociones y Publicaciones Universitarias.
Celaya, M.L. (2006) Lexical transfer and L2 proficiency: A longitudinal analysis of EFL written production. In A. Alcaraz-Sintes, C. Soto-Palomo and MC. Zunido-Garrido (eds) *Proceedings of the 29th AEDEAN Conference*. Jaen: Universidad de Jaen.
Celaya, M.L. and Torras, M.R. (2001) L1 influence and EFL vocabulary: Do children rely more on L1 than adult learners? *Proceedings of the 25th AEDEAN Meeting, University of Granada, 13–15 December* (pp. 1–14).
Celaya, M.L. and Ruiz de Zarobe, Y. (2008) CLIL, age, and L1 influence. Paper presented at the XXXII AEDEAN Conference, Palma de Mallorca, 13–15 November.
Celce-Murcia, M. (1978) The simultaneous acquisition of English and French in a two year old child. In E. Hatch (ed.) *Second Language Acquisition: A Book of Readings* (pp. 38–54). Rowley, MA: Newbury House.
Cenoz, J. (2001) The effect of linguistic distance, L2 status and age on cross-linguistic influence in third language acquisition. In J. Cenoz, B. Hufeisen and U. Jessner (eds) *Cross-Linguistic Influence in Third Language Acquisition: Psycholinguistic Perspectives* (pp. 8–20). Clevedon: Multilingual Matters.
Cenoz, J. (2002) Age differences in foreign language learning. *ITL Review of Applied Linguistics* 135–136, 125–142.
Cenoz, J. (2003) The influence of age on the acquisition of English: General proficiency, attitudes and code mixing. In M.P. García Mayo and M.L. García Lecumberri (eds) *Age and the Acquisition of English as a Foreign Language* (pp. 77–93). Clevedon: Multilingual Matters.
Cervero, M.J. and Pichardo Castro, F. (2000) *Aprender y enseñar vocabulario*. Madrid: Edelsa.
Chandler, J. (2003) The efficacy of various kinds of error feedback for improvement in the accuracy and fluency of L2 student writing. *Journal of Second Language Writing* 12, 267–296.
Channell, J. (1988) Psycholingusitc considerations in the study of L2 vocabulary acquisition. In R. Carter and M. McCarthy (eds) *Vocabulary and Language Teaching* (pp. 83–96). London: Longman.
Chastain, K. (1988) *Developing Second-Language Skills: Theory to Practice* (2nd edn). New York: Harcourt Brace Jovanovich.
Cherry, R. and Meyer, P. (1993) Reliability issues in holistic assessment. In M.W. Williamson and B. Hout (eds) *Validating Holistic Scoring for Writing Assessment: Theoretical and Empirical Foundations* (pp. 109–141). Cresskill, NJ: Hampton Press.
Chiang, S. (2003) The importance of cohesive conditions to perceptions of writing quality at the early stages of foreign language learning. *System* 31, 471–484.
Cho, Y. (2003) Assessing writing: Are we bound by only one method? *Assessing Writing* 8, 165–191.
Cho, K.-S. and Krashen, S. (1994) Acquisition of vocabulary from the Sweet Valley Kids Series: Adult ESL acquisition. *Journal of Reading* 37, 662–667.

Clark, E. (1993) *The Lexicon in Acquisition*. Cambridge: Cambridge University Press.
Clark, M. and Ishida, S. (2005) Vocabulary knowledge differences between placed and promoted EAP students. *Journal of English for Academic Purposes* 4, 225–238.
Coady, J. (1995) Research on ESL/EFL vocabulary acquisition: Putting it in context. In T. Huckin, M. Haynes and J. Coady (eds) *Second Language Reading and Vocabulary Learning* (pp. 3–24). Norwood, NJ: Ablex Publishing Corporation.
Coady, J., Magoto, J., Hubbard, P., Graney, J. and Mokhtari, K. (1995) High frequency vocabulary and reading proficiency in ESL readers. In T. Huckin, M. Haynes and J. Coady (eds) *Second Language Reading and Vocabulary Learning* (pp. 217–226). Norwood, NJ: Ablex Publishng Corporation.
Coady, J. and Huckin, T. (eds) (1997) *Second Language Vocabulary Acquisition*. Cambridge: Cambridge University Press.
Cobb, T. (2000) One size fits all? Francophone learners and English vocabulary tests. *The Canadian Modern Language Review* 57 (2), 295–324.
Cobb, T. (2003) Analyzing late interlanguage with learner corpora: Quebec replication of three European studies. *The Canadian Modern Language Review* 59, 393–423.
Cobb, T. and Horst, M. (1999) Vocabulary sizes of some City University students. *City University (HK) Journal of Language Studies* 1, 59–68.
Cobb, T. and Horst, M. (2004) Is there room for an academic word list in French? In P. Bogaards and B. Laufer (eds) *Vocabulary in a Second Language* (pp. 15–38). Amsterdam: John Benjamins.
Codina Espurz, V. and Usó Juan, E. (2000) Influencia del conocimiento previo y del nivel de una segunda lengua en la comprensión escrita de textos académicos. In C. Muñoz (ed.) *Segundas lenguas. Adquisición en el aula* (pp. 299–315). Barcelona: Ariel Lingüística.
Consejo de Europa (2001) *Marco común europeo de referencia para las lenguas: aprendizaje, enseñanza y evaluación*. Estrasburgo (Spanish version by Instituto Cervantes, 2002). [English version: Council of Europe (2001). *Common European Framework of Reference for Languages: Learning, Teaching, Assessment*. Cambridge: Cambridge University Press.]
Connor, U. (2003) Changing currents in contrastive rhetoric: Implications for teaching and research. In B. Kroll (ed.) *Exploring the Dynamics of Second Language Writing* (pp. 218–241). Cambridge: Cambridge University Press.
Cook, V. (1991/1996) *Second Language Learning and Language Teaching*. London: Edward Arnold.
Corder, S.P. (1967) The significance of learner's errors. *IRAL* 5, 161–170.
Corder, S.P. (1973) *Introducing Applied Linguistics*. Middlesex: Penguin Books.
Corporate Author Cambridge ESOL (2004) http://www.cambridge.org/aus/browse/browse_samples.asp?subjectid=55
Crusan, D. (2002) An assessment of ESL writing placement assessment. *Assessing Writing* 8, 17–30.
Crystal, D. (1980) *A First Dictionary of Linguistics and Phonetics*. London: André Deutsch.
Cumming, A. (2001) Learning to write in a second language: Two decades of research. *International Journal of English Studies* 1 (2), 1–23.

Cumming, A. (2003) Experienced EFL/ESL writing instructors conceptualizations of their teaching: Curriculum options and implications. In B. Kroll (ed.) *Exploring the Dynamics of Second Language Writing* (pp. 71–92). Cambridge: Cambridge University Press.
Cumming, A., Kantor, R., Baba, K., Erdosy, U., Eouanzoui, K. and James, M. (2005) Differences in written discourse in independent and integrated prototype tasks for next generation TOEFL. *Assessing Writing* 10, 5–43.
Curtis, M. (1987) Vocabulary testing and vocabulary instruction. In M. McKeown and M. Curtis (eds.) *The Nature of Vocabulary Acquisition* (pp. 37–51). Hillsdale, NJ: Erlbaum.
Da Rocha, F.J. (1980) On the reliability of error analysis. *Studia Anglica Posnaniensia* 12, 83–90.
Dagneaux, E., Denness, S. and Granger, S. (1998) Computer-aided error analysis. *System* 26, 163–174.
Dagut, M.B. (1977) Incongruencies in lexical 'gridding' – An application of contrastive semantics analysis to language teaching. *IRAL* 15, 221–229.
Dagut, M., and Laufer, B. (1982) How intralingual are 'intralingual errors'? In G. Nickel and D. Nehls (eds) *International Review of Applied Linguistics: Error Analysis, Contrastive Linguistics and Second Language Learning* (pp. 19–41).
De Angelis, G. and Selinker, L. (2001) Interlanguage transfer and competing linguistic systems in the multilingual mind. In J. Cenoz, B. Hufeisen and U. Jessner (eds) *Cross-Linguistic Influence in Third Language Acquisition: Psycholinguistic Perspectives* (pp. 42–58). Clevedon, UK: Multilingual Matters.
De Bot, K. and Schreuder, R. (1993) Word production and the bilingual lexicon. In R. Schreuder and B. Weltens (eds) *The Bilingual Lexicon* (pp. 191–214). Amsterdam: John Benjamins.
De Cock, S. and Granger, S. (2005) Computer learner corpora and monolingual learners dictionaries: The perfect match. In W. Teubert and M. Mahlberg (eds) *The Corpus Approach to Lexicography* (pp. 72–86). Special issue of *Lexicographica* 20. Berlin, New York: Walter de Gruyter.
De Groot, A.M.B. (1993) Word-type effects in bilingual processing tasks: Support for a mixed-representational system. In R. Schreuder and B. Weltens (eds) *The Bilingual Lexicon* (pp. 27–51). Amsterdam: John Benjamins.
De Haan, P. and van Esch, K. (2005) The development of writing in English and Spanish as foreign languages. *Assessing Writing* 10, 100–116.
Delisle, H. (1982) Native speaker judgement and the evaluation of errors in German. *Modern Language Journal* 66, 39–48.
Deschamps, A. (1992) From spelling to sound: English graphematics as an aid to vocabulary acquisition. In P. Arnaud and H. Bejoint (eds) *Vocabulary and Applied Linguistics* (pp. 182–195). London: MacMillan.
Dewaele, J.M. (1998) Lexical inventions: French interlanguage as L2 versus L3. *Applied Linguistics* 19 (4), 471–490.
Dewaele, J.M. (2001) Activation or inhibition? The interaction of L1, L2 and L3 on the language mode continuum. In J. Cenoz, B. Hufeisen and U. Jessner (eds) *Cross-linguistic Influence in Third Language Acquisition: Psycholinguistic Perspectives* (pp. 69–89). Clevedon: Multilingual Matters.
Díaz Galán, A. and Fumero Pérez, M.C. (2004) The problem–solution pattern: A tool for the teaching of writing? *BELLS: Barcelona English and Literature*

Studies 12. ON WWW at http://www.publicacions.ub.es/revistes/bells12/ PDF/art03.pdf. Accessed XX.XX.XX.
Djokic, D. (1999) Lexical errors in L2 learning and communication. *Rassegna Italina di Linguistica Aplicata* 1, 123–135.
Dordick, M. (1996) Testing for a hierarchy of the communicative interference value of ESL errors. *System* 24 (3), 299–308.
Dušková, L. (1969) On sources of errors in foreign language learning. *IRAL* 7, 11–35.
Ecke, P. (2001) Lexical retrieval in a third language: Evidence from errors and tip-of-the-tongue states. In J. Cenoz, B. Hufeisen and U. Jessner (eds) *Cross-Linguistic Influence in Third Language Acquisition: Psycholinguistic Perspectives* (pp. 90–114). Clevedon, UK: Multilingual Matters.
Eisterhold, J.C. (1990) Reading–writing connections: Towards a description for second language learners. In B. Kroll (ed.) *Second Language Writing: Research Insights for the Classroom* (pp. 88–102). Cambridge: Cambridge University Press.
Ellis, N. (1997a) Vocabulary acquisition: Word structure, collocation, word-class, and meaning. In N. Schmitt and M. McCarthy (eds) *Vocabulary: Description, Acquisition and Pedagogy* (pp. 122–139). Cambridge: Cambridge University Press.
Ellis, N. (2004) The processes of SLA. In B. VanPatten, J. Williams, S. Rott and M. Overstreet (eds) *Form-Meaning Connections in Second Language Acquisition* (pp. 139–154). Mahwah, NJ: Erlbaum.
Ellis, N. and Beaton, A. (1993) Psycholinguistic determinants of foreign language vocabulary learning. *Language Learning* 43 (4), 559–617.
Ellis, R. (1985) *Understanding Second Language Acquisition*. Oxford: Oxford University Press.
Ellis, R. (1994) *The Study of Second Language Acquisition*. Oxford: Oxford University Press.
Ellis, R. (1997b) *Second Language Acquisition Research and Language Teaching*. Oxford: Oxford University Press.
Ellis, R. and Heimbach, R. (1997) Bugs and birds: Children's acquisition of second language vocabulary through interaction. *System* 25 (2), 247–259.
Engber, C.A. (1995) The relationship of lexical proficiency to the quality of ESL compositions. *Journal of Second Language Writing* 4 (2), 139–155.
Enkvist, N.E. (1973) Should we count errors or measure success? In J. Svartvik (ed.) *Errata: Papers in Error Analysis* (pp. 16–23). Lund: GWE Gleerup.
Erdmenger, M. (1985) Word-acquisition and vocabulary structure in third-year EFL learners. *IRAL* 23 (2), 159–164.
Faerch, C. and Kasper, G. (1983) Plans and strategies in foreign language communication. In C. Faerch and G. Kasper (eds) *Strategies in Interlanguage Communication* (pp. 20–60). London: Longman.
Fan, M. (2000) How big is the gap and how to narrow it? An investigation into the active and passive vocabulary knowledge of L2 learners. *RELC Journal* 31 (2), 105–119.
Fathman, A.K. and Whalley, E. (1990) Teacher response to student writing: Focus on form versus content. In B. Kroll (ed.) *Second Language Writing: Research Insights for the Classroom* (pp. 178–190). Cambridge: Cambridge University Press.

Fayer, J.M. and Krasinski, E. (1987) Native and nonnative judgements of intelligibility and irritation. *Language Learning* 37 (3), 313–326.

Fernández, S. (1995) Errores e interlengua en el aprendizaje del español como lengua Extranjera. *Didáctica* 7, 203–216.

Fernández, S. (1997) *Interlengua y análisis de errores en el aprendizaje del español como lengua extranjera*. Madrid: Edelsa.

Ferris, D. and Hedgcock, J.S. (1998) *Teaching ESL Composition: Purpose, Process and Practice*. Mahwah, NJ: Erlbaum.

Fisher, R. (1984) Testing written communicative competence in French. *Modern Language Journal* 68, 13–20.

Fitzgerald, J. (1995) English-as-a-second-language learners' cognitive reading processes: A review of research in the United States. *Review of Educational Research* 65, 145–190.

Flower L. and Hayes, J. (1981) A cognitive process theory of writing. *College Composition and Communication* 32, 365–387.

Frantzen, D. (1995) The effects of grammar supplementation on written accuracy in an intermediate Spanish content course. *Modern Language Journal* 79, 329–344.

Freidlander, A. (1990) Composing in English: Effects of a first language on writing in English as a second language. In B. Kroll (ed.) *Second Language Writing: Research Insights for the Classroom* (pp. 109–125). Cambridge: Cambridge University Press.

Gabryś-Barker, D. (2006) The interaction of languages in the lexical search of multilingual language users. In J. Arabski (ed.) *Cross-Linguistic Influences in the Second Language Lexicon* (pp. 144–166). Clevedon: Multilingual Matters.

García Lecumberri, M.L. and Gallardo, F. (2003) English FL sounds in school learners of different ages. In M.P. García Mayo and M.L. García Lecumberri (eds) *Age and the Acquisition of English as a Foreign Language* (pp. 115–135). Clevedon: Multilingual Matters.

García Mayo, M.P. (2003) Age, length of exposure and grammaticality judgements in the acquisition of English as a foreign language. In M.P. García Mayo and M.L. García Lecumberri (eds) *Age and the Acquisition of English as a Foreign Language* (pp. 94–114). Clevedon: Multilingual Matters.

García Mayo, M.P. and García Lecumberri, M.L. (eds) (2003) *Age and the Acquisition of English as a Foreign Language*. Clevedon: Multilingual Matters.

Gass, S. (1988) Second language vocabulary acquisition. *Annual Review of Applied Linguistics* 9, 92–106.

Gass, S. and Schachter, J. (1990) *Linguistic Perspectives in Second language Acquisition*. Cambridge: Cambridge University Press.

Gearhart, M., Herman, J.L., Novak, J.R. and Wolf, S.A. (1995) Toward the instructional utility of large-scale writing assessment: Validation of a new narrative rubric. *Assessing Writing* 2 (2), 207–242.

Gleitman, L., and Landau, B. (1996) *The Acquisition of the Lexicon*. Amsterdam: MIT/Elsevier.

Glenwright, P. (2002) Language proficiency assessment for teachers: The effects of benchmarking on writing assessment in Hong Kong schools. *Assessing Writing* 8, 84–109.

Goldfield, B.A. and Reznick, J.S. (1990) Early lexical acquisition: Rate, content, and the vocabulary spurt. *Journal of Child Language* 17, 171–183.

Goldsmith, P. (1995) The development of spelling and word knowledge in older students (Years 5–11). *Australian Review of Applied Linguistics* 18 (1), 109–128.
González Álvarez, E. (2004) *Interlanguage Lexical Innovation*. Munich: Lincom Europa.
Goodfellow, R., Jones, G., Lamy, M-N. (2002) Assessing Learners' Writing Using Lexical Frequency. *ReCALL* 14 (1), 129–142.
Gost, C. and Celaya, M.L. (2005) Age and the use of L1 in EFL oral production. In M.L.Carrió Pastor (ed.) *Perspectivas Interdisciplinares de la Lingüística Aplicada* (pp. 129–136). València: Universitat Politècnica de València – AESLA, Asociación Española de Lingüística Aplicada.
Grabe, W. (2001) Notes towards a theory of second language writing. In T. Silva and P.K. Matsuda (eds) *On Second Language Writing* (pp. 39–58). Hillsdale, NJ: Erlbaum.
Grabe, W. (2003) Reading and writing relations: Second language perspective on research and practice. In B. Kroll (ed.) *Exploring the Dynamics of Second Language Writing* (pp. 242–262). Cambridge: Cambridge University Press.
Grabe, W. and Stoller, F. (1997) Reading and vocabulary development in a second language: A case study. In J. Coady and T. Huckin (eds) *Second Language Vocabulary Acquisition* (pp. 98–122). Cambridge: Cambridge University Press.
Grace, C. (2000) Gender differences: Vocabulary retention and access to translations for beginning language learners in CALL. *The Modern Language Journal* 84 (2), 214–224.
Grant, L. and Ginther, A. (2000) Using computer-tagged linguistic features to describe L2 writing differences. *Journal of Second Language Writing* 9 (2), 123–145.
Gu, P.Y. (2003) Vocabulary learning in a second language: Person, task, context and strategies. *Teaching English as a Second or Foreign Language* 7 (2), 1–24. On WWW at www.writing.berkeley.edu/TESL-EJ/ej26/toc.html.
Gu, Y. and Leung, C. (2002) Error patterns of vocabulary recognition for EFL learners in Beijing and Hong Kong. *Asian Journal of English Language Teaching* 12, 121–141.
Haastrup, K. and Phillipson, R. (1983) Achievement strategies in learner/native speaker interaction. In C. Faerch and G. Kasper (eds) *Strategies in Interlanguage Communication* (pp. 140–158). London: Longman.
Hakuta, K., Bialystok, E. and Wiley, E. (2005) Critical evidence: A test of the critical period hypothesis for second language acquisition. *Psychological Science* 14 (1), 31–38. On WWW at www.faculty.ucmerced.edu/khakuta/docs/Critical Evidence.pdf. Accessed 14.12.05.
Halden-Sullivan, J. (1996) Reconsidering assessment: From checklist to dialectic. *Assessing Writing* 3 (21), 173–195.
Hamp-Lyons, L. (1990) Second language writing: Assessment issues. In B. Kroll (ed.) *Second Language Writing: Research Insights for the Classroom* (pp. 69–87). Cambridge: Cambridge University Press.
Hamp-Lyons, L. (1991) Scoring procedures for ESL contexts. In L. Hamp-Lyons (ed.) *Assessing Second Language Writing in Academic Contexts* (pp. 241–276). Norwood, NJ: Ablex Publishing Corporation.
Hamp-Lyons, L. (1992) Holistic writing assessment for LEP students. *Proceedings of the Second National Research Symposium on Limited English Proficient Student*

Issues: Focus on Evaluation and Measurement. OBEMLA. On WWW at http://www.ncela.gwu.edu/pubs/symposia/second/vol2/holistic.htm.
Hamp-Lyons, L. (2001) Fourth generation writing assessment. In T. Silva and P.K. Matsuda (eds) *On Second Language Writing* (pp. 117–128). Hillsdale, NJ: Erlbaum.
Hamp-Lyons, L. (2003) Writing teachers as assessors of writing. In B. Kroll (ed.) *Exploring the Dynamics of Second Language Writing* (pp. 162–190). Cambridge: Cambridge University Press.
Hancin-Bhatt, B. and Nagy, W. (1994) Lexical transfer and second language morphological development. *Applied Psycholinguistics* 15, 289–310.
Hansen, L., Umeda, Y. and McKinney, M. (2002) Savings in the relearning of second language vocabulary: The effects of time and proficiency. *Language Learning* 52 (4), 653–678.
Harklau, L. (2002) The role of writing in classroom second language acquisition. *Journal of Second Language Writing* 11, 329–350.
Harley, B. (1986) *Age in Second Language Acquisition*. Clevedon: Multilingual Matters.
Harley, B. (1995) Introduction: The lexicon in second language research. In B. Harley (ed.) *Lexical Issues in Language Learning* (pp. 1–28). Ann Arbor, MI: Research Club in Language Learning.
Harley, B., Allen, P., Cummins, J. and Swain, M. (eds) (1990) *The Development of Second Language Proficiency*. Cambridge: Cambridge University Press.
Harley, B. and King, M.L. (1989) Verb lexis in the written compositions of young L2 learners. *Studies in Second Language Acquisition* 11, 415–439.
Hartman, G.W. (1946) Further evidence of the unexpected large size of recognition among college students. *Journal of Educational Psychology* 37, 436–439.
Hatzidaki, A. and Pothos, E. (2008). Bilingual language representations and cognitive processes in translation. *Applied Psycholinguistics* 29, 125–150.
Hawkey, R. and Barker, F. (2004) Developing a common scale for the assessment of writing. *Assessing Writing* 9, 122–159.
Hazenberg, S. and Hulstijn, J. (1996) Defining a minimal receptive second-language vocabulary for non-native university students: An empirical investigation. *Applied Linguistics* 17, 145–163.
Helms-Park, R. and Stapleton, P. (2003) Questioning the importance of individualised voice in undergraduate L2 argumentative writing: An empirical study with pedagogical implications. *Journal of Second Language Writing* 12, 245–265.
Hemchua, S. and Schmitt, N. (2006) An analysis of lexical errors in the English compositions of Thai learners. *Prospect* 21 (3), 3–25.
Henning, G.H. (1973) Remembering foreign language vocabulary: Acoustic and semantic parameters. *Language Learning* 23 (2), 185–197.
Herwig, A. (2001) Plurilingual lexical organization: Evidence from lexical processing in L1–L2–L3–L4 translation. In J. Cenoz, B. Hufeisen and U. Jessner (eds) *Cross-Linguistic Influence in Third Language Acquisition: Psycholinguistic Perspectives* (pp. 115–137). Clevedon: Multilingual Matters.
Hirsh, D. and Nation, P. (1992) What vocabulary size is needed to read unsimplified texts for pleasure? *Reading in a Foreign Language* 8, 689–696.

Hirvela, A. and Sweetland, Y.L. (2005) Two case studies of L2 writers' experiences across learning-directed portfolio contexts. *Assessing Writing* 10, 192–213.
Horst, M., Cobb, T. and Meara, P. (1998) Beyond a clockwork orange: Acquiring second language vocabulary through reading. *Reading in a Foreign Language* 11 (2), 207–223.
Huckin, T., Haynes, M. and Coady, J. (eds) (1995) *Second Language Reading and Vocabulary Learning*. Norwood, NJ: Ablex Publishing Corporation.
Hudson, W. (1990) Semantic theory and L2 lexical development. In S. Gass and J. Schachter (eds) Linguistic Perspectives in Second language Acquisition (pp. 222–238). Cambridge: Cambridge University Press.
Hughes, A. and Lascaratou, C. (1982) Competing criteria for error gravity. *ELT Journal* 36 (3), 175–182.
Hulstijn, J. and Laufer, B. (2001) Some empirical evidence for the involvement load hypothesis in vocabulary acquisition. *Language Learning* 51 (3), 539–558.
Hyland, K. (2003) *Second Language Writing*. Cambridge: Cambridge University Press.
Hyltenstam, K. (1988) Lexical characteristics of near-native second-language learners of Swedish. *Journal of Multilingual and Multicultural Development* 9, 67–84.
Itoh, H. and Hatch, E. (1978) SLA: A case study. In E. Hatch (ed.) *Second Language Acquisition: A Book of Readings* (pp. 76–91). Rowley, MA: Newbury House.
Jacobs, H., Zinkgraf, S., Wormuth, D.R., Hartfiel, V.F. and Hughey, J.B. (1981) *Testing ESL composition: A Practical Approach*. Rowley, MA: Newbury House.
James, C. (1977) Judgements of error gravities. *ELT Journal* 31 (2), 116–124.
James, C. (1998) *Errors in Language Learning and Use: Exploring Error Analysis*. London: Longman.
Janopoulos, M. (1993) Comprehension, communicative competence and construct validity: Holistic scoring from an ESL perspective. In M.W. Williamson and B. Hout (eds) *Validating Holistic Scoring for Writing Assessment: Theoretical and Empirical Foundations* (pp. 303–325). Cresskill, NJ: Hampton Press.
Jarvis, S., Grant, L., Bikowski, D. and Ferris, D. (2003) Exploring multiple profiles of highly rated learner compositions. *Journal of Second Language Writing* 12, 377–403.
Jiang, N. (2000) Lexical representation and development in a second language. *Applied Linguistics* 21 (1), 47–77.
Jiménez Catalán, R.M. (1992) *Errores en la producción escrita del inglés y posible factores condicionantes*. Colección Tesis Doctorales n° 73/92, Editorial de la Universidad Complutense.
Jiménez Catalán, R.M. and Ojeda Alba, J. (2007) The English vocabulary of girls and boys: Evidence from a quantitative study. In L. Litosseliti, H. Sauton, K. Harrington and J. Sunderland (eds) *Theoretical and Methodological Approaches to Gender and Language Study*. London: Palgrave Macmillan.
Jiménez Catalán, R.M. and Terrazas Gallego, M. (2008) The receptive vocabulary of English foreign language young learners. *Journal of English Studies* 5, 173–192.
Johansson, S. (1978) Problems in studying the communicative effect of learner's errors. *SSLA* 1 (10), 41–52.
Johns, A.M. (1990) L1 composition theories: Implications for developing theories of L2 composition. In B. Kroll (ed.) *Second Language Writing: Research Insights for the Classroom* (pp. 24–36). Cambridge: Cambridge University Press.

Johns Ann M. and P. Mayes. (1990) An analysis of summary protocols of university ESL students. *Applied Linguistics* 11, 253–271.

Katznelson, H., Perpignan, H. and Rubin, B. (2001) What develops along with the development of second language writing? Exploring the 'by-products'. *Journal of Second Language Writing* 10, 141–159.

Källkvist, M. (1998) How different are the results of translation tasks? A study of lexical errors. In K. Malmkjær (ed.) *Translation and Language Teaching: Language Teaching and Translation* (pp. 77–87). Manchester: St. Jerome Publishing.

Kepner, C. (1991) An experiment on the relationship of types of written feedback to the development of second language writing skills. *Modern Language Journal* 75, 305–313.

KET Handbook (2004) Read/Write Sample Test 2. Available online http://www.candidates.cambridgeesol.org/cs/digitalAssets/105923_Sample_Paper_R_W_KET.pdf.

Khalil, K. (1985) Communicative error evaluation: Native speakers evaluation and interpretation of written errors of Arab EFL learners. *TESOL Quarterly* 19 (2), 335–352.

Khalil, K. (1985) Communicative error evaluation: Native speakers evaluation and interpretation of written errors of Arab EFL learners. *TESOL Quarterly* 19 (2), 335–352.

Kobayashi, H. and Rinnert, C. (1992) Effects of first language on second language writing: Translation versus direct composition. *Language Learning* 42, 182–215.

Kobayashi, H. and Rinnert, C. (2002) High school student perceptions of first language literacy instruction: Implications for second language writing. *Journal of Second Language Writing* 11, 92–116.

Kormos, J. and Csizér, K. (2008) Age-related differences in the motivations of learning English as a foreign language: Attitudes, selves and motivated learning behaviour. *Language Learning* 58 (2), 327–355.

Krapels, A.R. (1990) An overview of second language writing process research. In B. Kroll (ed.) *Second Language Writing: Research Insights for the Classroom* (pp. 37–56). Cambridge: Cambridge University Press.

Krashen, S. (1993) *The power of reading*. Englewood, Colorado: Libraries Unlimited.

Krashen, S. (2004) *The Power of Reading* (2nd edn). Portsmount, NH: Heinemann Publishing Company.

Kroll, B. (1990) What does time buy? ESL student performance on home versus class composition. In B. Kroll (ed.) *Second Language Writing: Research Insights for the Classroom* (pp. 140–154). Cambridge: Cambridge University Press.

Kroll, J.F. (1993) Assessing conceptual representations for words in a second language. In R. Schreuder and B. Weltens (eds) *The Bilingual Lexicon* (pp. 53–81). Amsterdam: John Benjamins.

Kroll, B. (2003) Introduction: Teaching the next generation of second language writers. In B. Kroll (ed.) *Exploring the Dynamics of Second Language Writing* (pp. 1–10). Cambridge: Cambridge University Press.

Kroll, J., Michael, E., Tokowicz, N. and Dufour, R. (2002) The development of lexical fluency in a second language. *Second Language Research* 18 (2), 137–171.

Kubota, R. (1998) An investigation of L1–L2 transfer in writing among Japanese university students: Implications for contrastive rhetoric. *Journal of Second Language Writing* 7 (1), 69–100.

Kucera, H. and Francis, W.N. (1967) *Computational Analysis of Present-Day American English*. Providence, RI: Brown University Press.
Kuiken, F. and Vedder, I. (2007) Task complexity and measures of linguistic performance in L2 writing. *IRAL* 45, 261–284.
Kumaravadivelu, B. (1988) Communication strategies and psychological processes underlying lexical simplification. *IRAL* 26 (4), 309–319.
Kweon, S. and Kim, H. (2008) Beyond raw frequency: Incidental vocabulary acquisition in extensive reading. *Reading in a Foreign Language* 20 (2), 191–215.
Larsen-Freeman, D. and Long, M. (1991) *An Introduction to Second Language Research*. London: Longman.
Lasagabaster, D. and Doiz, A. (2003) Maturational constraints on foreign-language written production. In M.P. García Mayo and M.L. García Lecumberri (eds) *Age and the Acquisition of English as a Foreign Language* (pp. 136–160). Clevedon: Multilingual Matters.
Laufer, B. (1990a) 'Sequence' and 'order' in the development of L2 lexis: Some evidence from lexical confusions. *Applied Linguistics* 11 (3), 281–296.
Laufer, B. (1990b) Why are some words more difficult than others? Some intralexical factors that affect the learning of words. *IRAL* 28, 293–307.
Laufer, B. (1991a) Some properties of the foreign language learner's lexicon as evidenced by lexical confusions. *IRAL* 29 (4), 317–330.
Laufer, B. (1991b) The development of L2 lexis in the expression of the advanced learner. *Modern Language Journal* 75, 440–448.
Laufer, B. (1992) How much lexis is necessary for reading comprehension? In P. Arnaud and H. Béjoint (eds) *Vocabulary and Applied Linguistics* (pp. 126–132). London: Macmillan.
Laufer, B. (1996) The lexical threshold of second language reading comprehension. In K. Sajavaara and C. Fairweather (eds) *Approaches to Second Language Acquisition* (pp. 55–62). Jyväskylä: Jyväskylä University Printing House.
Laufer, B. (1997a) The lexical plight in second language reading. In J. Coady and T. Huckin (eds) *Second Language Vocabulary Acquisition* (pp. 20–34). Cambridge: Cambridge University Press.
Laufer, B. (1997b) What's in a word that makes it hard or easy: Some intralexical factors that affect the learning of words. In N. Schmitt and M. McCarthy (eds) *Vocabulary: Description, Acquisition and Pedagogy* (pp. 140–155). Cambridge: Cambridge University Press.
Laufer, B. (1998) The development of active and passive vocabulary in a second language: Same or different? *Applied Linguistics* 19, 255–271.
Laufer, B. (2003) Vocabulary acquisition in a second language: Do learners really acquire most vocabulary by reading? Some empirical evidence. *The Canadian Modern Language Review* 59 (4), 567–587.
Laufer, B. (2005) Lexical competence: What is it and how can it be measured? Paper presented at the Universidad de La Rioja, 11 May 2005.
Laufer, B. (2006). Comparing focus on form and focus on forms in second-language vocabulary learning. *The Canadian Modern Language Review* 63 (1), 149–166.
Laufer, B. and Nation, P. (1995) Vocabulary size and use: Lexical richness in L2 written production. *Applied Linguistics* 16, 307–322.
Laufer, B. and Nation, P. (1999) A vocabulary-size test of controlled productive ability. *Language Testing* 16, 33–51.

Laufer, B. and Paribakht, T.S. (1998) The relationship between active and passive vocabularies: Effects of language learning context. *Language Learning* 48 (3), 365–391.
Lee, S.H. (2003) ESL learners' vocabulary use in writing and the effects of explicit vocabulary instruction. *System*, 31, 537–561.
Lee, S.H. and Muncie, J. (2006) From receptive to productive: Improving ESL learners' use of vocabulary in a postreading composition task. *TESOL Quarterly* 40 (2), 295–320.
Legenhausen, L. (1975) *Fehleranalyse und Fehlerbewertung*. Berlin: Cornelsen-Velhagen & Klasing.
Lehmann, M. (2007). Is intentional or incidental vocabulary learning more effective? *The International Journal of Foreign Language Teaching* 3 (1), 23–28. On WWW at http://www.tprstories.com/ijflt/IJFLTJuly07.pdf. Accessed 22.10.07.
Leki, I. and Carson, J.G. (1994) Students' perceptions of EAP writing instruction and writing needs across the disciplines. *TESOL Quarterly* 28 (1), 81–101.
Lennon, P. (1991a) Error: Some problems of definition, identification, and distinction. *Applied Linguistics* 12 (2), 180–195.
Lennon, P. (1991b) Error and the very advanced learner. *IRAL* 29 (1), 31–43.
Lennon, P. (1996) Getting 'easy' verbs wrong at the advanced level. *IRAL* 34 (1), 23–36.
Leopold, W.F. (1978) A child's learning of two languages. In E. Hatch (ed.) *Second Language Acquisition: A Book of Readings* (pp. 23–33). Rowley, MA: Newbury House.
Li, P. (2009). Lexical organization and competition in first and second languages: Computational and neural mechanisms. *Cognitive Science* 33 (4), 629–664.
Li, L., Mo, L., Wang, R., Luo, X. and Chen, Z. (2008). Evidence for long-term cross-language repetition priming in low fluency Chinese–English bilinguals. *Bilingualism: Language and Cognition* 12 (1), 13–21.
Lin, J. and Wu, F. (2003) Differential performance by gender in foreign language testing. Poster for the 2003 Annual Meeting of NCME, Chicago.
Lindell, E. (1973) The four pillars: On the goals of a foreign language teaching. In J. Svartvik (ed.) *Errata: Papers in Error Analysis* (pp. 90–101). Lund: GWE Gleerup.
Linnarud, M. (1986) *Lexis in Composition: A Performance Analysis of Swedish Learner's Written English*. Malmö, Sweden: Liber Förlag Malmö.
Littlewood, W.T. (1984) *Foreign and Second Language Learning: Language-Acquisition Research and Its Implications for the Classroom*. Cambridge: Cambridge University Press.
Liu, M., and Braine, G. (2005) Cohesive features in argumentative writing produced by Chinese undergraduates. *System* 33, 623–636.
LoCoco, V. (1975) An analysis of Spanish and German learners' errors. *Working Papers in Bilingualism* 7, 96–124.
López-Mezquita Molina, M.T. (2005) *La Evaluación de la Competencia Léxica: Tests de Vocabulario. Su Fiabilidad y Validez*. Doctoral dissertation, Universidad de Granada.
López Guix, J.G. and J. Wilkinson (2001) *Manual de traducción: inglés-castellano*. Barcelona: Gedisa.
López Morales, H. (1993) En torno al aprendizaje del léxico. Bases psicolingüísticas de la planificación curricular. *Proceedings of the III Congreso Nacional de ASELE. El español como lengua extranjera: De la teoría la aula* (pp. 9–22).

MacIntyre, P., Baker, S., Clément, R. and Donovan, L. (2002) Sex and age effects on willingness to communicate, anxiety, perceived competence, and L2 motivation among junior high school French immersion students. *Language Learning* 52 (3), 537–564.
Manchón, R.M., Roca, J. and Murphy, L. (2000) La influencia de la variable 'grado de dominio de la L2' en los procesos de composición en lengua extranjera: hallazgos recientes de la investigación. In C. Muñoz (ed.) *Segundas lenguas. Adquisición en el aula* (pp. 277–297). Barcelona: Ariel Lingüística.
Manchón, R.M., Roca de Larios, J. and Murphy, L. (2007) Second and foreign language writing strategies: Focus on conceptualization and impact of the first language. In D. Cohen and E. Macaro (eds) *Language Learners Strategies: 30 Years of Research and Practice*. Oxford: Oxford University Press.
Marinova-Todd, S. (2003) Know your grammar: What the knowledge of syntax and morphology in an L2 reveals about the critical period for second/foreign language acquisition. In M.P. García Mayo and M.L. García Lecumberri (eds) *Age and the Acquisition of English as a Foreign Language* (pp. 59–73). Clevedon: Multilingual Matters.
Marsden, E. and David, A. (2008) Vocabulary use during conversation: A cross-sectional study of development from year 9 to year 13 among learners of Spanish and French. *Language Learning Journal* 36 (2), 181–198.
Martínez Arbelaiz, A. (2004) Índices de progreso en la producción escrita de estudiantes de español en situación de inmersión. *RAEL* 3, 115–145.
Matera, C. and M. Gerber (2008) Effects of a literacy curriculum that supports writing development of Spanish-speaking English learners in head start. *NHSA Dialog* 11 (1), 25–43.
Matsuda, P.K. (2003) Second language writing in the twentieth century: A situated historical perspective. In B. Kroll (ed.) *Exploring the Dynamics of Second Language Writing* (pp. 15–34). Cambridge: Cambridge University Press.
McCarthy, M. (2006) Spoken fluency in theory and in practice. Plenary talk held at the BAAL/IRAAL Conference, Cork, 7–9 September 2006.
McKeown, M. and Curtis, M. (1987) *The Nature of Vocabulary Acquisition*. Hillsdale, NJ: Erlbaum.
McNeill, A. (1990) Second language vocabulary: Problems caused by the formal representation of words. *Perspectives* 2, 104–122.
McNeill, A. (1996) Vocabulary knowledge profiles: Evidence from Chinese-speaking ESL teachers. *Hong Kong Journal of Applied Linguistics* 1, 39–63.
Meara, P. (1983) Word associations in the foreign language: A report on the Birkbeck Vocabulary Project. *Nottingham Linguistic Circular* 11, 29–38.
Meara, P. (1984) The study of lexis in interlanguage. In A. Davies, C. Criper and A.P.R. Howatt (eds) *Interlanguage* (pp. 225–239). Edinburgh: Edinburgh University Press.
Meara, P. (1992) Network structures and vocabulary acquisition in a foreign language. In P. Arnaud and H. Béjoint (eds) *Vocabulary and Applied Linguistics* (pp. 62–70). London: MacMillan Academic and Professional Ltd.
Meara, P. (1996) The dimensions of lexical competence. In G. Brown, K. Malmkjaer and J. Williams (eds) *Performance and Competence in Second Language Acquisition* (pp. 35–53). Cambridge: Cambridge University Press.
Meara, P. and Bell, H. (2001) P_Lex: A simple and effective way of describing the lexical characteristics of short L2 texts. *Prospect* 16 (3), 5–17.

Meara, P. and English, F. (1987) Lexical errors and learners' dictionaries. Reports-Research/Technical 143. On WWW at http://www.eric.ed.gov/ERICDocs/data/ericdocs2sql/content_storage_01/0000019b/80/1c/4b/98.pdf.
Meara, P. and Fitzpatrick, T. (2000) Lex30: An improved method of assessing productive vocabulary in an L2. *System* 28, 19–30.
Meara, P. and Jones, G. (1987) Tests of vocabulary size in English as a foreign Language. *Polyglot* 8, Fiche 1.
Meara, P., Rodgers, C. and Jacobs, G. (2000) Vocabulary and neural networks in the computational assessment of texts written by second-language learners. *System* 28, 345–354.
Mecartty, F. (1998) The effects of proficiency level and passage content on reading skills assessment. *Foreign Language Annals* 31 (4), 517–534.
Medina Bellido, M. (1997) Actitudes de los alumnos ante el aprendizaje de la gramática, el léxico y la pronunciación de la lengua inglesa. *Lenguaje y Textos* 10, 67–78.
Medgyes, P. and Ryan, C. (1996) The integration of academic writing skills with other curriculum components n teacher education. *System* 24 (3), 361–373.
Meijers, G. (1992) The foreign language vocabulary acquisition of mono- and bilingual children and teachers' evaluation ability. In P. Arnaud and H. Bejoint (eds) *Vocabulary and Applied Linguistics* (pp. 146–155). London: MacMillan.
Milton, J. and Meara, P. (1998) Are the British really bad at learning foreign languages? *Language Learning Journal* 18, 68–76.
Min, H.T. (2008) EFL vocabulary acquisition and retention: Reading plus vocabulary enhancement activities and narrow reading. *Language Learning* 58 (1), 73–115.
Miralpeix, I. and Celaya, M.L. (2002) The use of P_Lex to assess lexical richness in compositions written by learners of English as an L3. *Proceedings of the 26th AEDEAN Meeting* (pp. 399–406).
Moon, J. and Nikilov, M. (2000) *Research into Teaching English to Young Learners*. Pécs: University of Pécs.
Morris, L. (2001) Going through a bad spell: What the spelling errors of young ESL learners reveal about their grammatical knowledge. *The Canadian Modern Language Review/La Revue canadienne des langues vivantes* 58 (2), 273–286.
Morris, L., and Cobb, T. (2004) Vocabulary profiles as predictors of the academic performance of teaching English as a second language trainees. *System* 32, 75–87.
Morrissey, M. (1983) Toward a grammar of learners' errors. *IRAL* 21 (3), 193–207.
Moskovsky, C. (2001) The critical period hypothesis revisited. *Proceedings of the 2001 Conference of the Australian Linguistic Society*.
Moya Guijarro, A.J. (2003) La adquisición/ aprendizaje de la pronunciación, del vocabulario y de las estructuras interrogativas en lengua inglesa. Un estudio por edades. *Didáctica* 15, 161–177.
Mukattash, L. (1986) Persistence of fossilization. *IRAL* 24, 187–203.
Muncie, J. (2002) Process writing and vocabulary development: Comparing lexical frequency profiles across drafts. *System* 30, 225–235.
Muñoz, C. (2000) Bilingualism and trilingualism in school students in Catalonia. In J. Cenoz and U. Jessner (eds) *English in Europe: The Acquisition of a Third Language* (pp. 157–178). Clevedon: Multilingual Matters.

Muñoz, C. (2001) Factores escolares e individuales en el aprendizaje formal de un idioma extranjero. In S. Pastor Cesteros and V. Salazar García (eds) *Estudios de Lingüística. Anexo 1. Tendencias y Líneas de Investigación en Adquisición de Segundas Lenguas.* Alicante: Departamento de Filología Española, Lingüística General y Teoría de la Literatura, Universidad de Alicante.

Muñoz, C. (2003) Variation in oral skills development and age of onset. In M.P. García Mayo and M.L. García Lecumberri (eds) *Age and the Acquisition of English as a Foreign Language* (pp. 161–181). Clevedon, UK: Multilingual Matters.

Muñoz, C. (2008) Symmetries and asymmetries of age effects in naturalistic and instructed L2 learning. *Applied Linguistics* 29 (4), 1–19.

Muñoz, C., Pérez, C., Celaya, M.L., Navés, T., Torras, R.M., Tragant, E. and Victori, M. (2005) En torno a los efectos de la edad en el aprendizaje escolar de una lengua extranjera. On WWW at www.ub.es/ice/portaling/educaling/cat/n_1/munoz-article-n1.pdf. Accessed 20.12.05.

Muñoz Basols, J. (2005) Aprendiendo de los errores de la abuela Dolores: el error como herramienta didáctica en el aula de ELE. Paper delivered at FIAPE. I Congreso Internacional: El español lengua del futuro, Toledo, Spain, 20–23 March.

Mutta, M. (1999) The role of vocabulary in language learning: A study of entrance examination compositions. *Diálogos hispánicos de Amsterdam* 23, 333–348.

Myles, F. (2005) The emergence of morpho-syntactic structure in French L2. In J. Dewaele (ed.) *Focus on French as a Foreign Language* (pp. 88–113). Clevedon: Multilingual Matters.

Nagy, W. and Herman, P. (1987) Breadth and depth of vocabulary knowledge: Implications for acquisition and instruction. In M.G. McKeown and M.E. Curtis (eds) *The Nature of Vocabulary Acquisition* (pp. 19–35). Hillsdale, NJ: Lauwrence Erlbaum.

Nation, P. (1990) *Teaching and Learning Vocabulary.* Boston: Heinle and Heinle Publishers.

Nation, P. (1993a) Vocabulary size, growth and use. In R. Schreuder and B. Weltens (eds) *The Bilingual Lexicon* (pp. 115–134). Amsterdam: John Benjamins.

Nation, P. (1993b) Measuring readiness for simplified material: A test of the first 1,000 words of English. In M.L. Tickoo (ed.) *Simplification: Theory and Application.* RELC Anthology Series 31 (pp. 193–203).

Nation, P. (2001) *Learning Vocabulary in Another Language.* Cambridge: Cambridge University Press.

Nation, P. (2004) A study of the most frequent word families in the British National Corpus. In P. Bogaards and B. Laufer (eds) *Vocabulary in a Second Language* (pp. 3–13). Amsterdam: John Benjamins.

Nation, P. (2006) How large a vocabulary is needed for reading and listening? *The Canadian Modern Language Review/La revue canadienne des langues vivantes* 63 (1), 59–81.

Nation, P. and Waring, R. (1997) Vocabulary size, text coverage and word lists. In N. Schmitt and M. McCarthy (eds) *Vocabulary: Description, Acquisition and Pedagogy* (pp. 6–19). Cambridge: Cambridge University Press.

Nattinger, J. (1988) Some current trends in vocabulary teaching. In R. Carter and M. McCarthy (eds) *Vocabulary and Language Teaching* (pp. 62–82). London: Longman.

Naves, T. and Miralpeix, I. (2002) Short-term effects of age and exposure on writing development. In I. Palacios Martínez, M.J. López Couso, P. Fra López and E. Seoane Posse (eds) *Fifty Years of English Studies in Spain (1952–2002): A Commemorative Volume. Proceedings of the XXVI Congreso de AEDEAN, Santiago de Compostela, 12–14 December 2002* (pp. 407–416). Universidad de Santiago de Compostela: Santiago de Compostela.

Naves, T., Miralpeix, I. and Celaya, M.L. (2005) Who transfer more ... and what? Cross-linguistic influence in relation to school grade and language dominance in EFL. *International Journal of Multilingualism* 2 (2), 113–134.

Neff, J. (2006) A rhetorical analysis approach to English for academic purposes. *Revista de Lingüística y Lenguas Aplicadas* 1, 63–72. On WWW at http://ojs.upv.es/index.php/rdlla/article/viewFile/683/670.

Ninio, A. (1995) Expression of communicative intents in the single-word period and the vocabulary spurt. In K.E. Nelson and Z. Reger (eds) *Children's Language* (Vol. 8, pp. 103–124). Hillsdale, NJ: Erlbaum.

Nippold, M.A. (1998) *Later Language Development: The School-Age and Adolescent Years* (2nd edn). Austin, TX: Pro-Ed.

Niżegorodcew, A. (2006) Assessing L2 lexical development in early L2 learning: A case study. In J. Arabski (ed.) *Cross-Linguistic Influences in the Second Language Lexicon* (pp. 167–176). Clevedon: Multilingual Matters.

Nurweni, A. and Read, J. (1999) The English language knowledge of Indonesian university students. *English for Specific Purposes* 18 (2), 161–175.

Odlin, T. (1989) *Language Transfer*. Cambridge: Cambridge University Press. (Second Edition, 1996.)

Oliver, R. (2000) Age differences in negotiation and feedback in classroom and Pairwork. *Language Learning* 50 (1), 119–151.

Olsen, S. (1999) Errors and compensatory strategies: A study of grammar and vocabulary in texts written by Norwegian learners of English. *System* 27, 191–205.

Olsson, M. (1973) The effects of different types of errors in the communication situation. In J. Svartvik (ed.) *Errata: Papers in Error Analysis* (pp. 153–160). Lund: GWE Gleerup.

Palapanidi, K. (2009) Análisis de errores léxicos en la lengua escrita de los aprendientes griegos de español. Unpublished MPhil Dissertation, Universidad Antonio de Nebrija.

Palmberg, R. (1987) Patterns of vocabulary development in foreign-language learner. *SSLA* 9, 201–220.

Pavičić Takač, V. (2008) *Vocabulary Learning Strategies and Foreign Language Acquisition*. Clevedon: Multilingual Matters.

Pearson, B., Fernández, S. and Oller, D.K. (1995) Lexical development in bilingual infants and toddlers: Comparison to monolingual norms. In B. Harley (ed.) *Lexical Issues in Language Learning* (pp. 31–57). Ann Arbor, MI: Research Club in Language Learning.

Penny, J., Johnson, R. and Gordon, B. (2000) The effect of rating augmentation on inter-rater reliability: An empirical study of a holistic rubric. *Assessing Writing* 7, 146–164.

Pérez Basanta, C. (1999) La enseñanza del vocabulario desde una perspectiva lingüística y pedagógica. In M.S. Salaberri Ramiro (ed.) *Lingüística aplicada a la enseñanza de lenguas extranjeras* (pp. 262–306). Almería: Universidad de Almería.

Pérez Basanta, C. (2005) Assessing the receptive vocabulary of Spanish students of English philology: An empirical investigation. In J.L. Martínez-Dueñas Espejo, N. Mclaren, C. Pérez_Basanta and L. Quereda Rodríguez-Navarro (eds) *Towards an Understanding of the English Language: Past, Present, and Future. Studies in Honour of Fernando Serrano* (pp. 457–486). Granada: Universidad de Granada.
Philp, J., Oliver, R. and Mackey, A. (2008) *Second Language Acquisition and the Young Learner. Child's Play?* Amsterdam: John Benjamins.
Picó, E. (1987) Error tolerance and error gravity: A report. In M. DeJuan (ed.) *New Horizons in TEFL*. Cinquemes Jornelas Pedagogiques d'Angles. Febrer-Març.
Pigada, M. and Schmitt, N. (2006) Vocabulary acquisition from extensive reading: A case study. *Reading in a Foreign Language* 18 (1), 1–28. On WWW at http://nflrc.hawaii.edu/rfl/April2006/pigada/pigada.htm.
Polio, C. (1997) Measures of linguistic accuracy in second language writing research. *Language Learning* 47 (1), 101–143.
Polio, C. (2001) Research methodology in second language writing research: The case of text-based studies. In T. Silva and P.K. Matsuda (eds) *On Second Language Writing* (pp. 91–116). Hillsdale, NJ: Erlbaum.
Polio, C. and Glew, M. (1996) ESL writing assessment prompts: How students choose. *Journal of Second Language Writing* 5 (I), 35–49.
Polio, C., Fleck, C. and Leder, N. (1998) "If I only had more time": ESL learners' changes in linguistic accuracy on essay revisions *Journal of Second Language Writing* 7 (I), 43–68.
Politzer, R.L. (1978) Errors of English speakers of German as perceived and evaluated by German natives. *Modern Language Journal* 62, 253–261.
Poulin-Dubois, D. (1995) Object parts and the acquisition of the meaning of names. In K.E. Nelson and Z. Reger (eds) *Children's Language* (Vol. 8, pp. 125–143). Hillsdale, NJ: Erlbaum.
Poulisse, N. (1993) A theoretical account of lexical communication strategies. In R. Schreuder and B. Weltens (eds) *The Bilingual Lexicon* (pp. 157–189). Amsterdam: John Benjamins.
Qian, D. (1999) Assessing the role of depth and breadth of vocabulary knowledge in reading comprehension. *Canadian Modern Language Review* 56, 282–307.
Qian, D. (2002) Investigating the relationship between vocabulary knowledge and academic reading performance: An assessment perspective. *Language Learning* 52 (3), 513–536.
Raimes, A. (1985) What unskilled ESL students do as they write: A classroom study of composing. *TESOL Quarterly* 19, 229–258.
Read, J. (1997) Vocabulary and testing. In N. Schmitt and M. McCarthy (eds) *Vocabulary: Description, Acquisition and Pedagogy* (pp. 303–320). Cambridge: Cambridge University Press.
Read, J. (2000) *Assessing Vocabulary*. Cambridge: Cambridge University Press.
Read, J. (2004) Plumbing the depths: How should the construct of vocabulary knowledge be defined? In P. Bogaards and B. Laufer (eds) *Vocabulary in a Second Language* (pp. 209–227). Amsterdam: John Benjamins.
Reid, J. (1990) Responding to different topic types: A quantitative analysis from a contrastive rhetoric perspective. In B. Kroll (ed.) *Second Language Writing: Research Insights for the Classroom* (pp. 191–210). Cambridge: Cambridge University Press.

Reynolds, D. (2001) Language in the balance: Lexical repetition as a function of topic, cultural background, and writing development. *Language Learning* 51 (3), 437–476.
Richards, J. (1971) A non-contrastive approach to error analysis. *English Language Teaching* 25, 204–219.
Ringbom, H. (1981) The influence of other languages on the vocabulary of foreign language learners. In G. Nickel and D. Nehls (eds) *Error Analysis, Contrastive Analysis and Second Language Learning* (pp. 85–96). Heidelberg: Julios Groos Verlag.
Ringbom, H. (1983) Borrowing and lexical transfer. *Applied Linguistics* 4, 207–212.
Ringbom, H. (1987) *The Role of the First language in Foreign Language Learning*. Clevedon, UK: Multilingual Matters.
Ringbom, H. (2001) Lexical transfer in L3 production. In J. Cenoz, B. Hufeisen and U. Jessner (eds) *Cross-Linguistic Influence in Third Language Acquisition: Psycholinguistic Perspectives* (pp. 59–68). Clevedon: Multilingual Matters.
Ringbom, H. (2006) The importance of different types of similarity in transfer studies. In J. Arabski (ed.) *Cross-Linguistic Influences in the Second Language Lexicon* (pp. 36–45). Clevedon: Multilingual Matters.
Robinson, P. (1989) A rich view of lexical competence. *ELT Journal* 43 (4), 274–281.
Robinson, P. (1995) Procedural and declarative knowledge in vocabulary learning: Communication and the language learners' lexicon. In T. Huckin, M. Haynes and J. Coady (eds) *Second Language Reading and Vocabulary Learning* (pp. 229–262). Norwood, NJ: Ablex Publishing Corporation.
Robinson, P. and Ellis, N.C. (eds) (2008) *Handbook of Cognitive Linguistics and second Language Acquisition*. New York: Routledge.
Roca de Larios, J., Machón, R.M. and Murphy, L. (2007) Componentes básicos y evolutivos del proceso de formulación en la escritura de textos en lengua materna y lengua extranjera. *RESLA* 20, 159–183.
Rokita, J. (2006) Code-mixing in early L2 lexical acquisition. In J. Arabski (ed.) *Cross-Linguistic Influences in the Second Language Lexicon* (pp. 177–190). Clevedon: Multilingual Matters.
Ruiz de Zarobe, Y. (2002) Edad y tipología pronominal en la adquisición del inglés como tercera lengua. In I. Palacios Martínez, M.J. López Couso, P. Fra López and E. Seoane Posse (eds) *Fifty Years of English Studies in Spain (1952–2002): A Commemorative Volume. Procreedings of the XXVI Congreso de AEDEAN, Santiago de Compostela, 12–14 December 2002* (pp. 417–428). XXX: XXX.
Ruiz de Zarobe, Y. (2005a). Age and third language production: A longitudinal study. *International Journal of Multilingualism* 2 (2), 105–112.
Ruiz de Zarobe, Y. (2005b) Perspectiva longitudinal de la edad en producción escrita. *Proceedings of the II Simposio Internacional de Bilingüismo* (pp. 333–341).
Sajavaara, K. and Fairweather, C. (eds) (1996) *Approaches to Second Language Acquisition*. Jyväskylä: Jyväskylä University Printing House.
San Mateo Valdehíta, A. (2003/2004). Aprendizaje de léxico en español como segunda lengua. Investigación sobre tres métodos. Unpublished MPhil Thesis, UNED. On WWW at http://www.mec.es/redele/biblioteca2005/san_mateo.shtml.
Sánchez Rodríguez, S. (2002). El léxico en la construcción de la expresión creativa en la edad infantil. *Textos de Didáctica de la Lengua y de la Literatura* 31, 24–34.

Sánchez Jiménez, D. (2006) Análisis de errores ortográficos de estudiantes filipinos en el aprendizaje del español como lengua extranjera. Unpublished Masters Thesis, Universidad de Salamanca. On WWW at http://www.mec.es/redele/Biblioteca2006/DavidSanchez.shtml.

Santiago, R. and Repáraz, C. (1993) La incorporación temprana de un segundo idioma: Análisis de errores ortográficos en lengua inglesa. *Bordon* 45 (2), 207-219.

Santos, T. (1988). Professor's reactions to the academic writing of non-native-speaking students. *TESOL Quarterly* 22, 69-90.

Santos Gargallo, I. (1993) *Análisis Contrastivo, Análisis de Errores e Interlengua en el marco de la Lingüística Contrastiva*. Madrid: Síntesis.

Santos Rovira, J.M. (2007) Errores en el proceso de aprendizaje de la lengua española. Un estudio sobre alumnos chinos. *IDEAS- Investigación y Estudios Hispánicos Aplicados* 4, 19-30.

Sanz, C. (2000) Bilingual education enhances third language acquisition: Evidence from Catalonia. *Applied Psycholinguistics* 21 (1), 23-44.

Scarcella, R. and Higa, C. (1982) Input and age differences in second language Acquisition. In S.D. Krashen, R.C. Scarcella and M.H. Long (eds) *Child–Adult Differences in Second Language Acquisition* (pp. 175-201). Rowley, MA: Newbury House Publishers.

Scarcella, R. and Zimmerman, C. (1998) Academic words and gender: ESL student performance on a test of academic lexicon. *Studies in Second Language Acquisition* 20, 27-49.

Schmitt, N. (1995) A fresh approach to vocabulary using a word knowledge framework. *RELC Journal* 26, 86-94.

Schmitt, N. (1998) Tracking the incremental acquisition of second language vocabulary: A longitudinal study. *Language Learning* 48, 281-317.

Schmitt, N. (2000) *Vocabulary in Language Teaching*. Cambridge: Cambridge University Press.

Schmitt, N. and McCarthy, M. (eds) (1997) *Vocabulary. Description, Acquisition and Pedagogy*. Cambridge: Cambridge University Press.

Schmitt, N. and Meara, P. (1997) Researching vocabulary through a word knowledge Framework: Word associations and verbal suffixes. *Studies in Second Language Acquisition* 19, 17-36.

Schmitt, N., Schmitt, D. and Clapham, C. (2001) Developing and exploring the behaviour of two new versions of the vocabulary levels test. *Language Testing* 18 (1), 55-89.

Schreuder, R. and Weltens, B. (eds) (1993) *The Bilingual Lexicon*. Amsterdam: John Benjamins.

Seashore, R.H. and Eckerson, L.D. (1940) The measurement of individual differences in general English vocabularies. *Journal of Education Psychology* 31, 14-38.

Selinker, L. (1972) Interlanguage. *IRAL* 10, 209-230.

Selinker, L., Swain, M. and Dumas, G. (1975) The interlanguage hypothesis extended to children. *Language Learning* 25 (1), 139-152.

Silva, T. (1990) Second language composition instruction: Developments, issues and directions in ESL. In B. Kroll (ed.) *Second Language Writing: Research Insights for the Classroom* (pp. 11-23). Cambridge: Cambridge University Press.

Silva, T. and Matsuda, P.K. (eds) (2001) *On Second Language Writing*. Hillsdale, NJ: Erlbaum.

Silva, T., Reichelt, M., Chikuma, Y., Duval-Couetil, N., Mo, R.P.J., Vélez Rendón, G. and Wood, S. (2003) Second language writing up close and personal: Some success stories. In B. Kroll (ed.) *Second Language Writing: Research Insights for the Classroom* (pp. 93–114). Cambridge: Cambridge University Press.
Singleton, D. (1989) *Language Acquisition: The Age Factor*. Clevedon: Multilingual Matters.
Singleton, D. (1996) Formal aspects of the L2 mental lexicon: Some evidence from university-level learners of French. In K. Sajavaara and C. Fairweather (eds) *Approaches to Second Language Acquisition* (pp. 79–85). Jyväskylä: Jyväskylä University Printing House.
Singleton, D. (1999) *Exploring the Second Language Mental Lexicon*. Cambridge: Cambridge University Press.
Singleton, D. (2000) *Language and the Lexicon: An Introduction*. London: Edward Arnold.
Singleton, D. (2003) Critical period or general age factor(s)? In M.P. García Mayo and M.L. García Lecumberri (eds) *Age and the Acquisition of English as a Foreign Language* (pp. 3–22). Clevedon: Multilingual Matters.
Singleton, D. and Little, D. (1991) The second language lexicon: Some evidence from university-level learners of French and German. *Second Language Research* 7 (11), 61–81.
Skehan, P. (1989) *Individual Differences in Second Language Learning*. London: Edward Arnold.
Skjær, S. (2004) El análisis de errores y su impacto en la comunicación en textos escritos por alumnos noruegos en su examen final de bachillerato. Unpublished Masters Thesis, Universidad Antonio Nebrija. On WWW at http://www.mec.es/redele/biblioteca2005/skjaer.shtml.
Smith, C. (1993) *Collins Spanish-English/English-Spanish Dictionary, Third Edition*. New York: HarperCollins.
Smith, M.D. and Locke, J.L. (1988) *The Emergent Lexicon. The Child's Development of a Linguistic Vocabulary*. San Diego: Academic Press.
Staehr, L.S. (2008) Vocabulary size and the skills of listening, reading and writing. *Language Learning Journal* 36 (2), 139–152.
Stoller, F. and Grabe, W. (1995) Implications for L2 vocabulary acquisition and instruction from L1 vocabulary research. In T. Huckin, M. Haynes and J. Coady (eds) *Second Language Reading and Vocabulary Learning* (pp. 24–45). Norwood, NJ: Ablex Publishng Corporation.
Stowe, L. and Sabourin, L. (2005) Imaging the processing of a second language: Effects of maturation and proficiency on the neural processes involved. *International Review of Applied Linguistics* 43, 329–353.
Sunderman, G. and Kroll, J. (2006) First language activation during second language lexical processing. *Studies in Second Language Acquisition* 28, 387–422.
Swan, M. (1997) The influence of the mother tongue on second language vocabulary acquisition and use. In N. Schmitt and M. McCarthy (eds) *Vocabulary: Description, Acquisition and Pedagogy* (pp. 156–180). Cambridge: Cambridge University Press.
Szulc-Kurpaska, M. (2000) Communication strategies in 11 year-olds. In J. Moon and M. Nikolov (eds) *Research into Teaching English to Young Learners* (pp. 345–359). Pecs: University Press Pecs.

Takala, S.J. (1984) *Evaluation of Students' Knowledge of English Vocabulary in the Finnish Comprehensive School.* Reports of the Institute of Educational Research 350. Jyväskylä: Institute of Educational Research.
Taylor, B. (1975) The use of overgeneralization and transfer learning strategies by elementary and intermediate students of ESL. *Language Learning* 25 (1), 73–107.
Taylor, G. (1986) Errors and explanation. *Applied Linguistics* 7, 144–166.
Tercanlioglu, L. (2004) Pre-service EFL teachers' beliefs about foreign language learning and how they relate to gender. *Electronic Journal of Research in Educational Psychology* 5–3 (1), 145–162.
Terrazas Gallego, M. and Agustín Llach, M.P. (2009) Exploring the increase of receptive vocabulary knowledge in the foreign language: A longitudinal study. *International Journal of English Studies* 9 (1), 113–133.
Terrebone, N.G. (1973) English spelling problems of native Spanish speakers. In R. Nash (ed.) *Reading in Spanish–English Contrastive Linguistics* (pp. 136–155). San Juan: Inter American University Press.
Thorndike, E.L. and Lorge, I. (1944) *The Teacher's Word Book of 30,000 Words.* New York: Teachers College, Columbia University.
Torras, R.M. and Celaya, M.L. (2001) Age-related differences in the development of written production: An empirical study of EFL school learners. *IJES* 1 (2), 103–126.
Tremblay, M.C. (2006) Cross-linguistic influence in third language acquisition: The role of L2 proficiency and L2 exposure. *Otawa Papers in Linguistics* 34, 109–120. On WWW at http://aix1.uottawa.ca/ ~ clo/Tremblay.pdf.
Tschihold, C. (2003) Error analysis and lexical errors. In C. Tschihold (ed.) *English Core Linguistics* (pp. 287–299). Bern: Peter Lang.
Umbel, V. and Oller, D.K. (1994) Developmental changes in receptive vocabulary in Hispanic bilingual school children. *Language Learning* 44 (2), 221–242.
Urquhart, A.H. and Weir, C.J. (1998) *Reading in a Second Language: Process, Product and Practice.* New York: Longman.
Valero Garcés, C., Mancho Barés, G., Flys Junquera, C. and Cerdá Redondo, E. (2000) Evolución de la Interlengua y analysis de textos: ENWIL y el análisis de errores en la expresión escrita en EFL. In F.J. Ruiz de Mendoza Ibañez (ed.) *Panorama actual de la lingüística aplicada* (pp. 1849–1857). Logroño: Universidad de la Rioja.
Valero Garcés, C., Mancho Barés, G., Flys Junquera, C. and Cerdá Redondo, E. (2003) *Learning to Write: Error Analysis Applied.* Alcalá de Henares: Universidad de Alcalá.
VanParys, J., Zimmer, C., Li, X. and Kelly, P. (1997) Some salient and persistent difficulties encountered by Chinese and francophone students in the learning of English vocabulary. *ITL Review of Applied Linguistics* 115–116, 137–164.
VanPatten, B., Williams, J., Rott, S. and Overstreet, M. (eds) (2004) *Form-Meaning Connections in Second Language Acquistion.* Mahwah, NJ: Erlbaum.
Vandrick, S. (2003) Literature in the teaching of second language composition. In B. Kroll (ed.) *Second Language Writing: Research Insights for the Classroom* (pp. 263–284). Cambridge: Cambridge University Press.
Vázquez, G. (1987) Didáctica de la comprensión lectora. *Hispanorama* 47 (Special issue): 84–139.

Vázquez, G. (1991) *Análisis de errores y aprendizaje de español lengua extranjera*. Frankfurt: Peter Lang.
Vázquez, G. (1992) La enseñanza del español como segunda lengua: El concepto de error: estado de la cuestión y posibles investigaciones. *Proceedings of the Spanish Language Conference*, Seville, 7–10 October 1992 (pp. 497–504).
Verhallen, M. and Schoonen, R. (1993) Lexical knowledge of monolingual and bilingual children. *Applied Linguistics* 14, 344–363.
Verhallen, M. and Schoonen, R. (1998) Lexical knowledge in L1 and L2 of third and fifth graders. *Applied Linguistics* 19 (4), 452–470.
Viberg, Å. (1996) The study of lexical patterns in L2 oral production. In K. Sajavaara and C. Fairweather (eds) *Approaches to Second Language Acquisition* (pp. 87–107). Jyväskylä: Jyväskylä University Printing House.
Victori, M. (1999) An analysis of writing knowledge in EFL composing: A case study of two effective and two less effective writers. *System* 27, 537–555.
Victori, M. and Tragant, E. (2003) Learner strategies: A cross-sectional and longitudinal study of primary and high-school EFL learners. In M.P. García Mayo and M.L. García Lecumberri (eds) *Age and the Acquisition of English as a Foreign Language* (pp. 182–209). Clevedon: Multilingual Matters.
Vihman, M.M. and Miller, R. (1988) Words and babble at the threshold of language acquisition. In M.D. Smith and J.L. Locke (eds) *The Emergent Lexicon: The Child's Development of a Linguistic Vocabulary* (pp. 151–183). San Diego: Academic Press.
Viladot, J. and Celaya, M.L. (2006) How do you say 'preparar'? L1 use in EFL oral production and task-related differences. Paper presented at the XXX AEDEAN Conference, University of Huelva, 14–16 December 2006.
Wang, L. (2003) Switching to first language among writers with differing second-language proficiency. *Journal of Second Language Writing* 12, 347–375.
Wang, W. and Wen, Q. (2002) L1 use in the L2 composing process: An exploratory study of 16 Chinese EFL writers. *Journal of Second Language Writing* 11, 225–246.
Waring, R. (1997) The negative effects of learning words in semantic sets: A replication. *System* 25 (2), 261–274.
Waring, R. (2002) Scales of vocabulary knowledge in second language vocabulary assessment. On WWW at http://www1.harenet.ne.jp/~waring/papers/scales.htm.
Warren, B. (1982) Common types of lexical errors among Swedish learners of English. *Moderna Språk* 76 (3), 209–228.
Webb, S. (2008) The effects of context on incidental vocabulary learning. *Reading in a Foreign Language* 20 (2), 232–245.
Weigle, S.C. (2002) *Assessing Writing*. Cambridge: Cambridge University Press.
Weinreich, U. (1974) *Languages in Contact: Findings and Problems*. The Hangue: Mouton & Co. (8th reprint, first published in 1953).
Weinreich, U. (1953) *Languages in Contact*. New York: Linguistic Circle.
Wen, Q. and Johnson, R.K. (1997) L2 learner variables and English achievement: A study of tertiary-level English majors in China. *Applied Linguistics* 18 (1), 27–48.
Wesche, M. and Paribakht, T.S. (1996) Assessing second language vocabulary knowledge: Depth versus breadth. *Canadian Modern language Review* 53 (1), 13–40.

West, M. (1953) *A General Service List of English Words*. London: Longman.
White, E.M. (1993) Holistic scoring: Past triumphs, future challenges. In M. Williamson and B. Hout (eds) *Validating Holistic Scoring for Writing Assessment: Theoretical and Empirical Foundations* (pp. 79–108). Cresskill, NJ: Hampton Press.
Williams, S. and Hammarberg, B. (1998) Language switches in L3 production: Implications for a polyglot speaking model. *Applied Linguistics* 19 (3), 295–333.
Williamson, M.M. (1993) An introduction to holistic scoring: The social, historical, and theoretical context for writing assessment. In M.M. Williamson and B. Hout (eds) *Validating Holistic Scoring for Writing Assessment: Theoretical and Empirical Foundations* (pp. 1–43). Cresskill, NJ: Hampton Press.
Williamson, M.M. and Hout, B. (1993) *Validating Holistic Scoring for Writing Assessment: Theoretical and Empirical Foundations*. Cresskill, NJ: Hampton Press.
Wolfe, E., Bolton, S., Feltovich, B. and Niday, D. (1996) The influence of student experience with word processors on the quality of essays written for a direct writing assessment. *Assessing Writing* 3 (2), 123–147.
Wolfe-Quintero, K., Inagaki, S. and Kim, H. (1998) *Second Language Development in Writing: Measures of Fluency, Accuracy, and Complexity*. Hawaii: University of Hawaii at Manoa.
Wolter, B. (2001) Comparing the L1 and L2 mental lexicon: A depth of individual word knowledge model. *Studies in Second Language Acquisition* 23, 41–69.
Wolter, B. (2002) Assessing proficiency through word associations: Is there still hope? *System* 30, 315–329.
Woodall, B. (2002) Language-switching: Using the first language while writing in a second language. *Journal of Second Language Writing* 11, 7–28.
Wray, A. (2002) *Formulaic Language and the Lexicon*. Cambridge: Cambridge University Press.
Yamada, J., Takatsuka, S., Kotake, N. and Kurusu, J. (1980) On the optimum age for teaching foreign vocabulary to children. *IRAL* 18 (3), 245–247.
Yang, Y. (2001) Sex and language proficiency level in color-naming performance: An ESL/EFL perspective. *International Journal of Applied Linguistics* 11 (2), 238–256.
Yoshida, M. (1978) The acquisition of English vocabulary by a Japanese-speaking child. In E. Hatch (ed.) *Second Language Acquisition: A Book of Readings* (pp. 91–99). Rowley, MA: Newbury House.
Zamel, V. (1983) The composing processes of advance ESL students: Six case studies. *TESOL Quarterly* 17, 165–187.
Zhang, S. (1987) Cognitive complexity and written production in English as a second language. *Language Learning* 37, 469–481.
Zhu, W. (2004) Faculty views on the importance of writing, the nature of academic writing, and teaching and responding to writing in the disciplines. *Journal of Second Language Writing* 13, 29–48.
Zimmermann, R. (1986a) Classification and distribution of lexical errors in the written work of German learners of English. *Papers and Studies in Contrastive Linguistics* 21, 31–40.
Zimmermann, R. (1986b) Semantics and lexical error analysis. *Englisch-Amerikanische Studien* 2, 294–305.

Zimmermann, R. (1987) Form-oriented and content-oriented lexical errors in L2 learners. *IRAL* 25, 55–67.
Zola, D. (1984) Redundancy and word perception during reading. *Perception and Psychophysics* 36 (3), 277–284.
Zughoul, M.R. (1991) Lexical choice: Towards writing problematic word lists. *IRAL* 29, 45–60.
Zydatiss, W. (1974) A 'kiss of life' for the notion of error. *IRAL* 12 (3), 231–237.

For Product Safety Concerns and Information please contact our EU Authorised Representative:

Easy Access System Europe

Mustamäe tee 50

10621 Tallinn

Estonia

gpsr.requests@easproject.com

www.ingramcontent.com/pod-product-compliance
Lightning Source LLC
Chambersburg PA
CBHW070559300426
44113CB00010B/1315